The Infinite Reservoir

The Infinite Reservoir

A New Beginning for Science, Theology,
and Human Meaning—Rooted in Divine Action

Kevin Michael Mc Guinness

WIPF & STOCK · Eugene, Oregon

THE INFINITE RESERVOIR
A New Beginning for Science, Theology, and Human Meaning—
Rooted in Divine Action

Copyright © 2025 Kevin Michael Mc Guinness. All rights reserved. Except for brief quotations in critical publications or reviews, no part of this book may be reproduced in any manner without prior written permission from the publisher. Write: Permissions, Wipf and Stock Publishers, 199 W. 8th Ave., Suite 3, Eugene, OR 97401.

Wipf & Stock
An Imprint of Wipf and Stock Publishers
199 W. 8th Ave., Suite 3
Eugene, OR 97401

www.wipfandstock.com

PAPERBACK ISBN: 979-8-3852-5340-1
HARDCOVER ISBN: 979-8-3852-5341-8
EBOOK ISBN: 979-8-3852-5342-5

VERSION NUMBER 09/19/25

Scripture quotations taken from the (NASB®) New American Standard Bible®, Copyright © 1960, 1971, 1977, 1995, 2020 by The Lockman Foundation. Used by permission. All rights reserved. lockman.org.

For

Maria Felix Lira Mc Guinness

You gave up your dreams so that ours could live.
While I disappeared for hours, days, and months into the logic
of this book, you remained steadfast, patient, unseen.
Though you were always on my mind, I know I failed to show it,
stealing time that belonged to you,
without explanation.
Still, you endured,
bearing the weight of our home, our children, and me—
your most difficult burden.

To Kieran, Joshua, Erin, and to me,
you gave everything.
Your quiet strength shaped this world more than my words ever will.
You are, to me,
an infinite reservoir
of restraint, of faith, of love,
structuring our universe,
and making this book—
and this life—possible.

Your brilliance, your sacrifice,
your career given up for our sake—
none of it forgotten.
This book is dedicated to you.

I am grateful to my brother Keith P. Mc Guinness Sr for his frequent
support and encouragement throughout the writing of this book.

What cannot not be gives itself by restraint.
In that restraint, the universe begins.

When the atheist declares, "There is nothing!"
He is, unknowingly, naming God—who is no thing.
Only his ignorance keeps him from seeing it.

—Kevin Michael Mc Guinness

Contents

List of Tables | xi
A Letter to Pope Leo XIV | xiii
Preface | xv
Introduction | xix

1. Establishing the Necessity of Being Per Se | 3
   Part One: The Fundamental Questions | 3
   Part Two: The Necessity of a Causal Joint | 9

2. The Emergence of Motion, Time, and Space | 13
   Part One: The Necessity of Motion in Infinite Actuality | 13
   Part Two: The Deceleration of Infinite Reciprocal Motion | 18

3. Deceleration as the Mechanism of Finite Reality | 28
   Part One: The Necessity of Deceleration for Sustaining Finite Reality | 28
   Part Two—Deceleration and the Structure of Individual Beings | 37

4. The Causal Joint of Divine Action: From Infinite Power to Finite Creation | 44
   Part One—Introduction and the Necessity of a Causal Joint | 44
   Part Two—The Causal Joint as the Act of Divine Potentiation | 50
   Part Three—The Causal Joint and the Structure of Finite Reality | 54
   Part Four—The Causal Joint and the Return of the Soul | 60

Contents

5   Omnipotence: The Power that Upholds Reality | 67

6   Omniscience: The Absolute Unity of Knowledge and
    the Relational Foundation of Rationality | 73

7   Omnipresence: The Boundless and
    Indivisible Presence of Being | 80

8   The Convergence of Science, Metaphysics, and Theology | 87

9   The Resolution of Divine Action in Light
    of Metaphysical Necessity | 95

10 The Unification of Divine Action and Human Purpose | 103

11 The Necessary Union of Intellect, Will, and Divine Truth | 109

12 Divine Action and the Structure of Reality | 116

13 Science, Theology, and the Convergence on Truth | 122

14 Participation in Divine Action | 127
    Part One: The Structure of Participation | 127
    Part Two: Imperfect Participation Cannot Fulfill Itself | 133
    Part Three: The Means of Participation | 139
    Part Four: The Logic of the Beatific Vision | 144
    Part Five: The Transition to Perfected Participation—
      The Process of Elevation | 150

15 The Waiting Soul: Structure, Time, and the Logic of Return | 157

16 The Fulfillment of Divine Action in the Logos | 163

17 The Hypostatic Union and the Rational Necessity
    of Decelerated Knowledge | 171

18 The Argument from Nonexistence as Unifying
    Classical Arguments for God | 177

19 The Logical Necessity of Divine Participation | 183

20 The Fulfillment of Rational Participation in Divine Truth | 189

21 The Metaphysical Necessity of Divine Elevation | 195

22 The Logos as the Bridge of Fulfillment | 201

Contents ix

23 The Cross as the Intersection of Justice and Mercy | 206

24 The Hope of the Christ: Justice and Mercy as
    the Foundation of Redemption | 212

25 The Problem of Evil and the Necessity of Divine Order | 218

26 From the Logic of Divine Redemption to the
    Logic of Divine Completion | 226

27 From Metaphysical Fulfillment to Empirical Revelation | 231

28 Theological Conflicts in the Absence of
    Metaphysical Clarity | 242

29 Political Philosophy, Justice, and the
    Misunderstood US Constitution | 249

30 The False Dilemma of Faith and Reason | 257

31 The Rational Foundation for a Just Society | 265
    Part One: The Role of Faith and Reason in Society | 265
    Part Two: The Roman Catholic Intellectual Tradition | 270
    Part Three: The Decline of Western Civilization | 273
    Part Four: Restoring the Proper Order | 276

32 Education as Participation in Divine Knowledge | 279

33 The Future of Metaphysical Integration | 287

34 The Metaphysical Restoration of Civilization | 294

35 The Ecclesial Restoration of Civilization | 310

36 The Synthesis: Truth as the Fulfillment of Civilization | 319

37 The Ties that Bind: Ecumenism and the
    Call to Christian Unity | 326

Afterword: Epilegomena to Any Future Physics | 333
Appendix: Metaphysical Concordance with Scripture | 341
Glossary of Metaphysical Physics Terms Used in the Afterword | 347
Preface to the General Glossary | 351
General Glossary | 353
Bibliography | 359

List of Tables

Table 2.1. Why Infinite Reciprocal Motion Is Unique | 15

Table 2.2. How Deceleration Structures the Universe | 24

Table 3.1. Why Finite Motion Requires Continuous Structuring | 30

Table 3.2. The Role of Negative Pressure in Finite Reality | 31

Table 3.3. Levels of Participation in Being | 38

Table 3.4. Free Will as Participation | 39

Table 5.1. Why Omnipotence is Not Just Extreme Power | 68

Table 5.2. How Omnipotence Sustains All Things Effortlessly | 70

Table 5.3. How Omnipotence Interacts with Creation | 71

Table 5.4. Why Omnipotence and Deceleration Are Inseparable | 71

Table 6.1. Common Misconceptions About Omniscience | 74

Table 6.2. Why Rationality Is Not a Divine Attribute but a Finite Expression | 75

Table 6.3. Why Divine Foreknowledge Does Not Eliminate Free Will | 76

Table 6.4. Why Deceleration is Necessary for Rationality | 78

Table 7.1. The Three False Views of Omnipresence | 81

Table 7.2. Why Divine Action Is Not Intervention | 82

Table 7.3. How Finite Beings Experience Omnipresence | 83

Table 7.4. How Omnipresence Structures Reality | 84

List of Tables

Table 8.1. Empirical Observation Must Reflect Metaphysical Necessity | 89

Table 8.2. Human Freedom Within Divine Knowledge | 91

Table 8.3. Three Perspectives on Reality | 93

Table 9.1. Understanding Miracles | 98

Table 9.2. Misconceptions about Divine Foreknowledge and Free Will Resolved | 100

Table 10.1. Common Misconceptions about Free Will | 105

Table 10.2. Spectrum of Participation in Divine Actuality | 106

Table 10.3. Alignment of Free Will with Divine Self-Expression | 107

Table 12.1. Revising the Concepts of General and Special Divine Action | 118

Table 12.2. Reality's Relationship with Divine Action | 119

Table 14.1. Hierarchy of Participation in Being | 129

Table 14.2. Why Imperfect Beings Cannot Perfect Themselves | 135

Table 14.3. Structured Hierarchy of Ascent Toward Participation | 140

Table 14.4. The Beatific Vision and the Nature of Ultimate Participation | 146

Table 14.5. Graduated Participation in Divine Actuality | 152

Table A-1. Confirmed Matches Between Unified Equation and Empirical Results | 338

A Letter to Pope Leo XIV

To His Holiness Pope Leo XIV,
Servant of the Servants of God,
Successor of Peter and Guardian of Communion in Truth:

Most Holy Father,

WITH REVERENCE FOR YOUR office and gratitude for your courage, I offer this book, not as a theological speculation but as a metaphysical act of service—a clarifying structure of truth through which communion may be restored, division dissolved, and the triune logic of God made more intelligible to reason.

Your election to the Chair of Peter has been marked by gestures that point beyond institutional reform. In your words, in your bearing, and in your Augustinian spirit, there is a quiet insistence that Truth is not something the church invents or revises, but something to which she must yield. In this, your pontificate begins, not with novelty but with fidelity to Being, to Love, to the One who is always before us.

This book is written in that same spirit.

It proposes no innovation, no new doctrine. It offers only a metaphysical clarity grounded in the logic of nonexistence's impossibility—the necessary triune structure of Being that reveals why creation exists, how participation is ordered, and why communion is not merely a theological hope but an ontological necessity.

From this structure, certain consequences follow:

- What appears fragmented in practice may yet be revealed as unified in structure. When the logic of divine action is rightly seen, what once seemed divergent can be recognized as ordered expression—differentiated not by contradiction, but by partial vision. Metaphysics does not erase distinction but shows how true distinction belongs within a greater unity already given.

- Faith and science are not at odds. The structure that makes the universe measurable is the same structure that grounds all being. What science observes—space, time, and motion—only exists because divine actuality has already made relation possible. The challenges faced by modern cosmology are not failures of data, but invitations to see the deeper order beneath all things.

- The human person is not an emergent thing but a metaphysical being structured in memory, intellect, and will called to return by the very pattern of their formation. Healing, education, vocation, family, and governance must all be restored to their metaphysical ground, lest they collapse under the weight of cultural fiction.

Your Holiness, these are not abstract conclusions. They are the necessary implications of divine order, seen clearly once the will submits to Truth. That clarity, I believe, is already animating your pontificate. What *The Infinite Reservoir* provides is its scaffolding.

If the church is to fulfill her mission—if the gospel is to be heard again, not as opinion but as structure, then we must speak metaphysically. We must recover the order of participation that modernity has obscured. That is what this book attempts: not to theologize but to show; not to assert but to unveil.

I place this work at your feet, not as an appeal for favor but as an act of filial submission to the Logos who speaks through the church when she is rightly ordered. I believe your voice may help the world to hear again, not merely about God but through him.

In truth, love, and communion,

Kevin Michael Mc Guinness
Author of *The Infinite Reservoir*
Feast of St. Augustine
August 28, 2025

Preface

FROM ANALOGY TO STRUCTURE: COMPLETING THE METAPHYSICAL VISION OF CLASSICAL THEISM

THIS WORK STANDS IN continuity with the metaphysical visions of St. Thomas Aquinas and St. Augustine. It affirms the foundational truths upheld by the Thomistic tradition: that God is pure act (*actus purus*), *ipsum esse subsistens*, the One in whom all things live and move and have their being. It shares with Augustine the conviction that our restless hearts are not seeking abstraction but communion—that the City of God is not a metaphor but the real destiny of rational creatures, a structured participation in the infinite life of Truth, Love, and reciprocal knowing.

It upholds the classical doctrines of divine simplicity, immutability, and omnipotence without dilution or compromise. But it also proceeds to identify the precise metaphysical impasse where Thomism, in safeguarding these truths, withholds what it elsewhere demands: an intelligible explanation of how the eternal, unchanging act of God results in real, temporal effects.

Aquinas rightly insists that God does not change in creating, that the act by which God creates is identical to his essence, and that no real relation arises in God from creation. But when pressed to explain how this changeless act yields time-bound effects, Thomism turns to analogy.[1]

---

1. Thomas Aquinas teaches that God's act of creation is eternal, unchanging, and identical with his essence (*Summa Theologiae* I.9.1; I.19.1; I.28.1–3; I.45.2; I.46.1). He rightly insists that no change occurs in God when he creates, but, lacking a metaphysical account to explain how this is possible, he concludes that the relation of the world to God is real only from the creature's side (I.13.7, ad 2). In *Summa Theologiae* 1.13.5, Aquinas states, "Therefore, such names are said of God and of creatures in an analogical sense, that is, according to a proportion." This framework of analogical naming—neither

God is said to be the cause of creatures, not univocally but analogously. The relation between Creator and creature is real in the creature, but—so it is said—only a "relation of reason" exists in God. Yet this phrasing is misleading, for if God is Truth and reason is our sequential participation in Truth, then there is no "reason in God" as if he possessed it in part. What is called a relation of reason is, in truth, the finite intellect's way of perceiving God's changeless and complete act. The metaphysical grammar remains impeccably ordered, but the causal how disappears from view.

This book seeks to supply what that analogy defers. Without departing from the classical doctrines of divine simplicity and pure act, it offers a deeper articulation of divine causality grounded in metaphysical logic, namely, that the act of creation is not an extrinsic imposition upon being but the structured self-suppression of infinite actuality. This clarifies what has long been referred to as the "causal joint"—the necessary structure through which finite forms are potentiated from infinite Being without change, sequence, or composition in God.

The eternal act of God is thus not merely timeless and changeless—it is also, and necessarily, structured. In God, the Three share themselves completely, at an infinite rate of exchange, such that the Three are indeed One. This Infinite Reciprocal Motion (IRM)—this absolute stillness of infinite relational self-giving—decelerates into finite form, not by transition or transformation but by the deliberate sequestering of change from the divine side. Creation does not arise from any external prompting but through divine foresight—the deliberate sequestering of change from within infinite actuality—so that time may unfold without introducing division into the One who acts. This is not the realization of divine potential (for there is none) but the potentiation of structured finitude from plenary act.

This is not a rejection of Thomism. It is an attempt to bring it to completion at the point of its highest tension. If the Thomistic vision is true—and I believe it is—then it must be completed not by revision but by metaphysical integration. The gap between eternity and time cannot be resolved by analogy alone. It must be shown that there exists a

---

univocal nor purely equivocal—reflects Aquinas's conviction that all language about God is derived from created effects. However, this analogical structure also introduces a well-known tension in Thomistic theology, particularly when attempting to explain how an eternal, immutable act can give rise to a temporal and contingent world (see also, I.13.6–7).

structure in the Truth of Being per se by which the divine can cause and communicate finite being without introducing either division or finite motion into himself, who is the One changeless Act. This book proposes that such a structure exists. This is the causal joint of Divine Action.

For some, it is perhaps the greatest irony; for others, the greatest vindication; for Thomists, no surprise at all—that the very mystery that classical theism professes but does not explicate—the Holy Trinity—turns out to be the metaphysical key to the Creator-creature distinction.

This book proposes that the difference between divine and finite substance is precisely the difference between IRM and Finite Reciprocal Motion (FRM). The divine substance—the triune actuality of Father, Son, and Spirit—is not the revelation of symbolic analogy but the disclosure of a metaphysical necessity: the only form in which infinite actuality can be relational without division. In IRM, there is no sequence, no distinction of time or part, but only the perfect simultaneity of self-giving, self-receiving, and the act that unites them. This is the life of God.

Finite beings emerge through the structured deceleration of IRM. God remains fully present to creatures who are sequestered from him, not by distance or division but by the very structure that makes their finitude possible. They are neither identical with God nor autonomous from him but sustained by participation in his act. Finite beings emerge through structured deceleration of this IRM. They exist through FRM—structured relationality that unfolds in space, time, and causal order. Thus, the structure of finite being is not arbitrarily imposed but necessarily triadic, because it is a participation in the very actuality of divine life. The difference between God and creature is not a difference in genus or essence but a difference in mode—between fully actual triune relationality and its structured limitation in finite form.

It should not be surprising—though it may be unsettling to systems that privilege analogy over explanation—that the doctrine of the Trinity was the answer all along, not just theologically but metaphysically. The Creator-creature relationship, the act of creation, the nature of causality, and the structure of consciousness all trace back to this triune actuality. It is the singular Truth that upholds the rest.

Yet even this—this metaphysical structure of IRM and FRM, this intelligible account of divine action and created form—does not exhaust the mystery of God. It only deepens it. For what is unveiled here is not a replacement for mystery but the unveiling of its form, the logic by which mystery becomes meaningful without ceasing to be mystery.

God remains infinitely beyond comprehension, not because he is unintelligible but because his intelligibility is infinite. Every act of understanding that draws closer to the Truth does not diminish divine mystery; it expands our capacity to revere it. The more the soul sees, the more it knows it cannot see all—and yet, that what it does see is real, ordered, and meant to be understood.[2]

This work proceeds from the conviction that metaphysics must do justice to both truth and mystery. It must explain what can be explained—not by analogy alone, but by structure—while never pretending that comprehension contains God. The Trinity is not solved here. It is shown to be the structuring actuality from which all finite intelligibility proceeds, and to which all rational creatures are ordered in return.

---

2. "[H]oly mother, the Church, holds and teaches that God, the principle and end of all things, can be known with certainty from the created world by the natural light of human reason" (*Dei Filius*, ch. 2, Denz. 3004 / DS 3026). *The Infinite Reservoir* satisfies this dogmatic declaration by grounding the certainty of God's existence in a metaphysical deduction that begins, not with essences, ideal forms, or observed structures but with the impossibility of nonexistence. From this starting point—the reality of the finite knower—it constructs a participatory metaphysics (which may be called "metaphysical existentialism" or "participationism"), that avoids circularity and fulfills the Roman Catholic Church's requirement of certainty through reason.

Introduction

HOW TO READ THIS BOOK

This book is not a commentary, nor is it a compilation of opinions or a reaction to contemporary debates. It is a first-order metaphysical argument, constructed from the ground up, rooted in logic, and oriented toward reality. Its goal is not merely to inform but to awaken. The reader is invited not only to consider its claims but to enter into the structure of Truth itself.

The Infinite Reservoir proceeds from one foundational insight: nonexistence is impossible. From this follows the necessity of Being, the structure of divine action, and the logic by which finite creation arises from infinite actuality. Every chapter unfolds a specific consequence of this starting point, clarifying the nature of causality, personhood, truth, time, and return.

You are not asked to agree immediately, nor to suspend disbelief as though this were a work of theology or speculative mysticism. What you are asked to do is more difficult: to think rigorously, to follow the argument step by step, and to allow your preconceptions to be tested by the clarity of logic itself.

Some chapters are metaphysically dense. Others are poetically reflective. This is by design. The structure of the book mirrors the structure of the soul: intellect, will, and relation—each participating in Truth, the Good, and Love. Read accordingly.

- If you are a philosopher, pay attention to the argument's necessity.
- If you are a scientist, observe how the empirical fits within the metaphysical.

- If you are a theologian, note how mystery is not denied but deepened—given a form that does not diminish its transcendence.
- If you are a seeker, read with the patience of one whose soul already intuits that reality is not arbitrary.

There are no shortcuts. But everything here is ordered and intelligible. The logic is not obscure, only unfamiliar, because it is not built on modern assumptions but on the actual structure of Being.

In the end, the best way to read this book is to let it read you. If the soul awakens, even in part, to the reality it describes, the work will have done its job.

This is not just a book. It is a path—a metaphysical return to what has always been true.

My Prayer

Merciful Lord come unto me
And grant that I may gaze
Upon thy sweet enduring face.
There, in the presence of thy countenance
To gain repose.

This respite ne'er to wrest from me
The fiery passion of thy essential ecstasy
When faith doth share and man doth touch
What only God first knows.

Hear my prayer, Lord.
Immerse my soul in the radiance of thy holy Word
As yet unseen in the image of thy blessed integrity.
The granting of my prayer to teach thy undeserving child
And all thou choosest through him to reach
The Power, the Passion, and the Presence there found
In the peaceful beauty of the Lord.

I die.
Each time a creature turns from thee
I die, it seems again.
And grief floods o'er my heart
As though my child, not thine alone
Didst not, my face, recall.

That soul deep hellish pain I spurn.
O'er that I'd sooner choose the stake
And gladly would I burn
If in my burning I could bring that soul to thee
For whom my soul does yearn.

There is no life in me, save thee.
Save thee?
No. No, t'was thee,
Who, in that sacrifice I ne'er couldst make,
Didst cross Hell's gate
To consecrate my soul.

—Kevin Mc Guinness

1

Establishing the Necessity of Being Per Se

PART ONE: THE FUNDAMENTAL QUESTIONS

The Unavoidable Question of Existence

BEFORE ANYTHING ELSE CAN be asked or known, one question must be faced.

Why is there existence rather than nonexistence?[1]

This is not a scientific question, nor merely a philosophical curiosity—it concerns the foundational *actuality* (the infinite, unchanging foundation of existence)[2] without which neither *reality* (the field of existing things as we encounter them) nor inquiry would be possible.

---

1. Though perhaps most famously posed by Leibniz in *Principles of Nature and of Grace* (in *Monadology*, 415) as the question "Why is there something rather than nothing?" the more precise formulation—*Why is there existence rather than nonexistence?*—more clearly expresses the foundational insight of metaphysics. This insight was already intimated by Parmenides of Elea and has echoed, in some form, through the work of every thinker who has seriously contemplated the nature of existence. See Kirk et al., eds., *Presocratic Philosophers*, 239–62.

2. Cf. Aquinas, *Summa contra Gentiles*, I.16. Aquinas argues that in God there is no potentiality whatsoever since anything that could potentially be could also potentially not be. As the first cause and necessary being, God must be pure actuality. While the present work arrives at a similar conclusion through a distinct metaphysical logic grounded in the impossibility of nonexistence, the affirmation of God as wholly actual

Science describes the physical mechanisms of becoming but not the necessity of *Being*. Philosophy explores the structure of *reality* but rarely confronts the impossibility of absolute nonexistence. Theology begins with what must be.

To understand anything about *reality*, we must first understand why *reality* exists at all rather than nonexistence. Before the subjects of logic, science, or theology can even arise, one question must be answered:

Can nonexistence ever be possible?

This chapter introduces the argument from nonexistence, showing that Nonexistence per se is logically impossible. From this, it follows that *Being per se*—not a being, not a thing but *existence itself*—must necessarily exist.

This is not merely a matter of metaphysical speculation; it is the foundation upon which all logic, science, and theology must stand.

If we are to understand anything about *reality*, we must first understand why *reality* is in the first place. And that inquiry begins here.

1. Why Does Anything Exist at All?

Throughout history, philosophers and scientists have sought to understand why any*thing* exists at all. Science explains how particular *things* come to be, but the deeper questions remain:

- Could there ever have been absolute nonexistence—a state in which not only things, but even the possibility of things—was absent?
- If absolute nonexistence is impossible, then does *existence itself* follow necessarily?
- Is there a necessary foundation of being that cannot fail to exist?

These are not abstract puzzles but fundamental questions about *reality*. If existing things exist now, then either they exist necessarily or they have been brought into existence by what is necessary—*Being itself*.

Is *Being itself* a thing, or is it something else entirely?

This inquiry is not merely an intellectual exercise—it underlies everything we experience, think, or do. *Reality*, as we observe it, consists of things that change, decay, and cease to exist. Yet beneath all change, we must ask: What is the foundation of all that exists?

(*actus purus*) resonates with this classical formulation.

Language at the Threshold of Being

Human language is naturally structured to describe finite beings: things with limits, properties, distinctions, and relations. It assumes categories, boundaries, and differentiation because it is born from and for finite *participation* in *Being*.

Yet *Being per se*—the infinite *actuality* that necessarily is—does not fit within any category or boundary. It is not a thing among things, nor a being among beings, but the source of all thingness and being. Indeed, *Being per se*—for lack of words that can embrace the infinite—*is not a being or thing at all*.

At the threshold of pure *Being*, language strains. If it is not guided by strict logical necessity, it risks either collapsing into silence (fearing misrepresentation) or falsely projecting creaturely structures onto what transcends all limitation.

This work proceeds by strict logic: by first establishing the impossibility of absolute nonexistence and then deducing the necessary structure of *Being per se* without distorting it through finite categories. Thus, while language remains an imperfect instrument, its use here, as will soon become clear, is governed by the logic that proceeds from Being per se—not by the habits of creaturely description.

In this way, *The Infinite Reservoir* honors the metaphysical insight that Being per se—pure actuality—infinitely exceeds beings while preserving the intelligibility necessary for true philosophy, theological interpretation, and scientific inquiry to proceed.[3]

---

3. Feser, *Five Proofs*, 17–68. While Feser rightly defends the Thomistic principle that God is not a being among beings but pure actuality, the traditional framework often retains linguistic and conceptual habits that risk obscuring the infinite difference between Being and beings. This work seeks to complete the classical defense of divine actuality by grounding it in the pure logical necessity of Being per se, thereby avoiding misinterpretation as either an anthropomorphic collapse or an apophatic retreat. See also Hart, *Experience of God*, 84–97. Hart has correctly emphasized the infinite ontological difference between Being and beings, critiquing systems that reduce divine actuality to a category among finite existents. This work acknowledges and affirms Hart's insight while supplying the rigorous logical foundation often absent in modern apophatic approaches, ensuring that the transcendence of Being is not preserved by negation alone but established by pure metaphysical necessity.

2. Is Absolute Nonexistence Possible?

It is common to assume that absolute nonexistence is possible. We can imagine an empty void, a universe that never was, or even the absence of everything. However, these are not true nonexistence but mental constructs that still contain aspects of being:

- What we call "empty space" or "the void" is not nonexistence; it presupposes extension, dimensionality, and relational structure.
- Even the concept of nothingness exists in our minds; it is itself a content of thought and not true nonexistence.

But what if we go further and ask: Could there be existence without things—no space, no time, no change, no field of *reality* at all? This question forces distinctions that are often overlooked:

- Absolute nonexistence is impossible.
- Absolute nothingness must be considered.

At first, the existence of absolute nothingness (no-thingness) may seem paradoxical, but the confusion arises from failing to distinguish nonexistence per se from nothingness per se.

- *Nonexistence per se* refers to *the absence of all being and all possibility of being.* But to be absent would already assume some reference to being.

Therefore, absolute nonexistence is impossible because it would have to be—in order to not be.

- *Nothingness per se* is absolute no-thingness. It is not nonexistence but rather the necessary ground of all existing things. It is not the lack of *Being* but the absence of finitude (finite things).

This distinction is crucial: finite *reality* does not stand in contrast to absolute nothingness but emerges as its structured expression. Absolute nothingness is not a mere negation of being; it is the foundation that potentiates structured *reality*. Finite, contingent beings emerge not from nonexistence, but from nothingness as the structured foundation of all existing things—a clarification of what theology has traditionally called *creatio ex nihilo*.

Therefore, far from being an empty void or a negation, absolute nothingness is what structures *reality* in the first place. Therefore, its nature and the question of its necessity must be examined more deeply, as we will fully develop next in "The Argument from Nonexistence."

3. *The Argument from Nonexistence*

Because nonexistence per se is impossible, existence per se must be—not as a thing, but as the necessary foundation of all things. However, this does not mean that contingent things—that is, things that depend on something else for their existence—must have always existed. Instead, it means that there must be a necessary foundation that cannot fail to be—identified in classical theology as pure act,[4] and, as revealed in Exod 3:14 as the "I Am,"[5] the metaphysical ground of all that is. This reasoning is formalized as follows in the *stepwise logical proof of necessary Being per se*:

Premise 1: Nonexistence per se is not a real state—it is a meaningless placeholder, an abstraction that does not correspond to anything actual.

Premise 2: Nonexistence per se cannot have properties, characteristics, or the capacity to produce anything.

Premise 3: If something possesses even the potential to exist, then it is not nonexistence per se.

Conclusion: Since nonexistence per se is impossible, then *Being per se* must be necessary—not as an object or thing, but as the absolute foundation of all *reality*.

This leads to a foundational principle: *something must exist necessarily, but this necessity is not the necessity of a thing*. Rather, it is the necessity of *Being per se*—pure *actuality* that does not arise, does not transform, and is not *contingent*. It is not an entity within existence; it is *existence itself*.

---

4. See Aquinas, *Summa Theologiae*, I, q. 3, art. 2, where he affirms that God is *actus purus*—pure actuality without potentiality.

5. See Exod 3:14: "This is what you shall say to the sons of Israel: 'I AM has sent me to you.'" This declaration, long interpreted in classical theology as identifying God with necessary being, grounds the metaphysical insight that God is *actus purus*—the self-sufficient actuality who cannot not be. See Aquinas, *Summa Theologiae*; Augustine, *De Trinitate*; Feser, *Five Proofs*; Hart, *Experience of God*.

Being per se is not a mere abstract principle; it is the absolute, self-sufficient *actuality* in which all things participate, and which itself is neither dependent nor derived. This is what is meant by God—not a being among beings, but the very act of *existence itself*.

4. What Kind of Existence Must Be Necessary?

Having established that something must exist necessarily, we must now ask: What must this necessary *actuality* be like?

- Can it be finite?
    - No, because finite things depend on something outside themselves.
- Can it be changing?
    - No, because change requires a prior state of non-actualization.
- Can it be *contingent*?
    - No, because contingency implies a cause beyond itself.

Thus, the necessary foundation of existence must be infinite, unchanging, and self-sufficient. It is not a thing—it is *Being per se*; pure *actuality* upon which all else depends.

This is what we mean by *Being per se—existence itself*.

5. Being Per Se as the Foundation of All Reality

Now that we have established that nonexistence per se is impossible and that *Being per se* must necessarily exist, we are compelled to take a further step.

What is the nature of this infinite *actuality*?

Being per se is not a thing, not a composite entity, not a product of causality. Yet if *Being per se* necessarily is, it cannot be wholly without structure. Its *actuality* must reveal certain necessary characteristics—features without which it would not be the self-sufficient source of all else.

We can thus proceed by strict deduction, unfolding what must pertain to *Being per se* without imposing any finite or creaturely limitations upon it. These necessary characteristics are as follows:

- It is infinite—it has no external limits because there is no existence outside of it.
- It is fully actual—it does not transition from possibility or potential to *actuality*; it is pure *actuality*.
- It is uncaused—since it is necessary, it is not produced.
- It is the source of all *contingent* things—anything that changes or depends on something else must ultimately derive from *Being per se*.

Being per se is not a set of principles or abstract truths but the absolute, self-sufficient *actuality* in which finite *reality* exists through structured *participation*.

6. Moving Forward: The Necessity of Structured Emergence

Since *Being per se* necessarily exists and absolute nonexistence is logically impossible, then what follows must also be necessary: that finite things do not emerge from nonexistence, nor from change within infinite *Being*, but through a particular *structured act*.

Part Two now examines this necessity. It explores how the emergence of finite *reality* requires, not just an ontological source but a metaphysical structure—one that allows *participation* without division and finitude without collapse. This is the logic of the *causal joint*.

PART TWO: THE NECESSITY OF A CAUSAL JOINT

The Origin of the Finite

Now that we have established the necessity of *Being per se* as the uncaused, infinite foundation of all *reality*, we must now ask:

How do finite, changing things emerge from the infinite, *Being per se*?

This is a crucial question because since *Being per se* is infinite, unchanging, and fully *actual*, then it lacks nothing. But if it lacks nothing: How can there be finite things that are limited and dependent? To answer this, we must demonstrate why finite *reality* requires a structured mechanism—what we call the *causal joint*—by which the finite is selected and sustained within the infinite.

1. Why Finite Reality Cannot Emerge by Accident or Necessity Alone

Many assume that if *Being per se* necessarily exists, then finite things must follow automatically. But this is a misunderstanding.

- If finite things arose from necessity, then Being per se would be forced to produce them, implying a lack of self-sufficiency.
- If finite things arose by accident, it would mean randomness exists within infinite actuality, contradicting its perfect actuality.

Thus, because neither necessity alone nor randomness can explain the existence of finite *reality*, we arrive at a critical principle:

The existence of finite things requires an intentional structuring—an act of selection—the deliberate choice of infinite *actuality*.

This brings us to the *causal joint*—a structured metaphysical process by which the finite is *potentiated* from the infinite.

2. The Necessity of a Causal Joint

Since *Being per se* is fully *actual* and unchanging, it does not transition or evolve.

But how, then, can finite *reality* arise?

Finite *reality* does not arise through transformation, but through structuring—a selective process that allows finitude to emerge without altering infinite *actuality*. This structured process is what has been called the *causal joint* of divine action—yet as we will see, it is not merely a mechanism, but the very foundation of all finite *participation* in *Being*.[6]

Because the finite does not emerge automatically but must be structured, we must now ask: What structured process allows finite, changing *reality* to emerge from infinite, unchanging *Being per se*?

This process must satisfy three conditions:

1. It cannot change the infinite. *Being per se* remains fully *actual* and does not transform into something else.

---

6. In theological contexts, Robert John Russell employed the term in discussions of divine action, asking how God's causality might interface with physical causality. See Russell, *Chaos and Complexity*. Here, however, the term is redeployed in a deeper metaphysical sense, describing the necessary structured potentiation through which infinite actuality sustains finite existence without division or transformation.

2. It must allow for structured selection. The finite does not emerge arbitrarily—it is structured according to a rational, intelligible order.
3. It must allow finite things to be distinct from the infinite. The finite does not become infinite, nor does the infinite dissolve into finitude.

The only process that satisfies these conditions is *deceleration* within infinite *actuality*—a structured selection that does not change the infinite but actively *potentiates* finitude within it.

But this raises important questions. What is there to *decelerate*? And, *Being per se* is already infinite and unchanging, so, how can anything be selected or structured within it?

The answer to these questions lies in the nature of infinite *actuality* itself. While the infinite does not change, it does not exclude *structured potentiation*. To understand this *deceleration*, we must first grasp the concept of *infinite reciprocal motion*, which will be explored in the next chapter. There, it will become clear that the *deceleration of infinite reciprocal motion*—occasionally abbreviated in this work as *Deceleration*—does not transform *Being per se* into something else, nor does it introduce a gap or an external cause. Instead, it is the self-suppression of the infinite—an intentional structuring that allows for the emergence of finite *reality* without altering or diminishing the infinite.

3. Being Per Se as the Perfectly Actual Potentiator

Thomistic theology describes God as pure act—that is, as fully actual and devoid of all potentiality.[7] While this formulation rightly establishes God as self-sufficient and immutable, it does not fully explain how finite *reality* emerges from infinite *actuality* without implying an unnecessary transition, division, or external causation. By contrast, in the present work, God is understood instead as the perfectly *actual potentiator*, whose very nature *potentiates* structured finitude through self-suppression, without any change or loss within infinite *Being itself*.

Rather than merely actualizing potential within creation, *Being per se* is best understood as the perfectly *actual potentiator*—not a being that

---

7. Aquinas, *Summa Theologiae*, I, q. 3, art. 1; cf. Aquinas, *On Being and Essence*, 51–59. Classical theism, especially in Aquinas, affirms that God is *actus purus*—pure actuality without potentiality. This work builds upon that foundation by clarifying how infinite actuality potentiates finite structure without transition, division, or external causation.

brings forth realities by externalizing its own *actuality* but one whose very nature *potentiates* structured finitude through self-suppression.

This is not a movement from *potentiality* to *actuality* (which would imply deficiency), but rather a movement from *actuality* to *structured potentiality*—a deliberate, self-structuring expression of infinite *actuality* that allows for finite differentiation without diminishing the infinite.

Thus:

- *Being per se* is not a passive ground of possibility but an active *potentiator*—structuring finitude rather than actualizing unrealized potential.
- The finite does not emerge from a lack within the infinite, nor from mere possibility but as a *structured limitation* within infinite *actuality*.
- This self-expression does not transform infinite *actuality* but structures a relation within it, ensuring finitude remains distinct yet dependent.

Hence, *Being per se* is the perfectly *actual* potentiator. Its self-expression does not transition from potentiality to *actuality* but instead selects limitation from infinite *actuality*. In doing so, it sustains finite *reality* as a structured participatory relationship without diminishing or altering its own infinite *actuality*.

4. Moving Forward: The Structure of Motion in the Act of Creation

Being per se must exist necessarily, and absolute nonexistence is logically impossible. Yet because *Being* is infinite, unchanging, and lacks nothing, it cannot change, divide, or become other than itself.

Still, the world exists—ordered, limited, and in motion.

How, then, can motion emerge from what is eternally actual?

To answer this, chapter 2 begins by examining the nature of motion, not as a change within *Being* but as a structured act by which *Being* gives rise to relation, distinction, and the *form* of the world.

2

The Emergence of Motion, Time, and Space

PART ONE: THE NECESSITY OF MOTION IN INFINITE ACTUALITY

From the Stillness of Being Per Se to the Commotion of Finite Reality

Having established that Being per se is the perfectly actual potentiator, we must now confront an apparent paradox: How can something unchanging be self-expressive?

Since Being per se is fully actual and lacks nothing, its self-expression cannot involve deficiency, growth, or change. This means its self-expression must be structured in a way that allows for relationality without implying contingency or transformation of Being itself. The resolution of this paradox lies in the necessity of motion—not motion as we experience it in time and space but a fundamental, infinite relationality.

We have established the following:

- Being per se exists necessarily and cannot be reduced to potentiality or contingency.
- Finite reality does not emerge automatically but must be a structured selection by infinite actuality.

- Being per se is the perfectly actual *potentiator* whose self-expression *potentiates* structured finitude without altering its own infinite actuality.

So, we must now ask: What is the nature of this self-expression? How does Being per se structure the transition from infinite actuality to finite being? To answer these questions, we must examine the necessity of motion within infinite actuality and its role in structuring finite reality.

1. The Necessity of Motion in Infinite Actuality

At first, it may seem that motion is not possible within Being per se because motion is typically understood as:

- Change over time
- Movement from one place to another
- A process requiring energy

Since Being per se is unchanging, indivisible, and independent of energy, it seems contradictory to say that motion can exist within it.

However, if Being per se had no motion whatsoever, it would imply a kind of static or frozen existence, which is not relationality but mere inertness. But we have already established that Being per se must be relational—it must be self-expressive while remaining unchanging. Therefore, the only kind of motion that can exist in infinite actuality must be:

- Fully actual, requiring no external cause
- Not a process, but an eternal, self-contained relational state
- Not dependent on time, space, or energy but intrinsic to the structure of Being itself

Infinite reciprocal motion (IRM) is the only possible source of the structured self-expression of Being per se. Without it, there would be no *structured relationality*, no foundation for differentiation, and no means for finite reality to emerge.

Table 2.1. Why Infinite Reciprocal Motion Is Unique

This table compares types of motion to demonstrate why only infinite reciprocal motion can structure finite relationality without requiring space, time, or energy.

Type of Motion	Requires Time?	Requires Space?	Requires Energy?	Possible in the Infinite?
Linear motion	Yes	Yes	Yes	No (requires space and time)
Rotational motion	Yes	Yes	Yes	No (requires spatial dimensions)
Vibrational motion	Yes	Yes	Yes	No (requires frequency over time)
Infinite reciprocal motion	No	No	No	Yes (fully actual, non-sequential)

2. Infinite Reciprocal Motion: Motion That Is Stillness

Rather than thinking of motion in the conventional sense, we must recognize that in Being per se, motion is not a process but an eternally actual relationality. It is not *movement* in the sense of change or transition but rather the structure of absolute relationality.

This means:

- *IRM* does not occur in a sequence but is fully actual as an eternal relational state.
- *IRM* does not require an external mover—it is self-existent.
- *IRM* is not a transition from one state to another but a perfect, unchanging exchange.

This is IRM—the necessary *form* of relational existence in the infinite.

Key Properties of IRM include:

- Unchanging—there is no before or after, only the eternal now.
- Perfectly unified—there are no distinct parts to move from one state to another.

- Indistinguishable from stillness—since motion is fully actual and non-sequential, no change occurs.

Thus, IRM is simultaneously absolute unity and perfect exchange.

3. The Triune Structure of Infinite Reciprocal Motion

Since motion is relational, it cannot consist of just one thing moving. Instead, motion must be structured as a relational unity. This means that all motion, even within infinite actuality, must necessarily involve three components:

1. A mover (that initiates motion)
2. A moved (that receives motion)
3. A medium of exchange (that unites the mover and the moved)

This is the triune necessity of *IRM*.

Thus, motion within Being per se is not arbitrary—it is necessarily structured in a triune relation.

- This triune structure is not imposed externally but is intrinsic to the nature of pure relationality.
- It is the only way that infinite actuality can express itself while remaining fully actual.

For motion to be relational without requiring change, it must be a structured triunity. This is because relationality presupposes differentiation—something given, something received, and a structure that unites them. This triune structure is not an imposed framework but an intrinsic feature of infinite actuality itself.

This establishes that Being per se must be structured relationally and as a triunity, and this structure is the foundation for all finite reality.

4. The Image and Likeness as Structural Participation

Because all finite reality exists by structured *participation* in infinite actuality, the triune relationality of Being per se must be reflected, in finite terms, as triadic relational structure. This is not an optional correspondence or imposed metaphor—it is the only possible *form* by which finite relationality can mirror the infinite without contradiction.

This triadic relational structure is not an arbitrary feature of finite reality but the necessary *form* of *participation* in the infinite. It reflects, in finite terms, the infinite triune relationality of Being itself. The unity, distinction, and relationality observed in all intelligible structure—especially in the human being—bear witness to this.

In theological terms, the human being is made in the image and likeness of God—not merely by moral resemblance but through structured *participation* in Truth itself and thus in the very order of Being.[1] The image is the structural *form*—intellect, will, and relational openness—while the likeness is the degree to which that structure is conformed to the source it reflects. Far from being a poetic metaphor, this image and likeness is the only possible *form* by which finite being can mirror the infinite without collapsing into contradiction.

5. The Emergence of Finitude Through Deceleration

Because *deceleration of infinite reciprocal motion* through the *causal joint* is the necessary self-expression of Being per se, we must now ask: How does finite motion, which is bound by time, space, and energy, emerge from infinite actuality?

The answer lies in the structured process by which finite reciprocal motion emerges as triadic structure—a decelerated expression of the triune relationality of infinite actuality, without alteration of that actuality.[2] Through this process the following occurs:

---

1. See Gen 1:26–27. On the *imago Dei* as rational participation in divine order, see Aquinas, *Summa Theologiae*, I, q. 93, art. 4.

2. Traditional appeals to divine *plenitude* or metaphysical *overflow* attempt to explain the emergence of creation as a consequence of divine fullness. While historically influential, these concepts introduce subtle but decisive contradictions that violate the simplicity of *Being per se*. To speak of *plenitude* implies stored or hidden actuality—as though God contains parts, powers, or potential awaiting release. To speak of *overflow* implies internal pressure or reactive diffusion. Even the notion of *latent potential* smuggles in composition, contingency, or passivity—all of which contradict the indivisible, purely actual nature of infinite Being.

In the metaphysical framework presented here, *Being per se* does not create by unfolding or discharging a surplus. It gives rise to finitude through the structured deceleration of infinite reciprocal motion—a self-suppressing act that selects limitation without change, loss, or division. Finitude is not released from fullness; it is *potentiated* as structured participation in relational actuality.

To invoke plenitude as the cause of creation is no more coherent than to speak of three Gods instead of the one God who is the singular Triune act. The error is not theological rebellion but metaphysical confusion—an error that the logic of infinite reciprocal motion, and its decelerated expression, corrects.

- *Finite reciprocal motion* is *potentiated* as a structured *participation in infinite reciprocal motion*, rather than a transformation of it. In other words, the infinite gives existence; we participate by receiving what is given.
- The triune structure of infinite actuality is expressed in finite relationality, maintaining the fundamental relational unity of Being per se.
- The absolute unity of Being per se allows for *structured differentiation* as finitude while remaining undiminished and unchanged.

6. Moving Forward: The Potentiation of Finite Motion

Because motion within finite reality is structured, it must be sustained—not by force or collision, but by the ordered limitation that gives rise to distinction and duration. The universe is not a passive result of infinite power, but a structured expression of that power through relation and restraint.

Part Two now turns to this structure more precisely. It examines how the *causal joint potentiates* finite motion through *Deceleration* and *negative pressure*—not as interruptions in Being, but as the very logic by which time, energy, and space are made coherent in limitation.

PART TWO: THE DECELERATION OF INFINITE RECIPROCAL MOTION

The Transition from Infinite Reciprocal Motion to Finite Reality

Having established that IRM is the only possible *form* of motion within infinite actuality, we now turn to the structured transition that gives rise to finite motion and the emergence of time, space, and energy as ordered consequences.

Since Being per se is fully actual and lacks nothing, its self-expression cannot involve deficiency, growth, or transformation. This means that the emergence of finite reality must be structured in a way that allows for relational differentiation without contingency or change within infinite actuality.

Thus, the necessity of motion arises, not as we experience it in time and space but as the fundamental relational structure of infinite actuality.

This relationality is neither imposed nor derived but is intrinsic to Being per se, manifesting as:

- The self-knowing actuality of the Knower
- The self-expressed actuality of the Known
- The perfect relational act of Knowing

Within infinite actuality, these remain perfectly one, but within *structured limitation*, they differentiate into the triadic structure of finite motion:

1. Mover
2. Moved
3. Medium of Exchange[3]

1. The Necessity of Structured Selection: Deceleration of Infinite Reciprocal Motion

Since finite reality does not emerge automatically, it must be a structured selection from infinite actuality—*potentiated* rather than *actualized*. This structured selection is accomplished by *deceleration from infinite reciprocal motion* as follows:

- Infinite reciprocal motion remains infinite; therefore, it may express its structure by self-limitation—through deceleration, which can neither add to nor subtract from its infinite actuality. In this way, finitude is potentiated as structured limitation.[4]

---

3. The triadic structure of infinite actuality—Knower, Known, and Knowing—bears historical resonance with classical Trinitarian theology, particularly in Augustine's *De Trinitate*, bk. X–XV:291–525 and in the metaphysical formulations of Aquinas, *Summa Theologiae*, I, q. 27–28. However, the structure presented here is not analogical but logically derived from the impossibility of nonexistence and the relational unity of infinite Being. The finite triad of Mover, Moved, and Medium of Exchange arises not as an imposed schema but as the decelerated participation of finite reality in that infinite structure. Nonetheless, the triune structure of God deduced here by metaphysical necessity and that revealed to Augustine through theological reflection ultimately converge—as one might expect of a God who hides neither from reason nor from faith.

4. At first glance, it may seem contradictory to say that the infinite One becomes visible as a relational Three. But in this metaphysical system, the infinite is not made of parts or powers. It is One because it is perfectly actual—indivisible, unchanging, and without potential. Yet it is not static: it is infinite reciprocal motion, a pure act of relation.

- This *potentiation* does not transform infinite actuality but instead structures a relational differentiation that manifests as finite motion.
- Time, space, and energy emerge as structured conditions of this differentiation, *sustaining* finitude while preserving relational unity within infinite actuality.

Therefore, the transition from infinite relationality to finite existence is not a rupture or transformation, but a structured *potentiation*—one that allows finite reality to emerge as a distinct yet dependent *participation* within the One.

2. Deceleration: The Structured Selection of Finite Motion

Deceleration of infinite reciprocal motion is not a slowing down of infinite actuality, nor does it imply a transformation of the infinite into the finite. Instead, *Deceleration* is the structuring process that allows for finite reality to emerge within infinite actuality without disrupting its unity.

Understanding Deceleration: The Emergence of Structured Differentiation

In infinite actuality, reciprocal motion occurs without sequence or separation—it is a perfectly unified, self-sustained relational structure in which all differentiation is fully actualized in perfect simultaneity. However, for finite reality to exist, relational exchanges must be *decelerated*, structured within limits of time, space, and energy and unfolding sequentially rather than being perfectly simultaneous.

Deceleration is the selection of limitation within infinite actuality, allowing for this *structured differentiation* to emerge. This means:

- IRM remains fully actual—it is neither diminished nor interrupted but is selectively potentiated as finite structure.

When this act is decelerated—that is, when it is expressed under limitation as finite reciprocal motion—its relational structure becomes visible as a triad. This is not a division, nor an emanation, nor three beings. It is the structured participation of finitude in the logic of relation that reveals what already is the infinite. In this sense, the One becomes known as Three not by changing, but by being received under limitation. As light becomes color when passed through a prism, so the invisible One becomes visible—not by fragmentation, but by relational self-limitation.

It is really Three, actually One.

- The limited existence given in finite reciprocal motion is sequestered from Being per se—not as a separated part but as a structured expression of infinite relation under limitation.
- This structured participation manifests as time, space, and energy—not as separate things but as the necessary conditions that allow finitude to persist.

Thus, *Deceleration* is the necessary structuring of potentiation that enables finite motion to exist while ensuring that infinite actuality remains unchanged. It does not create something external to the infinite but establishes an ordered relational differentiation that sustains finitude within it.

Deceleration and the Bubble Analogy

To understand how *Deceleration* structures finite reality within infinite actuality, imagine a bubble forming—not in space, but as a *structured differentiation* within the One itself.

The One as Infinite Reciprocal Motion

Infinite actuality (Being per se) is not extended through space, composed of parts, or dependent on anything outside itself for definition or existence. It is a perfect, undivided singularity, yet it can be conceptualized as an infinite triune relationality—mover, moved, and medium of exchange—in perfect *IRM*.

This infinite motion is not motion through space or time; rather, it is pure relational exchange occurring with perfect simultaneity—such that there is no distinction between the three. Because *IRM* is infinitely fast, perfectly one, and all-encompassing, the relational structure remains perfectly unified. This means:

- There is no dimensional separation within the infinite.
- There is no sequence—all relations occur in infinite simultaneity, beyond temporal distinction.
- There is no outside—Being per se is not a spatial entity.

The Emergence of the Bubble: The Selection of Limitation

Now, imagine that within this undivided relational unity, a structured deceleration occurs. This does not mean that something enters or exits pure actuality. Rather, pure actuality expresses its triune essence—triadically and without subtraction—not by stopping or diminishing but by deliberately slowing its infinite reciprocal motion into a finite, sequential mode of relational exchange, thereby giving rise to distinctly finite substance.

A mover, a moved, and a medium of exchange become distinct; physical dimensions manifest, and the expanding bubble of finite relationality emerges. This structured differentiation arises within the horizon of divine actuality, though not by alteration or composition of divine substance. Rather, it is a distinct, finite substance brought forth through a deliberate self-delimiting act of deceleration: the slowing of infinite reciprocal motion into structured relational form. It does not divide or alter the infinite, but it gives rise to a finite relational structure that is truly created *ex nihilo*—distinct in mode, structure, and substance from the Creator. This emergence is not an external object positioned alongside God but a metaphysically bounded yet physically unbounded expansion within divine actuality, though not by alteration or composition of divine substance: a bubble of finite substance suspended within the infinite by structured participation, not identity.

Within this expanding bubble of finitude is the following:

- The perfect simultaneity of infinite reciprocal motion breaks down into sequential interactions.
- What was once instantaneous exchange now requires time.
- What was once pure relational unity now unfolds within structured differentiation.

This is the emergence of finite reality—existing within infinite actuality, yet as a *structured limitation* that cannot return to the infinite by its own power (analogy is included in this callout to assist the reader, such are not literal metaphysical claims).

3. Deceleration as the Source of Time, Space, and Energy

Since *Deceleration* is the process that structures finite reality, it must introduce:

- Time—the ordering of motion into sequences
- Space—the structuring of relationality into distinct locations
- Energy—the introduction of resistance and limitation, allowing for measurable motion

Each of these emerges as a *structured limitation* of infinite actuality.

A. Time: The Ordering of Finite Motion

Time is not fundamental to Being per se because:

- In infinite actuality, there is no sequence—only the eternal now.
- *Deceleration* allows for a subset of motion to be structured sequentially, introducing a before and after, which we experience as time.
- This *structured limitation* does not change infinite actuality but allows for finite beings to experience motion within ordered sequences.

Thus, time is a *structured limitation* within which finite things move and change.

B. Space: The Structuring of Relationality

Space is not a separate container for reality because:

- In infinite actuality, there is no distance—everything is fully actual as a single unity.
- *Deceleration* allows relationality to be structured with distinction and separation, which we experience as space.
- Space is therefore not an independent reality but a necessary relational structure within which finite beings interact.

Thus, space is a structured consequence of how finite beings participate in relationality.

C. Energy: The Introduction of Resistance and Limitation

In infinite actuality, motion is instantaneous and total—there is no resistance, and therefore no need for energy. As infinite reciprocal motion is decelerated into finite motion, structured resistance emerges, and energy becomes the measurable expression of that resistance.

This resistance allows for:

- The transfer of motion between entities
- The conservation of momentum in dynamic systems
- The laws of causality that govern all finite interactions

Thus, energy is the necessary *structured limitation* that enables finite beings to engage in motion, causality, and change.

Table 2.2. How Deceleration Structures the Universe
This table shows how motion, time, space, and energy emerge as structured limitations of infinite actuality through deceleration.

Aspect of Reality	Infinite Actuality	Finite Reality (Through Deceleration)
Motion	Infinite reciprocal motion (instantaneous, relational, non-sequential)	Finite motion (sequential, directional, measurable)
Time	Eternal now (no past or future)	Structured progression (before and after)
Space	Non-local unity	Structured relationality (distinct locations)
Energy	Omnipotence (no resistance)	Structured limitation (interaction, causality, resistance)

4. The One-Way Separation Between Infinite and Finite

The boundary between the infinite and the finite is also one-way barrier:

- Infinite actuality remains undiminished and unaltered by the emergence of finitude.
- The finite is structured within the infinite but cannot reintegrate with pure actuality by its own power.

Thus, *Deceleration* does not generate something external to infinite actuality but structures finitude as a relational differentiation—one that, while maintaining a distinct mode of existence, remains incapable of reintegration by its own power yet is continuously sustained by its ever-present source as an ordered *participation* within the One.

5. The Necessity of Negative Pressure in Deceleration

A. What Is Negative Pressure?

Before defining *negative pressure* in the metaphysical sense, it is important to clarify its relation to physical phenomena. In modern physics, "negative pressure" describes tensile forces—relational structures that resist collapse or contraction, such as the expansive force attributed to dark energy or the tensile cohesion of fluids under stress. However, these physical and pseudo-physical expressions are not the foundation of the concept but its consequence. Here, *negative pressure* is understood as the metaphysical cause that makes such *structured relationality* possible at all. It is the act by which infinite actuality self-suppresses—*sustaining* finite relational structures without collapse into undifferentiated unity. Thus, while physical manifestations of *negative pressure* (in cosmology, material science, and fluid dynamics) echo this logic, the primary reality is metaphysical: *negative pressure* is the continuous act of relational structuring within Being per se that potentiates and sustains finite existence.

In physics, *negative pressure* refers to a tension or pulling force directed inward, rather than outward. But since there are no boundaries to space, the net effect of this inward tension is to stretch space, increasing the distance between the structures embedded within it. For example, dark energy is said to exert *negative pressure*, causing the accelerated expansion of space; and water under tensile stress exhibits *negative pressure* when stretched without breaking. In both cases, *negative pressure* is a counterintuitive but measurable phenomenon—not a vacuum, nor a mere absence, but a structured relational force resisting collapse or compression. Here, the term *negative pressure* is adapted and elevated to its metaphysical meaning—it describes the structured act by which infinite actuality restrains or self-suppresses, allowing finite beings to persist in distinct existence without collapsing back into the undifferentiated unity of infinite Being. It is important to recognize that *negative pressure* arises necessarily as the effect of *deceleration from infinite reciprocal motion*. *Deceleration* structures finite relational limitation; *negative pressure* sustains the persistence of that structure. The causal priority is clear: *Deceleration* precedes and necessitates *negative pressure*, not the other way around.

Negative pressure, in this metaphysical sense, is not an external force imposed on reality.

It is an intrinsic act of *structured limitation*—a necessary consequence of divine self-suppression within infinite actuality—establishing and maintaining the distinction between finite beings and the infinite.

Upon the *deceleration of infinite reciprocal motion, negative pressure* creates a structured boundary:

- It prevents finite motion from dissolving into instantaneous actuality.
- It sustains the relational tension necessary for finite beings to exist with ordered time, space, and causal interaction.
- It preserves differentiation, ensuring that finite beings retain their distinct identities without either collapsing into undifferentiated being or dispersing into formless potentiality.

Thus, *negative pressure* is the metaphysical tension by which infinite actuality restrains itself without division, *sustaining* structured finitude without loss or separation from the One. It is the *sustaining* act of relational distinction—an act of continuous self-suppression for the sake of finite *participation*.

B. How Negative Pressure Sustains Finitude

Within the *structured differentiation* of finitude, *negative pressure* ensures the following:

- Expansion—finite space remains structured rather than collapsing back into the unity of infinite actuality
- Differentiation—finite entities retain distinctness rather than dissolving into an undifferentiated whole
- Continuity—sequential motion is sustained within time rather than reverting to the simultaneity of infinite actuality

Thus, *negative pressure* is not a force of opposition but the *sustaining* condition of finitude. It ensures that structured reality does not arise arbitrarily but as a necessary, ordered *participation* within infinite actuality, allowing for the persistence of motion, relational distinction, and the intelligibility of creation.[5]

6. Moving Forward: The Continuous Structuring of Motion, Time, and Causality.

Because infinite actuality is undivided, unchanging, and lacking in nothing, the emergence of finite being cannot result from division, transformation, or addition. Yet finite beings undeniably exist, structured in time, space, and relation.

How, then, can finitude arise from what is fully actual?

How can limitation emerge without loss?

To answer these questions, we now turn to the logic of *Deceleration*, not as a weakening of Being but the *structured limitation* by which the infinite *potentiates* the finite.

---

5. Motion, time, space, and energy are not independent substances or pre-existing containers, but structured consequences of potentiation—that is, expressions of selected limitation within infinite actuality. They exist only by virtue of the ongoing act of Deceleration, which sustains them as intelligible aspects of finite participation. This understanding is essential for grasping the role of negative pressure as a structural condition rather than an opposing force.

3

Deceleration as the Mechanism of Finite Reality

PART ONE: THE NECESSITY OF DECELERATION FOR SUSTAINING FINITE REALITY

The Continuous Act That Holds Finitude Apart

IN CHAPTER 2, WE established the following:

- IRM is the necessary source of self-expression within Being per se.
- Deceleration is the structured process by which finite motion, time, space, and energy emerge.
- Negative pressure sustains finite existence, preventing it from collapsing back into unity.

Now, we must ask: Since finite reality is potentiated by Deceleration, does it require continual sustenance or is it self-*sustaining*?

At first, it may seem that once finite reality has emerged, it could continue independently as though it were set in motion and left to persist on its own. However, this assumption is false.

Unlike Being per se, which is fully actual and self-sufficient, finite motion, time, and energy are contingent—they do not persist by necessity but must be actively structured within actuality to remain distinct.

Thus, finite reality is not self-*sustaining*—it requires ongoing Deceleration to do the following:

- Prevent collapse into infinite actuality (ensuring structured separation)
- Maintain ordered differentiation (preventing dissolution into formless potential)
- Sustain motion, time, and energy (preserving *structured relationality*)

Therefore, Deceleration is not a one-time act but a continuous structuring that ensures finite reality remains distinct and coherent.

Refinement:

Whereas traditional formulations rightly conceive divine actuality as sustaining finite reality, they often describe sustenance as the continuous conservation of existence without fully specifying its structured operation. Here, we deepen that understanding: sustenance is an active, structured process of selection within infinite actuality. The continued existence of finite beings is not the mere persistence of things that were once created. It is an ongoing act of structured potentiation within Being per se, achieved through the continuous deceleration and self-suppression of infinite actuality.

Having established this necessity, we now examine how finite motion, time, space, and energy must be continuously structured through ongoing Deceleration.

1. Why Finite Motion Requires Continuous Structuring

A. The Contingency of Finite Motion

Unlike infinite actuality, which requires nothing external to sustain it, finite motion is always contingent on a structured framework. This is because finite motion:

- Requires an external source of energy to continue moving
- Depends on causal interactions within a structured system
- Is constrained by time and space, meaning it cannot exist in isolation

Thus, finite motion is not self-sustaining. It must be continually potentiated within *structured limitation*.

The following table summarizes why finite motion cannot be self-sustaining and must be continuously structured.

Table 3.1. Why Finite Motion Requires Continuous Structuring
This table explains why finite time, space, and energy cannot persist independently and must be sustained through active structuring.

Factor	Why It Must Be Sustained
Time	Without continuous selection, time would collapse into non-sequential actuality
Space	Without *structured limitation*, spatial differentiation would collapse
Energy	Without *structured resistance*, all interactions would become instantaneous actuality

B. The Role of Negative Pressure in Sustaining Finite Motion

Since negative pressure prevents finite reality from collapsing back into unity, it must also do the following:

- Sustain differentiation—ensuring that distinct entities remain distinct through structured separation

- Preserve causal relationships—maintaining structured interactions as an intrinsic feature of finitude

- Enable continued motion—acting as the necessary counterbalance to the structuring act of Deceleration, preventing entropy from dissolving finite existence

Without ongoing negative pressure, finite reality would either:

- Collapse back into infinite actuality, losing its *structured differentiation*; or

- Collapse into stasis, ceasing to exhibit motion, change, or relationality, but this is illogical.[1]

---

1. Stasis—understood as the total cessation of all motion, relation, and exchange—would signify the collapse of finite structured participation. In infinite actuality relational motion (IRM) is perfect and simultaneous; in finite reality, relational motion

Deceleration as the Mechanism of Finite Reality

The following table illustrates how negative pressure functions as an active structuring principle in finite reality.

Table 3.2. The Role of Negative Pressure in Finite Reality
This table illustrates how negative pressure actively preserves distinctness and relationality in finite structures.

Aspect of Reality	Without Negative Pressure	With Negative Pressure as an Active Structuring Principle
Time	All events collapse into simultaneity	Actively structures sequential differentiation of events
Space	All relationality collapses into unity	Provides the *structured resistance* necessary for interaction and causality
Energy	Motion becomes instantaneous actuality	Provides the *structured resistance* necessary for interaction and causality

Thus, negative pressure is not merely a boundary condition but the active structuring principle that ensures finite motion remains distinct from infinite actuality.

2. Negative Pressure as the Active Structuring Principle of Localized Reality

Since negative pressure ensures that finite reality remains distinct, deceleration must be a continual process that does the following:

- Maintain finite motion within *structured relationality*
- Prevent unstructured dissipation of energy and causality
- Allow for ongoing interactions without collapse into infinite unity

Thus, Deceleration is not a singular event but an ongoing structuring process of finitude.

(Finite Reciprocal Motion) necessarily unfolds across limits. To will absolute stasis would be to will the death of finite relationality—an entropic collapse incompatible with Truth itself. While stasis is hypothesized in physics (e.g., in models of entropic heat death), it is not a coherent metaphysical outcome. Finite beings must either continue in structured participation or return to infinite actuality there is no third state.

Refinement:

The very laws of motion, energy, and causality that govern the universe are not just empirical rules. They are the structured consequences of ongoing Deceleration. This leads us to a critical realization that the continued existence of finite reality is an ongoing act of structured potentiation.

Having established that motion requires continuous structuring and that negative pressure actively selects and sustains localized configurations, we must now explore how this *structured differentiation* extends beyond physical stability to the very order of causality. Just as finite motion is structured, then so, too, must be the relational framework governing all interactions within finitude. This leads us directly to the necessity of causal structuring as an extension of Deceleration, ensuring not only motion but also the coherence of finite beings within an ordered hierarchy of *participation*.

Negative Pressure: The Boundary That Sustains Finitude

Imagine the bubble analogy from earlier: a structured expansion of finite reality within infinite actuality.

But what prevents this bubble of finitude from collapsing back into infinite actuality or dissipating into unstructured potentiality?

The answer is negative pressure—the active structuring boundary that sustains finitude while preserving its distinction from the infinite.

What is Negative Pressure?

Negative pressure is not a physical force, nor is it a passive boundary. It is the necessary relational structure that sustains finite differentiation—preventing collapse while ensuring that finitude remains distinct within the infinite.

- It is not an external force holding reality together.
- It is not a vacuum pulling against existence.
- It is the structured limitation that ensures relational coherence within finitude.

Just as an air bubble's surface maintains structured separation between the air inside and outside, negative pressure maintains the *structured differentiation* of finite reality within the infinite.

How Negative Pressure Sustains Finite Reality

Within the bubble of finitude, negative pressure actively does the following:

1. Prevents collapse into infinite actuality

    - Without negative pressure, finite differentiation would collapse, reverting to instantaneous actuality.
    - This ensures that motion, time, space, and causality persist rather than vanishing into infinite simultaneity.

2. Sustains the distinct relationality of finite beings

    - Negative pressure allows finite beings to retain structured identity rather than becoming an undifferentiated whole.
    - This makes ordered interaction, energy exchange, and causal relationships possible.

3. Ensures continuous expansion without unraveling

    - Just as a bubble expands but maintains structural integrity, finite reality unfolds within the infinite without disintegrating.
    - This *structured limitation* permits finitude to exist in a stable, intelligible way.

(Analogy is included in this callout to assist the reader, such are not literal metaphysical claims.)

3. How Negative Pressure Explains Localized Configurations Without Dispersal

Negative pressure does not just sustain finite existence in general—it actively structures localized configurations of finite reality, such as matter, protons, planetary systems, black holes, and biological organisms. Unlike a purely expansive force that would disperse all finitude uniformly, negative pressure actively selects structured finitude, ensuring stability and relational coherence within the universe. This explains why localized formations persist rather than dissipating into an undifferentiated expansion.

A. Negative Pressure Is Directional and Differentiated

- It does not apply uniformly across all finitude but operates in a structured way that allows some regions of actuality to be more densely potentiated than others.
- This accounts for why the universe is not homogeneously expanding but instead structured into galaxies, stars, and stable systems capable of sustaining relational complexity.

B. Deceleration Introduces a Hierarchical Differentiation in Finitude

- Some structures (atoms, molecules, organisms) emerge through localized deceleration within a larger framework of expansion.
- This prevents everything from expanding uniformly and allows for stable interactions at different scales while preserving *structured differentiation*.

C. Relational Structuring Sustains Coherence

- Just as negative pressure allows for finite relationality without collapse, it also prevents excessive dispersal by structuring self-contained relational networks within finite being.
- Negative pressure does not just separate finite things—it actively enables the emergence of stable, interdependent systems. This ensures that distinct entities remain structured and relationally integrated rather than dispersive.

Thus, negative pressure is not merely expansive—it is a structured selection of limitation within actuality, allowing for stable differentiation and localized persistence within an otherwise expansive reality.[2]

Refinement:
This reveals that the very laws of motion, energy, and causality governing the universe are not merely empirical regularities but structured consequences of ongoing Deceleration.

4. *Deceleration and the Structure of Causality*

A. The Necessity of Causal Order

In a finite universe, motion is structured by causality—each event is related to prior events in a coherent sequence. This structure is necessary because:

- Without causality, motion would be random and unstructured.
- Without continuity, reality would lack coherence—finite beings would not persist over time.
- Without a relational framework, motion would not be possible in a structured way.

Refinement:
Traditional metaphysics assumes causality as a fundamental principle but does not fully explain why it exists. Here, we recognize that causality is structured by ongoing Deceleration—it is not merely a given but a consequence of the structured selection of finite motion. Thus, causality is not just a rule imposed on finite reality—it is a necessary condition of structured existence.

---

2. In physical cosmology, the rapid expansion of spacetime following the Big Bang—described in the theory of cosmic inflation and the observed accelerated expansion of the universe—may be interpreted as a physical expression of a deeper metaphysical principle: negative pressure. Within the present metaphysical framework, negative pressure is not a physical force but the intrinsic relational condition that sustains finite differentiation within infinite actuality, preventing collapse into simultaneity. Cosmic inflation and universal expansion thus temporally reflect what negative pressure sustains metaphysically: the persistence of ordered limitation within an expansive actuality.

B. The Triadic Nature of Causal Relations

Because infinite reciprocal motion is necessarily triune, finite causality must reflect this relational structure—causality is an imprint of infinite actuality within the finite. It reveals the following:

1. A cause (the initiator of motion)
2. An effect (that which undergoes motion)
3. A medium (the structure through which causality operates)

Refinement:
   While classical metaphysics recognizes the Aristotelian four causes, here we emphasize the necessity of a triadic structure—causality is not simply linear but emerges from the triune relational structure of actuality. Thus, even within finitude, we see the relational imprint of the infinite.

C. Why Finite Causality Requires Continuous Deceleration

Since causality is structured through motion and relationality, it must be:

- Sustained by negative pressure to prevent collapse into unity
- Governed by ongoing deceleration to maintain *structured differentiation*
- Continuously decelerated—without it, finite causality would:
    - Lose coherence—causal relations would no longer follow an ordered structure
    - Collapse into pure actuality—finite motion would become indistinguishable from infinite actuality
    - Fail to persist—the universe would become unsustainable as a structured system

Thus, causality is evidence that Deceleration is a continuous process. This brings us to the next key question:
   How does Deceleration structure, not just motion but also the very nature of finite existence? To answer this, we must explore how deceleration determines the structure of individual entities.

5. *Moving Forward: Deceleration and the Structure of Individual Beings*

Deceleration structures finite motion and causality, but it does not merely initiate movement. It sustains the *structured limitation* by which finite reality continues to exist without collapsing into undifferentiated actuality. Yet, since deceleration and negative pressure preserve motion, they must also determine the structure of the beings that participate in it.

We now turn to the structure of individual entities themselves in order to ask how deceleration shapes differentiation, free will, and consciousness, and why each finite being must exist as a structured *participation* in actuality.

PART TWO—DECELERATION AND THE STRUCTURE OF INDIVIDUAL BEINGS

How Differentiation Emerges and Persists

Now that we have established that Deceleration sustains motion and causality, we must explore how it determines the structure of individual entities.

THE NECESSITY OF STRUCTURED DIFFERENTIATION IN FINITE BEINGS

Unlike infinite actuality, finite beings must exist in *structured differentiation*.

Refinement:

Classical metaphysics often treats individuality as secondary, as an accidental property of finite beings. Here, we advance the argument by showing that differentiation is a necessary consequence of Deceleration. Since Deceleration structures reality through limitation, it must also structure how beings participate in actuality. This necessarily results in a hierarchy of participation in being.

Table 3.3. Levels of Participation in Being[3]
This table outlines the structured hierarchy of finite beings based on their participation in motion, perception, and rationality.

Level of Participation	Characteristics	Example
Existence + passive motion	Has being and participates in motion but does not initiate its own movement	Inanimate matter (rocks, atoms, stars)
Existence + self-motion	Has being and can initiate movement within itself but lacks perception	Plants, simple life forms
Existence + self-motion + perception	Has being, self-motion, and sensory awareness	Animals, sentient organisms
Existence + self-motion + rational thought	Has being, self-motion, perception, and rationality	Humans, rational beings
Existence + self-motion + rational thought + spiritual access	Has being, self-motion, rationality, and direct access to actuality	Spiritual beings, angels

Thus, the entire hierarchy of finite reality is not an arbitrary design but a structured selection of participation in actuality.

1. Why Negative Pressure Sustains Individual Differentiation

Because deceleration structures reality, negative pressure must sustain differentiation between individual beings.

Refinement:

Without negative pressure, finite things would not simply dissolve into infinite actuality—they would fail to be structured at all. This makes negative pressure an active principle of differentiation rather than merely a passive boundary. Negative pressure actively structures finitude by:

- Generating distinct entities as structured differentiations of actuality
- Sustaining continuity of existence by counteracting dissolution into actuality

---

3. The structure of participation outlined here draws upon the classical tradition of graded powers of soul, notably in Aristotle, *De Anima*, II.1–3.49–62. and Aquinas's *Summa Theologiae*, I, q. 75–78, where vegetative life, sensory perception, and rationality are distinguished as progressively higher acts of soul. The framework of participation in Being presented here follows a metaphysical logic of structured ascent, refining and extending these classical insights toward a more comprehensive account of structured finitude as participation in infinite actuality.

- Providing the structured relationality necessary for finite interaction without loss of identity

Thus, individual beings are not merely isolated objects but are structured participations in infinite actuality.

2. The Role of Free Will and Consciousness in Structured Participation

A. Free Will as Structured Participation in Actuality

Since rational beings participate in actuality through knowledge, they also participate in choice and volition.

Refinement:
   Free will is often conceived negatively—as an absence of determination. Here, we advance the view that free will is a structured participation in actuality. Thus, free will is not merely the power to choose. It is the necessary structure by which rational beings engage with actuality at their level of participation.

Table 3.4. Free Will as Participation[4]
This table illustrates the degrees of free will corresponding to levels of being, from inanimate matter to spiritual beings. As participation in actuality increases, so does the capacity for structured or perfect freedom.

Level of Being	Participation in Actuality	Degree of Free Will
Inanimate Matter	Exists, but does not move itself	None
Plants and simple Life	Moves, but does not know	None
Sentient beings	Moves and perceives, but does not reason	None
Rational beings	Knows and chooses	Structured free will
Spiritual beings	Knows and chooses in direct relation to actuality	Perfect free will

Thus, free will is not separate from divine selection. It is an aspect of it.

   4. The distinctions presented here draw upon classical metaphysics, particularly Aristotle's *De Anima* and Aquinas's *Summa Theologiae* I–II, q. 13, where self-motion, sensory awareness, and rational deliberation are associated with progressively higher forms of agency. The conception of free will as structured participation in actuality developed here extends these principles into a metaphysical framework grounded in the logic of finite participation.

B. Consciousness as Structured Self-Relation

Because rational beings have structured participation in infinite actuality, human consciousness is the finite, relational self-awareness of a being to its own structured participation in Being.

- Human consciousness is not a static property—it is a structured, relational act.
- It exists only in degrees of participation—higher beings exhibit deeper awareness of the order of Being.
- It is sustained by negative pressure, allowing distinct finite awareness to persist across time without collapsing into undifferentiated actuality.

Refinement:

Classical and some scientific theories of consciousness often treat it as emergent from matter. Here, we advance the view that human consciousness arises from finite participation in infinite self-knowing actuality. Thus, human consciousness is not a passive property, but an active, structured echo of the infinite relationality of Being itself.

3. The Causal Joint as the Necessary Link Between Infinite and Finite Reality

We have established that negative pressure actively structures finitude by the following means:

- Generating distinct entities as structured differentiations of actuality; not merely separating them from actuality but actively allowing them to cohere within *structured limitations*
- Sustaining continuity of existence by counteracting dissolution into actuality; stabilizing finite structures by balancing expansion with local coherence
- Providing the *structured relationality* necessary for finite interaction without loss of identity; ensuring that finite things remain distinct but relationally integrated rather than dispersive.

As a result, we must now ask:

What ultimately sustains finite existence as a structured reality?

The answer is the *causal joint*—the necessary metaphysical bridge between infinite actuality and finite being.

Refinement:

Traditional metaphysics recognizes God as the sustaining cause but does not fully articulate how finite being is actively selected. Here, we demonstrate that the *causal joint* of divine action is not just divine sustenance but structured potentiation. Thus, the *causal joint* is the necessary structuring process by which finite reality is potentiated from infinite actuality—actively sustained by ongoing Deceleration and negative pressure.

4. Summary of Chapter 3

- Deceleration is not just the emergence of finite reality. It is an ongoing structuring act.
- Negative pressure sustains *structured differentiation*, preventing collapse into unity.
- Finite beings exist in a hierarchy of participation in actuality, structured by Deceleration.
- Free will is the structured participation of rational beings in actuality.
- Human consciousness is the structured self-relation of finite beings to actuality.
- The *causal joint* is the necessary metaphysical bridge that sustains the structured distinction between infinite actuality and finite being.

5. Moving Forward: The Causal Joint as the Metaphysical Bridge

Chapter 3 established that finite beings do not persist on their own. Their continued existence requires not only deceleration and negative pressure, but a continuous structuring act that maintains their distinctness *as sequestered structure within* divine actuality. This act is not an interface, but a sustaining selection—neither imposed from without nor emerging from within the finite.

Chapter 4 now turns directly to this necessity. It introduces the *causal joint* as the structured act of divine power—an intentional potentiation by which infinite actuality gives rise to and sustains finite reality without division, diminution, or transition. The logic of creation begins here, with the structure that joins infinite power to finite limitation.

Crucibulum

(A Lamp Before the Cross)
If I am judged as good by man,
If all my deeds endure the scrutiny
Of man's most vigilant eye,
Ere days no longer flow as passers-by,
Will I be judged as good by God—as once by men?
If man's watchful gaze proves seducible,
Propending toward intensity and not intent,
Will man's path not be defined by what is rent
Between the ancient crucibulum and a crucible?

—Kevin Mc Guinness

4

The Causal Joint of Divine Action
From Infinite Power to Finite Creation

PART ONE—INTRODUCTION AND THE NECESSITY OF A CAUSAL JOINT

Why Finite Being Must Be Structured from Within

AT THE FOUNDATION OF reality lies a single logical necessity: the absolute, infinite power that is Being per se.

In the previous chapters, we established the following:

- Nonexistence per se is impossible. Therefore, Being per se must exist necessarily.
- Being per se does not undergo change or transition. It is fully actual.
- Finite reality does not emerge automatically. It must be structured through a process of selection.
- Deceleration is the structured self-limitation of infinite actuality through which finite motion, time, space, and energy are actively potentiated into existence.
- Negative pressure sustains the structured differentiation of finite reality.
- Free will and consciousness are structured participants in actuality.

Now, we must address a fundamental question:

How is finite reality sustained as a structured participation in infinite actuality?

Since finite reality does not emerge randomly, its structured existence must be continuously sustained by a necessary metaphysical link between infinite actuality and finite being. This link is the causal joint—the structured process by which Being per se actively sustains all finite existence.

In this chapter, we will demonstrate the following:

- Why the finite universe is not an accident of necessity but an intentional act of structured selection
- Why the causal joint is the only possible bridge between infinite actuality and finite being
- How omnipotence, omniscience, and omnipresence necessarily follow from infinity
- Why finite beings are not merely sustained but actively potentiated as structured participations in divine actuality

1. *The Fundamental Distinction Between Infinite Power and Finite Energy*

A. What Is Infinite Power?

Infinite power is not a force waiting to act, nor a vast reservoir of energy—it is the fullness of all being, the absolute actuality that underlies all existing things. Because it is fully actual, it possesses no unactualized potential and requires nothing outside itself to sustain or activate its power.

Key properties of infinite power are:

- Pure actuality—it does not transition between states or undergo change
- Self-sufficient—nothing external causes or sustains it; it is the unconditioned source of all reality
- Indivisible—it is not composed of measurable or transferable parts.

- Non-kinetic and non-potential—motion within infinite actuality is not sequential or constrained; rather, it is infinite reciprocal motion, pure relationality.

Thus, infinite power is omnipotence, not as a vast force within reality but as the structuring actuality from which all finite existence derives.

B. What Is Finite Energy?

In contrast to infinite power, finite energy is always constrained by limitation. It is a measure of motion within time and space, dependent on structured relationships and subject to change.

Key properties of finite energy are:

- Limited and measurable—unlike infinite power, energy is always quantifiable within a system
- Requires potentiality—energy operates within causal sequences; it always involves a transition from one state to another
- Transferable and exhaustible—it can be used, transferred, or dissipated, unlike the self-sufficient actuality of infinite power
- Structured within time and space—energy does not exist independently; it is meaningful only within a structured reality

Because finite energy depends on structured differentiation and limitation, it does not arise autonomously but is potentiated by infinite power as a structured participant in actuality.

C. Why Infinite Power Cannot Be Finite Energy

Since infinite power is absolute actuality, it cannot be identified with finite energy or reduced to any of its properties.

- If infinite power were kinetic or potential, it would require time and change. Therefore, it would not be absolute.
- Pure actuality is infinite reciprocal motion—perfect, non-transitional self-relation without kinetic or potential change that is logically prior to Deceleration.

- If infinite power were just an immeasurably large quantity of energy, it might still be exhaustible. Therefore, it would not be infinite.
- Energy is always finite, even if vast in amount, because it requires limitation and structure to be meaningful.
- If infinite power were divisible into parts, it would not be fully actual. Therefore, it would not be infinite.
- Divisibility implies composition, and composition implies contingency, which contradicts the indivisible nature of infinite actuality.

Thus, infinite power does not *convert* into finite energy. It actively potentiates finite energy as a *structured limitation* within actuality. The structured differentiation of energy, motion, and causality is not a fragmentation of infinite power but its deliberate potentiation of finitude.

2. The Necessity of a Causal Joint

Since finite reality does not emerge automatically, we must now address how it is structured and sustained within infinite actuality.

We already know that Deceleration is the structured process through which finite reality is potentiated. However, Deceleration alone does not account for the continuous sustenance of finite being as distinct from infinite actuality.

For this, we require a metaphysical bridge, a process that ensures the following:

- The finite remains distinct from infinite actuality.
- The finite is structured according to relational necessity.
- The finite is sustained as a coherent, intelligible reality.

This is the causal joint—the structured selection of finite being from within infinite actuality.

The causal joint is not a physical link but an active structuring process that ensures finite reality remains distinct while participating in Being per se. Thus, the causal joint is the necessary metaphysical bridge between infinite actuality and finite participation.

Since structured finitude requires continuous sustenance, the causal joint is not merely a point of distinction but an ongoing structuring that sustains the persistence of differentiated finite reality within actuality.

3. Why the Causal Joint Necessarily Structures Reality

The causal joint must follow certain conditions.

A. The Causal Joint Must Be Structured and Intentional

Since absolute actuality is fully self-sufficient, it lacks nothing and, therefore, would not create unless doing so were an intentional act of self-expression.

Things do not emerge by accident. Therefore, the causal joint cannot be a random or chaotic process. It is not the inevitable result of actuality but the freely chosen act by which actuality potentiates structured finitude, without which, finite reality would not and could not exist.

Finite reality does not merely persist—it is actively structured by divine intentionality, ensuring that it remains distinct yet relationally integrated. Thus, the causal joint is not a passive link but the ongoing, deliberate structuring of differentiated actuality.

B. The Causal Joint as the Structured Transition from Triune Actuality to Triadic Finitude

Since infinite actuality is necessarily relational, finite reality must inherit this triune relationality in finite form—not as an imposed pattern but as the only possible way structured differentiation can persist within actuality.

The triune structure of actuality is not a theological construct but a necessary consequence of the intrinsic relationality of Being per se.

- Every act of knowing follows the relation of subject, predicate, and object.
- Every act of motion follows the relation of mover, moved, and medium of exchange.
- Every causal interaction unfolds through the relation of cause, recipient (effect), and medium of causation.

Thus, finite reality does not simply "resemble" a triune form—its triadic structure is necessarily constituted by it. This ensures that differentiation is structured, rather than arbitrary, while preserving relational distinction within both infinite actuality and finite reality.

C. The Causal Joint as the Structured Potentiation of Finite Reality

The causal joint does not create the finite by altering infinite actuality; rather, it actively structures finite reality as a continuously sustained selection within Being itself, which is no-thing. Instead:

- It potentiates the finite by structuring it as a continuously sustained participation in actuality, ensuring its distinctiveness while maintaining its structured limitation.
- It sustains the finite by maintaining its structured differentiation.
- It ensures that finite being remains distinct while participating in actuality.

Thus, finite beings do not simply exist in isolation; their very being is a structured participation in infinite actuality.

4. Summary of Part One:

- The causal joint is the structured act of divine intentionality by which finite reality is potentiated through the limitation of infinite actuality.
- Infinite power does not become finite energy. It actively creates and sustains it.
- Finite reality does not emerge automatically. It is potentiated through structured limitation.
- The triune relational structure of Being per se is necessarily inherited by finite reality.
- The causal joint ensures that the finite remains distinct while participating in actuality.

Thus, the causal joint is neither a mere transition nor a boundary. It is the active structuring principle sustaining finite reality as distinct yet relational within Being itself.

5. Moving Forward: From Structured Selection to Sustained Potentiation

Part One established that finite reality does not emerge by necessity, nor by transformation within Being per se. It is instead continuously structured through the causal joint: the act by which infinite actuality potentiates finite being as distinct yet relational.

Part Two now develops this further by showing that the causal joint is not only the act of initial selection, but also the sustaining structure by which causality, motion, and time themselves are continuously ordered. This section demonstrates that omnipotence, omniscience, and omnipresence are not attributes that enable creation—they are the metaphysical preconditions from which creation necessarily follows.

PART TWO—THE CAUSAL JOINT AS THE ACT OF DIVINE POTENTIATION

How Infinite Attributes Necessitate the Finite Structure of the Universe

In Part One, we established the following:

- The Causal joint is the structured act by which finite reality is selected and sustained within infinite actuality.
- Finite reality does not emerge automatically. It is intentionally and continuously potentiated.
- The triune relational structure of Being per se is necessarily inherited by finite reality.
- The causal joint ensures that finite being remains structurally distinct yet necessarily participates in actuality.

Now, we must explore:

- How the causal joint structures causality, time, and relational motion
- How the causal joint follows necessarily from omnipotence, omniscience, and omnipresence
- Why finite beings are actively structured as participations in divine actuality

1. Why the Causal Joint Necessarily Follows from Omnipotence, Omniscience, and Omnipresence

Since Being per se is infinite actuality, it follows necessarily that omnipotence, omniscience, and omnipresence are intrinsic to divine actuality.

These attributes are not caused by or derived from the causal joint; rather, they precondition it. The causal joint follows necessarily from these attributes as the structured means by which finite reality is potentiated.

Thus, the attributes of omnipotence, omniscience, and omnipresence are not arbitrary descriptions of divine nature. They are logically necessary consequences of infinite actuality.

A. Omnipotence: Infinite Power as the Source of All Reality

Stepwise Proof of Omnipotence

1. Since infinite actuality lacks nothing, it is fully actual—complete in itself, without potentiality.
2. Since all power derives necessarily from actuality, and infinite actuality is fully actual and self-sufficient, there can be no external source of power independent of it.
3. Since all finite motion, energy, and being are potentiated through infinite actuality, no finite structure can impose limitation upon it.
4. If any principle, power, or being could restrict infinite actuality, it would have to exist externally—but existence external to infinite actuality is impossible.
5. Therefore, since infinite actuality originates all being, lacks nothing, and has no opposition, it must be omnipotent—there can be no reality apart from it.

B. Omniscience: The Infinite as Absolute Knowledge

Stepwise Proof of Omniscience

1. Since all relational actuality within infinite Being occurs infinitely and without succession, knowledge is immediate and total. There is no delay, fragmentation, or uncertainty.

2. In infinite actuality, knowledge and being are identical; there is no distinction between what infinite actuality is and what it knows.

3. Because all structured finitude emerges through limitation within infinite actuality, every finite being exists already as a relationally known participation.

4. Omniscience does not mean passively observing reality; in infinite actuality, knowledge is the structuring act itself, such that all finite differentiation is relationally integrated.

5. Since there is no knowledge external to infinite actuality, and all structured finitude follows from it, infinite actuality must be omniscient—knowing all because all knowledge is contained within its act.

C. Omnipresence: The Infinite as Indivisible and All-Encompassing

Stepwise Proof of Omnipresence

1. Since infinite actuality is not extended in space, it has no boundaries, locations, or divisions.

2. If any place existed where infinite actuality was absent, that place would have to exist externally to infinite actuality—but nothing external to infinite actuality is possible.

3. Since finite reality emerges through structured limitation within infinite actuality, infinite actuality must be fully present to every finite being, sustaining its relational participation even while finitude remains distinct.

4. Omnipresence does not mean diffusion throughout space, but infinite actuality being fully present as the sustaining ground of all finite existence.

5. Therefore, since there is no "outside" to infinite actuality, it must be omnipresent—fully present to all finite being as the act that structures and sustains their existence without spatial division or extension.

D. How These Attributes Structure Finite Reality

Since omnipotence, omniscience, and omnipresence follow necessarily from infinite actuality, they also define the structure of finite reality.

- Finite beings exist because omnipotence actively selects them to exist.
- All truth is structured by omniscience, meaning all knowledge in finitude participates in divine knowledge.
- Causality, motion, and existence are bound to omnipresence, since there is no outside to infinite actuality.

Thus, everything that exists is a structured participation in infinite actuality. This follows directly from the triune nature of infinite reciprocal motion, where knowledge, power, and presence are all unified without contradiction.

2. The Causal Joint as the Continuous Sustaining Link Between Infinite Actuality and Finite Reality

We have established the following:

- The finite emerges through structured selection by infinite actuality.
- Omnipotence, omniscience, and omnipresence are necessary attributes of infinite actuality.
- All finite being exists as structured participants in divine selection.

As a result, we must now explore how the causal joint actively sustains all finite reality.

Since finite reality does not self-sustain, its continued existence must be:

- Actively potentiated by infinite actuality
- Preserved through structured differentiation
- Sustained through continuous Deceleration and negative pressure

Thus, the causal joint is not merely a point of origin. It is a continuously potentiating structure that sustains the ordered differentiation of finite reality

3. Summary of Part Two

- Omnipotence, omniscience, and omnipresence are intrinsic to infinite actuality and precondition the structured act of the causal joint, which, through the deceleration of infinite reciprocal motion, structures all finite reality.
- Omnipotence means that all structured existence is selected, potentiated, and sustained through the causal joint of divine action.
- Omniscience means that all knowledge is contained and structured within absolute actuality.
- Omnipresence means that infinite actuality is fully present to all finite reality as the sustaining act underlying the causal joint without being distributed in space.
- The causal joint is the structured mediation between infinite actuality and finite being, sustaining relational participation without division or separation.

4. Moving Forward: The Sustaining Structure of Created Reality

Part Two established that omnipotence, omniscience, and omnipresence are intrinsic to infinite actuality and that the causal joint necessarily expresses these attributes. Finite beings are not created from absence or chance but from the structured act by which divine actuality potentiates limited existence.

Part Three now turns to the implications of this act. It explores how the causal joint sustains finite beings, not as passive objects but as structured participants in actuality, and why the laws of motion, energy, and causality are not imposed from outside but follow necessarily from divine selection.

PART THREE—THE CAUSAL JOINT AND THE STRUCTURE OF FINITE REALITY

Creation as Continuous Structuring, Not Once-For-All Origination

We have established the following:

The Causal Joint of Divine Action

- The causal joint structures the selection of finite limitation within infinite actuality, allowing for the sustained potentiation of finite being without division or change in the infinite.
- Omnipotence, omniscience, and omnipresence necessarily follow from infinite actuality.
- Finite beings are structured participants in divine selection.

Now, we must explore how the causal joint actively sustains all finite reality. Since finite reality does not emerge automatically, its continued existence must be:

- Continuously potentiated by infinite actuality
- Maintained through structured differentiation
- Sustained by ongoing Deceleration and negative pressure

Thus, the causal joint is not merely an initiating transition. It is the active structuring act that continuously potentiates and sustains finite reality, ensuring its structured distinction while integrating it within actuality.

1. Why Finite Beings Are Not Passive Recipients but Structured Participants in Divine Potentiation

A. The Nature of Participation in Being

Finite beings do not exist independently but as structured participants in divine potentiation, sustained as distinct yet relationally integrated within actuality.

The existence of a finite being is not a passive state but an active participation in divine actuality.

This means:

- Every finite entity is a selected, structured limitation within infinite actuality.
- Finite beings do not simply receive being, they actively exist within structured limitation.
- Each being participates in actuality according to its nature and degree of participation.

Thus, existence is not a static property—it is an ongoing structured relation within divine selection.

B. How the Causal Joint Sustains Participation in Being

Since finite beings are participants in actuality, the causal joint must do the following:

- Continuously sustain structured differentiation
- Prevent collapse into unity through negative pressure
- Maintain the relational structure that governs causality, motion, and existence

Without this structured selection, finite reality would collapse back into infinite actuality, losing its structured differentiation.

Thus, the causal joint is not a one-time act. It is a continuous structuring act that maintains the distinctness and participation of finite being.

2. Why the Laws of Motion, Energy, and Causality Are Structured Consequences of Divine Selection

Since finite reality is sustained by structured selection, we must now ask: Why do the laws of motion, energy, and causality follow structured patterns?

The answer is that all finite interactions must be structured triadically as a necessary participation in the triune actuality of infinite being. This means that motion, energy, and causality are not arbitrary. They are structured consequences of divine selection.

A. Motion as Structured Participation in Being

Motion in the finite universe is necessarily structured because:

- It is a relational expression of structured reality, reflecting the triune necessity of infinite reciprocal motion.
- It is actively potentiated within structured differentiation, maintaining distinction from infinite actuality.

- Its triadic structure is sustained as an ordered participation through its finite relationality, which is governed by time, space, and causality.

Thus, motion is not a random occurrence. It is the necessary structured expression of finite participation in actuality.

B. Energy as the Structured Limitation of Power

Since energy is a measure of finite motion, so it follows:

- Energy is not infinite; it is structured within limitation.
- Energy allows for structured differentiation, preventing collapse into unity.
- Energy follows laws because it is governed by structured participation in actuality.

Thus, energy is not an independent entity but a structured limitation of actuality, allowing for ordered interaction and maintaining the differentiation of finite motion.

C. Causality as the Structured Selection of Motion and Energy

Causality exists because:

- All motion and energy must be structured relationally.
- No finite event exists in isolation. It must be part of a structured sequence.
- Causal order ensures coherence and persistence of structured finitude.

Thus, causality is not imposed externally. It is the structured participation of finite motion in divine actuality. This means that the laws of physics, causality, and interaction are not random. They are structured selections that follow necessarily from the causal joint.

3. The Causal Joint as the Necessary Link Between Divine Knowledge and Finite Experience

Since omniscience means that all knowledge is already present in infinite actuality, we must now address the following question: How does finite experience participate in divine knowledge?

The answer is that finite beings do not add to divine knowledge. They participate in it according to their structured limitation.

A. The Necessity of Foreknown Participation

Since all knowledge is already present in infinite actuality, so it follows:

- Every finite being exists with its choices foreknown.
- Free will is not separate from divine selection. It is a structured aspect of it.
- Finite beings do not create new reality. They are real only through participation in divine actuality.

Thus, free will is not an independent force. It is the structured engagement of finite beings with actuality.

B. The Role of Consciousness in Structured Knowledge

Since consciousness is structured self-relation to actuality, so it follows:

- Conscious beings participate in divine Truth to different degrees.
- Knowledge is structured within finite limitation, allowing beings to engage with actuality.
- The awareness of reality is not passive. It is an active engagement with structured selection.

Thus, finite knowledge does not add to actuality but exists as the structured self-expression of omniscience in a foreknown reality in which we are graced to participate.

4. The Causal Joint as the Sustaining Act of Divine Creation

Since finite reality does not emerge automatically, its continued existence must be:

- Continuously potentiated by infinite actuality
- Sustained by ongoing Deceleration and negative pressure
- Structured relationally, ensuring coherent interaction

Thus, the causal joint is not merely an initial act—it is the continuous sustaining of all finite existence. This means:

- The universe is not a self-contained system. It is actively structured by divine selection.
- The persistence of reality is not an accident. It follows necessarily from the causal joint.
- Finite beings do not merely exist. They participate in actuality according to structured limitation.

Thus, creation is not an event in time. It is an ongoing act of structured potentiation.

Creation is not something that happened once in the past. It is an ongoing, structured act. God does not just set things in motion and step back. Instead, he actively sustains the structured differentiation of finite reality, ensuring that everything continues to exist as an ordered participation in actuality.

Since creation is not an event in time but an ongoing act of divine potentiation, structured finitude is continuously sustained through the causal joint, wherein relational differentiation is actively selected and maintained as a participation in divine actuality.

5. Summary of Part Three

- Finite beings do not passively exist. They are structured participants in actuality.
- Motion, energy, and causality are structured consequences of divine selection.
- The structured order of physics, causality, and interaction is not imposed externally but follows necessarily from the causal joint as the

sustaining act that ensures finite relationality remains distinct yet integrated within actuality.

- The causal joint sustains finite reality as a structured engagement with infinite actuality.
- Creation is not a one-time event. It is an ongoing act of structured potentiation.

6. Moving Forward: The Ongoing Act of Divine Creation

Part Three showed that finite beings do not simply exist. They are structured participants in actuality, sustained by the continuous act of divine potentiation. Motion, energy, and causality are not external conditions but ordered consequences of the causal joint, which structures all finite being in relation to infinite actuality.

Part Four now draws together these conclusions. It clarifies the full implications of the causal joint as the sustaining act of divine creation, showing why structured finitude necessarily follows from infinite actuality and how the universe is not a past event but a continuously structured expression of divine will.

PART FOUR—THE CAUSAL JOINT AND THE RETURN OF THE SOUL

Freedom and Knowledge as Structured Participation in the One

We have now established the following:

- The causal joint is the structured selection of finite reality from infinite actuality.
- Omnipotence, omniscience, and omnipresence necessarily follow from infinite actuality.
- Finite beings exist as structured participants in divine selection.
- Motion, energy, and causality are structured consequences of the causal joint.

The causal joint is not merely the point at which finite reality is potentiated; it is the continuous structuring act that sustains finite reality as distinct yet relationally integrated within actuality.

We are now ready to draw the final conclusions: What does it mean for finite reality to be continuously structured and sustained through the causal joint?

This means that creation is neither arbitrary nor accidental. Instead, it follows from divine selection—God chooses to potentiate a specific structured reality, fully knowing how all things unfold within it, including our free choices.

God does not create blindly or by chance. Rather, he knows all possible universes and selects the one that perfectly expresses his will while preserving the real freedom of its creatures. This universe is not necessary but follows necessarily from divine self-expression.

Because infinite actuality is necessarily relational and self-sufficient, structured finitude follows as its selected potentiation, not as an imposed necessity but as the freely chosen self-expression of infinite actuality, foreknowing the structured differentiation of all finite realities, including freely made choices within them.

The causal joint is the necessary act of divine potentiation—the structured differentiation of finitude from infinite actuality. This selection does not impose determinism but reflects the foreknown relational differentiation of all finite realities, ensuring that structured finitude follows necessarily from infinite actuality without violating free will.

We must now demonstrate why:

- The causal joint is the necessary sustaining act of divine creation.
- Structured finitude necessarily follows from infinite actuality.
- Creation is the divine potentiation of reality, not the realization or actualization of potentiality.

Creation is not about bringing possibilities into existence as if God were deliberating and then choosing between options he didn't already know. Instead, God potentiates a structured reality, meaning he selects and sustains a universe whose unfolding—including our free actions—is already foreknown.

Creation is not the realization of potential in any sense. It is the potentiation of structured reality in a sequential, apparently deliberative, sense—the selected differentiation of finite being from infinite actuality, sustained within the triadic structure of relational self-expression.

1. The Causal Joint as the Continuous Structuring of Finitude

A. Why Finite Reality Requires Continuous Structuring

Since finite reality is not self-sustaining, it must:

- Be continuously potentiated by infinite actuality
- Remain distinct from infinite actuality through structured limitation
- Be maintained through ongoing Deceleration and negative pressure

This means that finite reality is not a static product—it is an ongoing structured participation in divine actuality.

B. The Role of Negative Pressure in Sustaining Finitude

- Negative pressure is the structuring boundary that sustains finite differentiation, preventing its dissolution into infinite actuality. It ensures:
  - Differentiation between finite entities
  - The continued flow of time and causality
  - The maintenance of structured motion, energy, and interaction

Without negative pressure:

- All finite motion would collapse into pure actuality.
- All distinct beings would lose structured differentiation.
- Time and space would dissolve, reducing all to undifferentiated existence.

Thus, negative pressure is not a passive condition. It is the sustaining act that maintains finite reality within structured limitation.

2. The Universe as a Structured Act of Divine Potentiation

Since finite reality is sustained by structured potentiation, we must ask: What is the true nature of creation?

The answer is that creation is not the actualization of unrealized potential. It is the structured potentiation of finite reality within infinite actuality. This means the following:

- God does not actualize preexistent potential. Rather, God potentiates finite reality, structuring relational being through the self-limitation of infinite actuality without undergoing change or division.
- In time, creation is not a single event. It is the continuous sustaining of structured finitude.
  - God sees all time as a single structure of relation; man sees relation as divided by time.
- Reality is not arbitrary. It follows necessarily from the structured process of divine selection.

Thus, the universe is not merely allowed to exist. It is actively structured by the selection of finitude from infinite actuality.

Why Structured Finitude Necessarily Follows from Infinite Actuality

Since infinite actuality is necessarily relational, self-contained, and structured, so it follows:

- All finite expressions of reality must conform to this structure.
- The laws of motion, energy, and causality derive from the triune necessity of infinite actuality and are structured triadically within finite reality.
- All finite knowledge, communication, and meaningful exchange follows the same relational structure.

Thus, no reality can exist outside of the structured act of participation in infinite actuality. This means that all contingent being is necessarily structured participation in the absolute.

3. The Causal Joint as the Sustaining Act of Divine Creation

Creation is not something that happened once in the past. It is an ongoing, structured act—God does not just set things in motion and step back. Instead, he actively sustains the structured differentiation of finite reality, ensuring that everything continues to exist as an ordered participation in actuality.

Since creation is not an event in time but the continuous act of divine potentiation, structured finitude must be continuously sustained through the causal joint as the relational differentiation of finite being.

As a result:

- Being per se does not change, but it actively selects structured finitude.
- The causal joint is the sustaining link that continuously structures finite reality in time.
- Omnipotence, omniscience, and omnipresence necessarily follow from absolute actuality.
- All created beings emerge as structured participants in divine actuality, according to their degree of access to actuality.

Thus, the causal joint of divine action is not merely a transition—it is a structured act of selection, which defines the very nature of finite reality.

4. Implications of the Causal Joint and Divine Will

Because the causal joint actively structures all finite reality, we must conclude that nothing in finite existence is accidental. Everything exists as a structured selection.

Every part of reality—down to the smallest detail—exists within a structured framework. This does not mean that everything is predetermined in a way that eliminates free will, but rather that all possibilities were *foreknown and structured* within actuality in a way that ensures meaningful participation in the relational unfolding of Being.

Since the causal joint actively structures all finite reality, finitude is not accidental. It is a structured differentiation that follows necessarily from divine self-expression without negating the integrity of free causality.

- Free will is not separate from divine selection. It is a structured act of participation in actuality.
- The laws of physics, motion, and causality are not imposed. They emerge necessarily from structured limitation.

This means the following:

- Reality is structured, not arbitrary.
- Creation is intentional, not accidental.
- Finite beings do not exist in isolation—they are structured participants in divine actuality.

The causal joint is how finite reality remains distinct yet continuously structured within divine actuality. It ensures that the universe is not a chaotic or accidental system but a sustained participation in divine self-expression.

5. The Definition of the Causal Joint

With all logical steps established, we can now define the causal joint in its most complete form with respect to creation.

The causal joint is the structured potentiation of finite reality within infinite actuality, wherein relational differentiation is actively sustained through ongoing Deceleration and negative pressure, ensuring that finite beings remain distinct yet integrally related within divine knowledge, power, and presence. This definition captures:

- The necessity of structured selection
- The sustaining role of Deceleration
- The relational participation of all finite being in divine actuality

Thus, the causal joint is not merely an interface between infinite actuality and finite reality—it is the sustaining act that actively structures all contingent existence.

The triune structure of actuality is not an assumption but an unavoidable feature of Being per se. Any structured differentiation within finite reality must necessarily follow a triadic relational form, as demonstrated in motion, causality, and knowledge. The metaphysical necessity of triadic structuring ensures that finite reality is relationally integrated without erasing the distinction between it and infinite actuality.

6. Moving Forward: Omnipotence as the Actuality of Being

Chapter 4 concluded that creation is not a past event but an ongoing act—structured, sustained, and relational. The causal joint is not a mechanism external to God, but the very act by which finite beings are continuously selected and maintained in structured relation to infinite actuality. All creation is potentiated through this act, which is neither fragmented nor delayed but immediate and sustaining.

Chapter 5 now turns to the first of the divine attributes that follow necessarily from this structure: omnipotence. Not as unbounded force but as the actuality of Being itself, omnipotence is the absolute power that requires no energy, undergoes no exertion, and sustains all things as their ground and structure.

5

Omnipotence
The Power that Upholds Reality

Introduction: The True Meaning of Omnipotence

OMNIPOTENCE IS OFTEN MISUNDERSTOOD as mere *unlimited power*, as though it were the ability to do anything, including absurdities like making a square circle. But true omnipotence is not an arbitrary force—it is the very actuality of Being per se, the necessary foundation of all existence.

Since Being per se is fully actual, omnipotence does not mean raw power that can do anything but rather the absolute power that sustains and structures all reality.

In this chapter, we will clarify the following:

- Why omnipotence is not mere unlimited strength but the very substance of *existence itself*
- Why it requires no energy yet sustains all reality
- How omnipotence follows logically from the nature of infinite actuality
- Why common objections (such as logical paradoxes) misunderstand what omnipotence truly is

1. *The Logical Necessity of Omnipotence*

Being per se is absolute actuality. Therefore, omnipotence necessarily follows, not as a property added to God but as his very essence. This must be the case because omnipotence:

- Lacks nothing—there is no unrealized potential within it, meaning no external force is required to sustain its power
- Is unconditioned—nothing outside of it determines or limits its power because there is no "outside" to infinite actuality
- Is indivisible—it is pure actuality, lacking parts, composition, or any division within itself

Table 5.1. Why Omnipotence Is Not Just *Extreme Power*
This table clarifies why divine omnipotence is not measured by energy, contradiction, or coercion, but is the sustaining actuality of all finite existence.

Common Misconception	Why It's Incorrect	The True Nature of Omnipotence
Omnipotence means infinite energy.	Energy is finite, measurable, and exhaustible.	Omnipotence is not an amount of energy; it is the sustaining actuality of all that exists.
Omnipotence means God can do anything.	Logical contradictions are not acts of power but meaningless statements.	Omnipotence means God can do all that is possible according to his nature.
Omnipotence is about coercion.	If omnipotence were brute force, it would override free will and contingency.	Omnipotence sustains reality without overriding the freedom of rational beings.

Since omnipotence is not a quantity of power but the very actuality of Being, it therefore follows:

- All finite power derives from it. It is the only true source of existence.
- It cannot be limited. Limitation implies dependence on something external, but nothing is outside of Being per se.
- It does not compete with other forces. All other powers are contingent upon it.

Thus, omnipotence is not an optional attribute of God. It is a necessary truth about absolute Being.

2. Common Misconceptions and the Limits of Omnipotence

Many misunderstandings about omnipotence arise from improper definitions. Below, we examine common objections.

A. Logical Contradictions Do Not Apply

A common objection asks: If God is omnipotent, can he create a rock so heavy that he cannot lift it?

This question falsely assumes that omnipotence means the ability to perform nonsensical contradictions. However, logical impossibilities are not acts of power—they are meaningless statements. Omnipotence does not mean violating the nature of actuality but fully expressing it. Just as Being per se cannot *cease to exist*, God cannot act against his own nature because the expression of his power is not arbitrary—it is the necessary structuring of all reality.

Omnipotence means God can do all things that are possible according to the nature of *existence itself*.

B. Omnipotence Is Not Arbitrary Feats of Strength

Some imagine omnipotence as a brute force that imposes its will mechanically. However:

- Omnipotence is not coercion—it does not override free will or contingency.
- Omnipotence does not compete with natural forces—it is the sustaining actuality of all forces.
- God's power is not separate from reason or order—it is the very foundation of intelligibility.

C. Omnipotence Requires No Effort

Unlike human power, which depends on energy, effort, and action, divine omnipotence is effortless.

- God does not need to expend energy to sustain the universe.
- His sustaining power is not an exertion but a necessary actuality.
- All contingent existence depends on his power—he does not depend on anything.

Table 5.2. How Omnipotence Sustains All Things Effortlessly
This table contrasts human power with divine omnipotence, showing why only the latter can continuously sustain all reality without exertion.

Human Power	Divine Omnipotence
Requires effort and energy	Requires no exertion—fully actual
Is limited by external conditions	Is unconditioned and absolute
Can be lost or diminished	Cannot be depleted or measured
Depends on prior causes	Is the first cause of all reality

3. Omnipotence and the Sustaining of Reality

Since omnipotence is the actuality of Being per se, so it follows that omnipotence:

- Continuously sustains all existence; nothing persists independently of divine actuality
- Structures reality, rather than overriding it; the laws of physics and causality are expressions of divine order
- Allows for free will and contingency; it does not dictate every motion but sustains human choices

Omnipotence

Table 5.3. How Omnipotence Interacts with Creation
This table clarifies how omnipotence structures existence, laws, free will, and causality without overriding or replacing them.

Aspect of Reality	How It Relates to Omnipotence
Existence	Omnipotence is the sustaining actuality of all that is.
Laws of Nature	Omnipotence structures order rather than overriding it.
Free Will	Omnipotence sustains contingent choices rather than dictating them.
Causality	Omnipotence is the foundation of all causal interactions.

Thus, the very laws of motion, energy, and causality that govern the universe are structured consequences of ongoing divine omnipotence.

4. The Connection Between Omnipotence and Deceleration

Since omnipotence is not mere power but the sustaining actuality of reality, it necessarily structures the persistence of finite reality. This is where Deceleration comes in.

- Deceleration is the structured selection by which finite motion emerges from infinite actuality.
- Omnipotence is what sustains Deceleration—without it, structured limitation would collapse back into infinite actuality.
- Negative pressure is the necessary structuring boundary that prevents finite reality from collapsing.

Thus, omnipotence and Deceleration are not separate ideas but two aspects of the same sustaining act.

Table 5.4. Why Omnipotence and Deceleration Are Inseparable
This table shows how divine omnipotence sustains the structured limitation introduced by deceleration, preserving coherent reality.

Without Omnipotence	With Omnipotence
Deceleration would fail to sustain structure.	Deceleration remains structured and consistent.
Finite motion would collapse back into infinite actuality.	Negative pressure sustains limitation and distinction.
Causal relationships would not hold.	Omnipotence guarantees the rational order of reality.

Thus, omnipotence is not an arbitrary force. It is the active structuring principle of all reality.

5. Omnipotence as the Foundation of All Reality

Now that we have examined the true nature of omnipotence, we can conclude the following:

- Omnipotence is not about force—it is the actuality of Being itself.
- Omnipotence requires no energy or exertion because it is fully actual power.
- Omnipotence does not compete with natural forces but sustains them as structured selections within actuality.
- Omnipotence is not coercion but structuring potency, allowing for free will and relational contingency.
- Omnipotence is inseparable from Deceleration, ensuring finite differentiation persists rather than dissolving into unity.

6. Moving Forward: The Absolute Unity of Knowledge

Omnipotence, as the sustaining actuality of all that is, must also include the perfect unity of knowledge. God does not observe the world in time—he is the actuality that structures it. Omnipotence does not act in isolation; it is inseparable from omniscience and omnipresence. What is sustained must also be known and related.

In the next chapter, we examine omniscience, not as accumulation of facts but as the total, eternal self-knowledge of Being per se. We will see how all finite rationality arises through deceleration from this infinite actuality and how even our free will unfolds within the unchanging unity of divine knowledge.

6

Omniscience
The Absolute Unity of Knowledge and the Relational Foundation of Rationality

Introduction: What Is Omniscience?

OMNISCIENCE IS OFTEN MISUNDERSTOOD as knowing *everything* in a way similar to how humans accumulate knowledge—by observation, reasoning, and experience. However, omniscience is not an accumulation of facts but the perfect, unchanging unity of all knowledge within Being per se.

In this chapter, we will establish the following:

- Why omniscience is not a process of knowing but an eternal, unified actuality
- Why it is inseparable from omnipotence as the sustaining truth of reality
- How finite rationality emerges from omniscience through Deceleration
- Why omniscience does not conflict with human free will

Omniscience is not rational in the human sense of reasoning through problems. It is relational, meaning that all truth is eternally known in perfect unity. Let us now examine this more closely.

1. The Logical Necessity of Omniscience

Since Being per se is absolute actuality, so it follows:

- There is no truth external to it. All contingent reality exists within its sustaining actuality.
- It does not acquire knowledge over time. All truth is present in an eternal, unchanging act of knowing.
- Knowledge is not a collection of facts but the singular truth of Being itself.

2. Why Omniscience Is Not Passive Awareness but Active Sustenance

Table 6.1. Common Misconceptions About Omniscience
This table corrects popular misunderstandings by presenting omniscience as the triune act of self-knowing, not passive awareness.

Misconception	**Why It's Incorrect**	**True Nature of Omniscience**
Omniscience is like a database of facts.	Knowledge in God is not stored or accumulated.	Omniscience is the eternal triune act of self-knowing within infinite actuality, perfect reciprocal relation—Love itself.
Omniscience means predicting the future.	Prediction implies probability and time-sequence.	Omniscience knows all events in a timeless actuality.
Omniscience is passive observation.	Observation implies learning from an external source.	Omniscience is not observation—it sustains reality.

Thus, omniscience is not merely a property of God—it is identical to Being per se, just as is omnipotence. Without omniscience, reality would have no coherence, no intelligibility, and no rational order.

Since Truth is One and cannot be divided, omniscience is the unity of all Truth as a single, undivided actuality.

3. The Emergence of Rationality from Omniscience

Because omniscience is the eternal triune act of self-knowing within infinite actuality—Truth per se, perfectly known through perfect reciprocal relation—we must ask: How does rationality emerge? How can finite beings reason, distinguish, and learn through time, when divine knowing is eternally complete?

The answer is deceleration of IRM.

The deceleration of IRM is the metaphysical act by which infinite reciprocal knowing—immediate, indivisible, and complete—is made receivable by finite minds. It does not diminish Truth but structures it across limitation, allowing finite beings to engage Truth without collapse into totality. This structuring introduces delay, distinction, and direction, slowing simultaneity into sequence.

In infinite actuality, the Knower, Known, and Knowing are one: there is no before or after, no partiality, no inference. But in decelerated form, this perfect self-knowing is unfolded across time into the relational triad of subject, predicate, and object, allowing finite beings to encounter truth through reasoning, judgment, and experience.

Just as Deceleration structures motion into finite direction and space into relational distance, it structures knowing into rationality—a time-bound participation in eternal Truth.

Table 6.2. Why Rationality Is Not a Divine Attribute but a Finite Expression
This table contrasts infinite omniscience with rationality to show how finite knowledge is a structured limitation made possible through deceleration.

Omniscience (Infinite)	Rationality (Finite)
Non-sequential: no past, present, or future	Sequential: Truth is approached over time.
All truth is known as one unified whole, Truth per se.	Truth is grasped in part, through structured steps.
No deliberation or inference—Truth is identical with Being.	Reasoning involves comparison, inference, and selection.
Eternal and immediate	Temporal and progressive

God does not deliberate or compute options—he simply knows, eternally and without division. Rationality is not a divine attribute. It is the finite reception of Truth across limitation. It is how beings who exist in time come to participate in eternal actuality without being overwhelmed by it.

Rationality is necessary for finite creatures to engage a structured universe. It is not opposed to omniscience but is its decelerated form—structured participation rather than simultaneous possession. The triadic structure of knowledge—subject, predicate, object—is not arbitrary. It reflects the deeper triune nature of Being itself—Knower, Known, and Knowing—just as motion reflects the triadic relation of mover, moved, and medium.

Rationality is the decelerated *form* of divine self-knowing structured through limitation so that finite beings may enter into Truth without collapse or confusion.

4. How Omniscience and Free Will Coexist

A common concern is this: since God knows the future, does that mean human free will is an illusion?

This assumes that knowledge determines choices, which is a misunderstanding.

Table 6.3. Why Divine Foreknowledge Does Not Eliminate Free Will
This table clarifies the metaphysical compatibility between omniscience and human freedom by distinguishing knowledge from causation.

Misunderstanding	Why It's Incorrect	The True Relationship Between Omniscience and Free Will
Since God knows my choice, I am not free.	Knowledge does not cause action. Knowing what you will choose does not make you choose it.	Omniscience does not override free will—it contains it.
Because God foreknows an event, it must be necessary.	Necessary events are those that cannot be otherwise, but contingent events remain free even when known.	Omniscience includes both necessary and contingent truths.
Foreknowledge removes uncertainty, and without uncertainty there is no real choice.	Uncertainty exists only from the human perspective, not in divine actuality.	Free will exists fully within divine omniscience, just as motion exists within structured space.

5. The Key to Understanding Foreknowledge

- God does not predict future choices. All events—past, present, and future—are known in one unchanging act of knowledge.

- Knowing an event does not cause it. Free actions are truly free, even when known.
- From God's perspective, all choices are eternally present. From our perspective, we experience them sequentially.

Thus, divine omniscience fully encompasses free will, without contradiction.

6. *The Connection Between Omniscience and Deceleration*

We now connect omniscience to Deceleration in the following ways:

- Omniscience is absolute, unified, and timeless knowledge—it does not require sequential reasoning, learning, or energy expenditure.
- Deceleration introduces structured limitation, making rational engagement with knowledge possible.
- Negative pressure sustains structured limitation, ensuring that finite beings engage with Truth relationally rather than instantaneously.

Because omniscience is the undivided actuality, Truth per se, it does not involve sequential processing of information—all knowledge is present simultaneously, without fragmentation. In the absence of Deceleration, knowledge would remain instantaneous, total, and unified, meaning no distinction between events, no delay in understanding, and no progression of learning would be possible. However, with the deceleration of IRM, a key transition occurs:

- Information exchange, previously timeless, now occurs across space, consuming energy and requiring time.

This structured limitation is what allows rationality to emerge.

- Knowledge is no longer a single, indivisible actuality but becomes accessible in structured, finite exchanges.
- Truth is no longer grasped instantaneously but processed in sequences, allowing for distinctions and reasoning.
- Energy expenditure becomes necessary for information exchange, making knowledge something finite minds must acquire through structured participation rather than possess fully and immediately.

Through Deceleration, logic and rationality emerge as structured participation in Truth per se. Deceleration does not fragment Truth—it structures it rationally, ensuring that Truth is engaged relationally rather than absorbed as an undivided whole.

This means the following:

- Time emerges as the structured relationality of knowing—finite minds must process truth in steps rather than in totality.

- Space allows for the differentiation of information exchange, ensuring that truth is structured relationally as knowledge rather than as an undivided whole.

- Energy is required for cognition because information is no longer exchanged instantaneously but must be processed through structured participation in reality.

Thus, finite beings do not receive knowledge as omniscience does. Instead, they access it in structured relational participation, constrained by space, time, and energy.

Table 6.4. Why Deceleration Is Necessary for Rationality
This table contrasts divine omniscience with finite rationality to show how knowledge must be structured across limitation for reasoning to emerge.

Without Deceleration	With Deceleration
Knowledge would be instant and total.	Knowledge unfolds through structured relationality.
Rationality would not exist—only pure, immediate knowing.	Rationality emerges as a means of structuring truth finitely.
Information would not require time or energy to process.	Information exchange occurs across space, consuming energy and requiring time.
Finite beings could not engage with Truth relationally.	Logical sequences and reasoning become possible.

Closing Insight: Rationality as a Consequence of Structured Knowing

Since rationality is not a divine attribute but a structured limitation of omniscience, so it follows:

- The human mind does not contain Truth but participates in it sequentially, fragmentarily, and according to the structure by which Being is received.
- Time is not an external constraint on knowing—it is the structured limitation that makes reasoning possible.
- Energy expenditure in thinking is not incidental—it is a direct result of knowledge being structured relationally rather than accessed in totality.

This ensures that rationality, free will, and knowledge are meaningful participations in omniscience rather than deterministic inevitabilities. Thus, Deceleration does not weaken Truth—it makes structured knowing possible for finite beings.

7. Moving Forward: The Presence That Sustains All Things

Omniscience is not a passive awareness but the active, non-sequential unity of all knowledge within infinite actuality. It is not that God observes the world—he is the actuality in which all things are known and structured. But knowledge alone is not enough to sustain finite reality. Being must also be fully present to every aspect of creation, not as a spatial diffusion but as the indivisible source in which all things persist.

In the next chapter, we turn to omnipresence, not as divine extension in space but as the boundless and indivisible presence of Being itself. We will examine why there is no "distance" between God and creation, and how omnipresence follows necessarily from the same actuality that sustains all causality, motion, and personhood.

7

Omnipresence
The Boundless and Indivisible Presence of Being

Introduction: What is Omnipresence?

OMNIPRESENCE IS OFTEN MISUNDERSTOOD as God being spread out across space like a physical substance, as though he occupies every point in the universe in a spatial sense. However, omnipresence does not mean that God is everywhere as a part of creation—it means that nothing can exist apart from his sustaining actuality.

This chapter will establish the following:

- Why omnipresence is not a spatial extension but the necessary sustaining presence of Being per se
- Why there is no distance between God and creation
- How omnipresence logically follows from omnipotence and omniscience
- Why divine action is not intervention but continuous sustaining actuality
- How personhood arises through participation in the personal actuality of omnipresent Being

Rather than imagining omnipresence as a scattered presence throughout the cosmos, we must understand it as the very condition that makes all existence possible.

1. The Logical Necessity of Omnipresence

Since Being per se is infinite actuality, so it follows:

- There is no outside to its presence. If something could exist apart from infinite actuality, it would be self-existent, which is impossible.
- God does not occupy space—he sustains it. Space, like time, is a structured limitation introduced through deceleration of IRM.
- Everything that exists does so within the presence of Being per se, not as a separate reality.

Table 7.1. The Three False Views of Omnipresence
This table dispels common misconceptions of omnipresence by distinguishing it from spatial extension, absence, or episodic intervention.

False View of Omnipresence	Why It's Incorrect	The True Nature of Omnipresence
God is physically extended throughout space.	It means God has dimensions, contradicting infinite actuality.	Omnipresence is not spatial but is a sustaining presence.
God is separate from creation, only *watching* from afar.	This suggests God is limited to a location, which contradicts his necessity as the source of all being.	There is no *distance* between God and creation—he sustains all things directly.
God moves in and out of reality, *intervening* when needed.	This would imply God is sometimes present and sometimes not, which contradicts his unchanging nature.	Omnipresence means God continuously sustains all things, not merely intervening occasionally.

Thus, omnipresence is not about *where* God is—it is about the fact that there are no existing things without him. If omnipresence were not true, reality would not be present. Because Being per se is the sustaining source of all things, God's presence is not just everywhere—it is the reason anything exists at all.

2. The Connection Between Omnipresence and Divine Action

Because God is omnipresent, divine action is not about *intervention*. Instead, divine action is the following:

- The continuous sustaining of reality at every moment
- The structuring of all finite existence through Deceleration
- The foundation of all causality without being a cause among other causes

Table 7.2. Why Divine Action Is Not Intervention
This table distinguishes between common misconceptions of divine action and its true nature as continuous, non-local sustaining actuality.

Misunderstanding	Why It's Incorrect	The True Nature of Divine Action
God *intervenes* in the world like an external force.	This claim suggests God is outside of creation and only acts occasionally.	God continuously sustains all things, so divine action is never absent.
God's presence means everything is predetermined.	Omnipresence does not override free will or contingency.	Omnipresence allows finite beings to participate in perfect actuality while remaining distinct.
God is inside the universe like a physical entity.	Spatial limitations do not apply to infinite actuality.	Omnipresence is the sustaining foundation, not a localized presence.

Thus, omnipresence means that everything is continuously upheld by God's being—God's presence is not an occasional act but eternal, unchanging actuality.

3. Omnipresence and the Illusion of Distance from God

For traditions or individuals who might describe a felt separation from God, it is important to clarify that this sense of separation is an illusion of perception, not an actual distance. Since God sustains all things, it is impossible to be truly distanced from him. However, finite beings experience this as distance due to the following:

- The structured limitations of Deceleration
- The constraints of finite perception
- The consequences of free will

From God's perspective, there is no distance—only immediate, continuous sustenance. From our perspective, we experience finite knowledge and finite movement toward or away from Truth.

Table 7.3. How Finite Beings Experience Omnipresence
This table distinguishes between God's unchanging presence and the varying subjective experience of that presence in finite perception and moral awareness.

Perspective	Experience	Reality of Omnipresence
God's perspective	There is no distance—God sustains all things immediately.	God is fully present to all creation.
Finite perspective	Separation is felt due to limited perception and free will.	Omnipresence does not change; only our awareness of it does.
Moral perception	People experience *closeness* or *distance* from God psychologically based on their actions.	Omnipresence does not fluctuate; human perception does.

Thus, we do not move closer or farther from God in reality—we only experience degrees of awareness of his omnipresent actuality.

This sense of separation, however real it may feel, is psychological—it is not metaphysical. There is no actual distance between God and the *soul*, for all things are sustained at every moment by the omnipresent actuality of Being per se. Yet because the finite *intellect* cannot comprehend infinite presence all at once, and because the will may resist participation in the *Good*, the *soul* can come to perceive absence where there is only presence unreceived. This misperception—conditioned by the finite structure of reality and the wounds of disordered relation—can give rise to a spiritual desolation that many take as evidence against a personal God. But the logic of Being reveals the opposite: personhood, and the very capacity to feel such distance, is only possible because we are sustained by a personal God. The illusion of distance is thus not proof of God's absence. Much to the contrary, it is the echo of a personal presence we are structurally made to receive, even when it exceeds our present awareness.

4. Omnipresence and the Structure of Reality

Omnipresence is the sustaining framework that allows all finite beings to exist within structured reality. This means the following:

- Being per se is not spatial, but space is structured within it.
- There is no beyond God's presence—only different levels of participation in actuality.
- Thus, the triunity of one God in three persons—not merely personalization—makes us persons via the triadic relational structure of finite reality.
- Negative pressure ensures that finite beings remain distinct while fully sustained.

Table 7.4 How Omnipresence Structures Reality

This table explains how space, time, energy, and consciousness emerge as structured expressions of divine presence through deceleration.

Aspect of Reality	Role of Omnipresence
Space	All spatial structures exist within the sustaining presence of Being per se.
Time	All temporal sequences unfold within the unchanging actuality of omnipresence.
Energy	All finite motion and causality are upheld by omnipotent sustaining presence.
Consciousness	All knowledge and awareness are structured within the relational unity of omniscience.

Thus, omnipresence is not merely an attribute—it is the structured participation of all things in Being per se.

5. Omnipresence as the Sustaining Presence of All Reality

- We now conclude that omnipresence is not spatial but the sustaining actuality of all things.
- Omnipresence is not intervention but continuous sustenance.
- Omnipresence is not something that fluctuates—only perception of it changes.

- Omnipresence is the very reason space, time, and motion exist as structured realities.
- Omnipresence is the foundation of all finite existence, ensuring that nothing exists apart from Being per se.

In the next chapter, we will examine how science, metaphysics, and theology converge to affirm these truths, resolving the false divide between empirical knowledge and divine actuality.

6. Personhood as the Finite Echo of Omnipresent Being

To understand omnipresence rightly is not only to recognize that God sustains all things but to realize that some beings are capable of knowing, loving, and responding to that presence. This is not true of all creatures. A rock exists but does not consciously know. An animal senses but does not love through will. A machine computes but does not commune. Only the person—structured in Truth, Love, and Communion—is capable of receiving Being in a way that reflects and participates in its source.

In this metaphysical framework, a person is not defined by self-awareness, social behavior, or cognitive development. These are expressions of something deeper. A person is a finite being whose very structure reflects the triune actuality of Being itself: Truth as *intellect*, Love as *will*, and Communion as *relation*. This structure is not emergent; it is given. Personhood is the consequence of Being received as structure through the act of Deceleration.

Deceleration is what renders the infinite shareable. It introduces structured limitation without division, making it possible for finite beings to exist without fragmenting the infinite. In this way, the person is not an emanation from God, nor a self-standing being. The person is a structured participation in the personal nature of God's omnipresence, an echo of divine actuality made receivable through form.

Thus, personhood is not a human achievement but a metaphysical act of reception. It is not a function of matter, not reducible to brain states or social systems. The person is irreducible precisely because it is a metaphysical act of communion with Being per se. Were God not personal—capable of relation, will, and knowledge—there would be no triune structure to give and no beings capable of receiving it. There would be no persons at all.

This is why the illusion of distance from God is ultimately the echo of nearness. The capacity to feel separation implies a structure ordered toward presence, one too often interpreted as its opposite.[1] The finite *soul* does not drift from an impersonal force, but wavers in its participation in the One who sustains it at every moment. The person is thus not only upheld by omnipresence but is its highest finite expression: the structured likeness of personal Being in time.

7. Moving Forward: The Integration of All Knowledge

Omnipresence is not spatial extension but the indivisible actuality that sustains all things at every moment. Space, time, causality, and personhood persist only because they participate in this presence. But this sustaining structure is not confined to theology alone—it shapes the logic of every rational discipline.

In the next chapter, we will examine how science, metaphysics, and theology are not rivals but participants in the same ordered truth. Rather than dividing human understanding, we will see that each field reflects the same necessary structure of Being, and that true knowledge must ultimately converge in the actuality of divine self-expression.

---

1. Julian of Norwich, in her *Revelations of Divine Love*, recounts a vision in which she sees "a little thing the size of a hazelnut." When she asks what it is, she is told, "It is all that is made. It lasts and ever shall because God loves it." Though mystical in tone, this vision expresses a profound metaphysical truth. "It is all that is made" points to the shared finitude of creation: all things are structured through Deceleration and exist as recipients of limited form. "It lasts and ever shall because God loves it" is no sentimentalism; it is a metaphysical axiom. Being is given and sustained by Love, and God's love is not a feeling but the eternal act of sustaining what is finite without ceasing to be infinite.

Yet this vision stands in sharp contrast to the dominant impulse of modernity. Where Julian sees that even the smallest and most dependent thing is sustained by divine Love, our age often sees smallness, difference, or dependency as reasons to withdraw recognition—or to eliminate. This is not to say that an acorn is a person. But since God sustains what he has made simply because he loves it, how much more must he love those structured to know and return that love. As Christ taught, "Notice how the lilies of the field grow. . . . But if God so clothes the grass . . . will He not much more clothe you?" (Matt 6:28–30).

To be a person is to be a finite image of that sustaining Love, not only upheld by it but capable of returning it. The modern failure is to mistake the veiling of that capacity for the absence of worth. See Julian of Norwich, *Revelations*, long text, 47–48.

8

The Convergence of Science, Metaphysics, and Theology

Introduction: The Unity of Knowledge

Having established the logical necessity of Being per se and the divine attributes of omnipotence, omniscience, and omnipresence, it is now necessary to examine how these principles relate to the broader domains of scientific inquiry and theological understanding.

A common but false assumption is that science, metaphysics, and theology offer competing explanations of reality. This assumption is historically, philosophically, and logically flawed. The divide between these disciplines is an artificial construct that has arisen from an incomplete or fragmented approach to knowledge.

A truly integrated framework reveals a fundamental truth:

- Science, metaphysics, and theology are not separate domains of inquiry but distinct modalities of the same structured reality.
- They do not merely align—they are inseparably united in a single logical structure, grounded in the necessary actuality of Being per se.
- Metaphysics does not compete with science or theology—it is the logical foundation upon which both stand.

This chapter will demonstrate the following:

- How metaphysical necessity integrates scientific discoveries rather than deferring to them
- How theological truths do not merely align with scientific understanding but presuppose it
- Why an infinite foundation (Being per se) is a necessary precondition for all rational inquiry
- How the artificial separation of these disciplines weakens scientific, philosophical, and theological discourse alike
- Why this unification is the only viable resolution to the unresolved question of divine action

Rather than assuming a divide between reason and faith, this system puts an end to the false dichotomy, demonstrating the following:

- Science investigates what reality does.
- Metaphysics explains how and why reality is.
- Theology expresses this reality through divine revelation.

Each mode of inquiry is structured within Truth per se. They do not merely *interact*; they are necessarily integrated.

1. Science as the Study of Contingent Reality

Science is the empirical study of how the universe behaves. It constructs models based on observation, measurement, and predictive accuracy. However, science does not explain why the universe exists or why it follows logical and mathematical laws—it assumes these conditions as pre-given.

Thus, science is dependent on a deeper reality, one that metaphysics and theology do not merely describe but logically establish.

The Limits of Scientific Explanation

Science successfully describes reality within its domain, but it cannot answer the following questions:

- Why does anything exist at all?
- Why does the universe follow rational, predictable laws?

- Why do mathematical principles correspond to physical reality?
- Why can the human mind grasp reality intelligibly?

These foundational assumptions—that the universe is intelligible and structured—are not scientific conclusions but metaphysical necessities. Order must precede observation; reality is structured before it is studied.

Table 8.1. Empirical Observation Must Reflect Metaphysical Necessity
This table demonstrates how foundational assumptions in science presuppose metaphysical realities such as order, structure, and intelligibility.

Metaphysical Necessity	Scientific Observation
Order must preexist the universe—laws do not emerge from chaos.	The universe follows laws.
Rather than being an arbitrary human construct, mathematics must reflect the expressed rational order.	Mathematical structures describe physics.
Intelligibility must be embedded within reality.	The human mind can grasp reality.

Being per se is not mathematical. In the One who is—the infinite actuality from which all structure proceeds—there are no numbers, no formulas, no quantities. Mathematics, like logic, arises only through the act of Deceleration, by which infinite actuality is made receivable as structured limitation. Truth per se is not governed by logic; it is the ground from which all logic and order arise. What science studies as law or quantity is not a property of God, but the echo of intelligibility structured for finite minds. Mathematics is not eternal in itself—it is a mode of participation in the eternal.

Since metaphysical truths are tautologically necessary, they provide the logical foundation for science.

Thus:

- If science contradicts metaphysical necessity, science must adjust its models.
- Metaphysics does not defer to science—science conforms to logical necessity.

2. Theological Integration: Divine Sustenance, Not Intervention

If science describes how the universe functions and metaphysics explains why it exists, then theology does not merely affirm these truths—it expresses them through divine revelation. For those with eyes to see, even science becomes a kind of revelation—not in the mode of prophecy or dogma, but in the unveiling of structured reality sustained by God.

The laws of physics, the harmony of natural constants, the intelligibility of motion and relation—all these are signs of a deeper rationality. But this rationality is not abstract or impersonal; it is the visible echo of the infinite *Logos*. What science perceives as structure is the result of decelerated IRM—God's self-giving rendered receivable. Thus, when science is rightly ordered, it does not oppose theology—it silently testifies to it.

A. The Causal Joint and Divine Action

A unified metaphysical system resolves the longstanding problem of divine action.

- God does not intervene in creation as an external force—he sustains it at every moment.
- Divine omnipresence ensures that all things exist relationally within Being per se.
- Scientific inquiry is possible only because the universe is upheld by a rational, coherent order.

Thus, divine action is not supernatural interference but the necessary sustaining actuality of all contingent reality.

B. Free Will, Divine Foreknowledge, and Quantum Mechanics

A common theological objection is that if God knows the future, human free will must be an illusion. A similar scientific paradox appears in quantum mechanics: How do quantum probabilities resolve into determinate realities?

The Convergence of Science, Metaphysics, and Theology

Table 8.2. Human Freedom Within Divine Knowledge
This table corrects philosophical misconceptions about omniscience, free will, and quantum uncertainty through metaphysical clarity.

Misunderstanding	Why It's Incorrect	True Understanding of Divine Knowledge
Because God knows everything, human choices must be predetermined.	This assumes that knowledge causes events, confusing knowing with determining.	Divine knowledge is not causal; it knows free acts as they are—freely chosen yet eternally known.
Free will requires total unpredictability.	This equates freedom with randomness and denies the *soul's* structured nature.	Freedom is structured participation in Being—ordered, intentional, and self-directed.
Quantum uncertainty proves the universe is fundamentally indeterminate.	This misreads epistemological limits as ontological ones.	Uncertainty arises only within finite knowledge; in divine actuality, Truth is fully structured as self-knowing, without division between knower, known, and act of knowing.
Divine foreknowledge eliminates human responsibility.	This reduces persons to passive executors of a plan.	Persons are finite agents whose choices are truly free within God's sustaining presence.
Mathematics describes divine logic directly.	This projects finite symbolic systems into divine actuality.	Mathematics models aspects of structure but does not define or contain divine knowledge.
Possibility is a property of the universe.	This misunderstands potential as real apart from act.	All possibility exists only as structured potential—ordered participation in actuality made receivable through Deceleration.

Thus, free will is not a violation of determinism but a higher-order participation in structured reality.

3. The Necessary Infinite: Why Science Presupposes God

Materialist assumptions in modern science suggest that scientific discovery negates the need for God. However, careful metaphysical reflection reveals the opposite: science requires the principles that theology affirms.

A. The Rational Order of the Universe

Science is founded on the following assumptions:

- The universe follows consistent, rational laws.
- The human mind is capable of grasping these laws.
- Mathematics and physics correspond to reality.

None of these assumptions are self-explanatory—they only make sense if:

- Order is fundamental to reality, not an accident.
- The human *intellect* participates in a greater rational structure.
- Mathematics and physics reflect a deeper metaphysical unity.

Thus, science does not eliminate the need for God—it presupposes him as the necessary foundation of order and intelligibility.

B. The Metaphysical Necessity of Being Per Se

- The universe is contingent—it could have been otherwise or not existed at all.
- The principles governing it must be grounded in non-contingent actuality.
- Being per se is the only logically necessary foundation for all rational inquiry.

4. The True Convergence of Science, Metaphysics, and Theology

The following is now clear:

- Science assumes order and rationality, which must be metaphysically grounded.

The Convergence of Science, Metaphysics, and Theology

- Metaphysics does not just explain the necessity of structure—it establishes its foundation.
- Theology does not just affirm this reality—it expresses it through divine revelation.
- Scientific conclusions must conform to metaphysical necessity unless a logical flaw is found.
- The question of divine action finds resolution in this unified metaphysical system.

Thus, science, metaphysics, and theology are not separate paths of knowledge. They are modalities of the same structured reality; and all knowledge—scientific, philosophical, and theological—converges upon Being per se.

Table 8.3. Three Perspectives on Reality
This table compares science, metaphysics, and theology as convergent approaches to understanding structured reality.

Domain	Primary Concern	Ultimate Answer
Science	Describes how reality behaves	Requires an underlying metaphysical order
Metaphysics	Explains why reality exists as it does	Necessarily points to an infinite foundation (Being per se)
Theology	Expresses truths through divine revelation	Affirms God as the necessary actuality and source of intelligibility

5. Moving Forward: The Actuality of Divine Action

Science describes the behaviors of reality, metaphysics establishes their necessity, and theology reveals their fulfillment. Each discipline, when rightly understood, converges on the same Truth: Being per se is not merely the foundation of existence—it is the triune actuality from which all order proceeds. This being true, the question must be asked: How does God act?

In the next chapter, we will resolve the deepest tension in philosophy and theology—how infinite actuality can sustain, order, and act within finite creation without contradiction. Divine action is not intervention or exception. It is the continuous structuring of all reality, and it must be understood not through analogy to human causality but through the metaphysical necessity of the causal joint.

9

The Resolution of Divine Action in Light of Metaphysical Necessity

Introduction: The Problem of Divine Action

FOR CENTURIES, THEOLOGICAL AND philosophical discourse has struggled to articulate how God acts within creation.

- The central issue is often framed as follows:
  - If God is infinite, unchanging, and omnipotent, how does he interact with the finite, dynamic universe without contradicting his nature?
  - If all things are sustained by divine omnipresence, what distinguishes divine action from natural causality?
  - If God's foreknowledge is absolute, does divine action allow for human freedom or does it imply determinism?
- Traditional theological models often fall erroneously into two camps:
  - *Occasionalism*—the view that all causal activity is directly willed by God, making natural laws merely apparent rather than real.
  - *Deism*—the belief that God created the universe but does not engage with it, rendering divine action functionally irrelevant.

- Both views fail to resolve the proper metaphysical issues:
  - Divine action is not intervention, disruption, or periodic engagement—it is the singular, continuous structuring of all reality.
  - The term "miracle" is a psychological distinction, not a metaphysical one—there is no fundamental difference between the laws of gravity and an event traditionally considered supernatural.

This chapter will demonstrate the following:

- Divine action is not a separate intervention but the seamless unfolding of foreknown reality.
- God does not enter creation; creation exists entirely within his sustaining actuality.
- What is called special divine action is simply structured reality, foreknown and potentiated from the beginning.
- Human free will exists within divine omniscience without contradiction. Thus, the resolution of divine action is found not in intervention but in the structured potentiation of divine selection.

1. *The Causal Joint as the Singular Act of Divine Action*

A. All Existence Is a Structured Participation in Being Per Se

This means the following:

- Creation is not a one-time event—it is the ongoing potentiation of structured reality.
- All causality is sustained through divine selection—there is no distinction between ordinary and extraordinary events.
- What appears as natural causation and what appears as divine action are indistinguishable in actuality—they are psychological categories imposed by finite beings.

B. Divine Action Is Not Intervention—It Is the Continuous Structuring of Reality

A flawed understanding of divine action assumes one of the following:

- That God intervenes in the world as an external force
- That God leaves creation to operate independently, stepping in occasionally

Both assumptions are false because they mischaracterize the nature of divine actuality.

Properly understood:

- God does not act within time—he is the source of all temporality.
- God does not respond to events—he foreknows all events as structured realities.
- God does not violate natural law—he is the source of its intelligibility.

Rather than thinking of God acting on the universe, we must recognize the following:

- The universe exists as an ongoing act of divine selection.
- What appears to be natural and what appears to be miraculous are structurally identical—both are part of structured reality, sustained by infinite actuality.
- There is no need for supernatural exceptions because everything is already foreknown and structured within divine omniscience.

Thus, divine action is not a supernatural force imposed upon a natural system—it is the system itself.

2. The Misconception of "Miracles" as Disruptions of Natural Law

A major theological problem has been the assumption that miracles represent exceptions to natural order. This error stems from the false belief that divine action occurs alongside natural laws rather than structuring them from within.

Miracles Are Not "Interruptions" but Foreknown Selections

What is typically called a miracle is simply a structured event within foreknown reality.

Table 9.1. Understanding Miracles
This table clarifies why miracles are not violations of nature but structured selections within foreknown reality sustained by divine omniscience.

Common View of Miracles	Why It's Incorrect	Proper Understanding
Miracles are violations of natural law.	If miracles violated nature, then nature would be arbitrary.	Miracles are not violations, but structured realities potentiated in divine selection.
Miracles are supernatural interventions.	This assumes a division between *natural* and *supernatural*.	There is no such division—all reality is structured within divine actuality.
Miracles prove divine action in a special way.	This assumes that divine action occurs in degrees rather than as a singular actuality.	All of creation is equally an act of divine selection—there are no levels or ranks of divine causality.

Thus, the concept of special divine action is a human construct, not a metaphysical reality.

3. The Ego and the Miracle: The Psychological Impact of Misreading Divine Action Through the Desire for Specialness

A major theological error has long distorted the meaning of miracles: the belief that miracles represent divine exceptions to natural order—interventions in an otherwise closed system. As previously shown, this stems from the false metaphysical assumption that God operates alongside natural laws, rather than sustaining them as their structured ground. But beneath this theological mistake lies a deeper psychological pattern: the ego's desire for centrality, recognition, and uniqueness in the eyes of God.

Human beings have long struggled to accept that we are not the center of the universe (which, in fact, has no physical center). From

Copernicus and Galileo to contemporary cosmology, the displacement of Earth from the physical center of creation has been mirrored by an existential resistance to the idea that one's life is not the axis of meaning. This resistance easily transposes into a theology of miracles: if a person is touched by something extraordinary—if something impossible happens to them or through them—it is taken as evidence of divine favoritism. Miracles, in this view, become signs of being chosen, of being more loved, more important, or more holy than others.

This psychology mirrors broader cultural patterns. People seek proximity to celebrities as if something of their significance might "rub off." They crowd around fame, interpret coincidence as cosmic validation, and interpret suffering as punishment or rejection. In religious psychology, this often becomes spiritual exceptionalism—the belief that one can earn divine love by being better, holier, or more obedient than others. The miraculous is no longer the unveiling of divine structure; it is interpreted as a spotlight of divine approval.

But in truth, this is a projection of finite anxiety onto infinite Love. Miracles are not rewards. They are not merit badges. They are not interruptions of nature but revelations of deeper structure—moments in which divine sustaining presence becomes transparent. And such moments are not reserved for the especially favored. They are selective, not exclusive—manifestations of order, not symbols of hierarchy.

Those who seem to suffer endlessly, who endure invisibly, who are never touched by the visibly miraculous—they participate just as fully in the eschatological structure of creation *(that is, the divinely ordered fulfillment of all creation in its final form and purpose)*. Their lives, too, are held in the same sustaining logic. In many cases, *souls* who never receive what many would call an *obvious* miracle bear within themselves a deeper participation in Love, precisely because they are not protected from the full weight of finitude. Their hidden fidelity is itself a miracle, structured silently within Being.[1]

---

1. Julian of Norwich writes of the apostles' suffering during Christ's passion: "Then said our good Lord Jesus Christ: 'Art thou well pleased that I suffered for thee?' I said: 'Yea, good Lord, I thank thee.' Then said Jesus, our kind Lord: 'If thou art pleased, I am pleased. It is a joy, a bliss, an endless delight to me that ever I suffered Passion for thee; and if I might suffer more, I would suffer more.'" She goes on to describe how those who loved Jesus most—his mother and his disciples—suffered more deeply because they loved him: "The more loving, the more grieving." Their love increased both their suffering and their union with him.

This insight confirms a metaphysical truth: love does not alleviate the structure of suffering—it deepens it through participation. Those who suffer without reward or

Thus, the miracle is not a mark of divine affection withheld from others. It is not a token of cosmic favor. It is a structural event—a revealing of the same self-giving actuality that sustains the entire world. To seek miracles in order to feel significant is to misread both God and the *soul*. Divine significance is not earned by being noticed; it is received by being sustained. And those who are never noticed, never healed, never elevated, play no less a role in the story of creation than those through whom the structure shines for a moment.

4. Divine Foreknowledge and Free Will: The Resolution of an Apparent Contradiction

A final challenge in discussing divine action is the false dilemma of determinism vs. freedom.

Since God knows all things, is human freedom negated? If free will is real, does this imply that God lacks control?

This is not a real paradox but an illusion of perspective—it arises only because humans conceive of knowledge sequentially, while divine omniscience is non-sequential.

Foreknowledge Does Not Impose Necessity

A common error assumes that knowing an event in advance causes that event to occur. This is false.

Table 9.2. Misconceptions about Divine Foreknowledge and Free Will Resolved
This table dispels misunderstandings about the relationship between God's foreknowledge and human freedom by affirming foreknowledge as timeless, not deterministic.

Misconception	Why It's Incorrect	Proper Understanding
If God knows my choices, I am not free.	Knowledge does not cause action—foreknowing a choice is not the same as forcing it.	Foreknowledge does not determine events—it simply reflects their certainty.

---

miracle may share most intimately in divine Love, not as a sign of absence but of profound communion. See Julian of Norwich, *Revelations*, 72–74.

Misconception	Why It's Incorrect	Proper Understanding
Free will means God does not control creation.	This assumes that freedom and divine causality are mutually exclusive.	Free will operates within divine omniscience as a structured participation in actuality.
If humans are free, they can act outside divine knowledge.	This assumes that knowledge must be acquired rather than inherent.	All choices exist within divine omniscience from eternity.

Thus, human freedom does not contradict divine omniscience—it is an integral aspect of it.

5. The Full Resolution of Divine Action

Having removed the false distinction between general and special divine action, we now see the following:

- All divine action is a single, continuous potentiation of structured reality.
- Miracles are not disruptions—they are foreknown participations in structured reality.
- God does not enter creation—creation exists entirely within his sustaining actuality.
- Free will is fully compatible with divine omniscience, as all choices exist within structured selection.

6. Closing Insight: Divine Action as the Singular Foundation of All Reality

There is no hierarchy of divine action. There are no separate types of divine engagement with reality. Everything that exists is foreknown reality structured within divine actuality. Thus, divine action is not something that happens within the universe—divine action is the reason the universe exists at all.

7. Moving Forward: The Purpose of Human Participation in Reality

Since divine action is not external intervention but the continuous structuring of all reality through the causal joint, then every facet of existence—from motion to consciousness—unfolds within a relational order. But such order demands more than passive existence. It requires response.

In the next chapter, we will examine the unique role of human beings within this divine act of structuring. Far from being bystanders, we are participatory agents in the unfolding of actuality. Chapter 10 explores how freedom, responsibility, and the teleological structure of creation converge, revealing the human vocation as the deliberate alignment of finite will with divine intelligibility. Here, metaphysics becomes ethics, and ontology becomes purpose.

10

The Unification of Divine Action and Human Purpose

Introduction: The Integration of Divine Action, Freedom, and Purpose

IN PREVIOUS CHAPTERS, WE established that divine action is not an external intervention but the structured potentiation of reality. Rather than acting as an outside force, God's self-expression unfolds through the causal joint, which selects and sustains structured reality from infinite actuality. This understanding leads us to a critical question: What is the purpose of human existence within this structured reality?

The universe is neither random nor deterministic but instead an intentional act of divine self-expression. Therefore, human existence cannot be accidental. It must play a necessary role in the unfolding of reality.

This chapter will establish the following:

- Human beings are not passive observers but active participants in the potentiation of reality.
- Free will is not simply the ability to choose—it is the means by which finite reality unfolds toward its full expression.
- The structure of reality implies human responsibility in shaping its teleological completion.

- The highest fulfillment of human existence is found in aligning free will with divine intelligibility.

Thus, the resolution of divine action is not only metaphysical. It is also existential. The very structure of reality demands that human life be purposeful, relational, and participatory.

1. *The Purpose of Free Will in Divine Potentiation*

A. Freedom as Participation in Reality

A common misconception is that free will exists for its own sake, as though having choices is the highest good. However, within the metaphysical structure we have developed, free will is not an end in itself—it is a means by which finite beings participate in divine self-expression.

Unlike an arbitrary ability to make choices, free will is the means by which we engage. Every action, every choice, every moment of recognition or rejection of truth is a mode of participation in structured reality.

This means the following:

- Freedom is necessary for relational intelligibility.
- Reality is structured by relational differentiation—the capacity to recognize distinctions and act accordingly is foundational to existence.
- Freedom is not randomness—it is meaningful participation.
- Every choice operates within a foreknown range of possibilities yet remains truly free.
- Freedom allows genuine engagement with divine self-expression.
- Without free will, human existence would be mechanistic, reducing our role in reality to mere automatic processes. This would contradict the triadic nature of reality, which requires relational participation.

Thus, free will is not separate from divine order—it is an intrinsic part of it.

The Unification of Divine Action and Human Purpose

B. Clarifying Misconceptions About Free Will

A structured understanding of free will requires clearing up common misconceptions.

Table 10.1. Common Misconceptions About Free Will

This table corrects distorted views of freedom by showing that free will is not an isolated faculty but a structured mode of participation in divine potentiation.

Common View of Free Will	Why It's Incorrect	Corrected Understanding
Free will is independent from divine action.	This assumes free will operates outside divine knowledge.	Free will is a participatory aspect of divine self-expression, not an independent force.
Free will exists for its own sake.	This assumes choice has no ultimate purpose.	Free will is the means by which human beings participate in divine potentiation.
Freedom means unlimited possibility.	This assumes all choices are equally valid or meaningful.	Free will operates within divine omniscience, where some choices align with actuality while others diminish participation in it.

C. Degrees of Participation in Being

Since human free will is not independent from reality but rather a form of participation within it, so it follows:

- Different beings participate to different degrees.
- The more a being aligns with divine self-expression, the more fully it participates in Being itself.
- Freedom is meaningful only when exercised in accordance with the intelligibility of reality.

We can think of participation in Being as occurring along a spectrum.

Table 10.2. Spectrum of Participation in Divine Actuality
This table outlines the degrees to which different beings participate in Being, showing that free will entails responsibility to align with divine self-expression.

Degree of Participation	Mode of Existence	Relationship to Divine Self-Expression
Full Participation	Beings that are fully aligned with divine actuality	Direct, unimpeded participation in the divine order
Partial Participation	Finite rational beings (humans)	Structured freedom allowing for choice and moral responsibility
Minimal Participation	Inanimate matter and non-human biological life	Sustained by divine actuality but lacking rational participation

The key takeaway is this: the highest function of free will is not simply to choose but to choose in accordance with reality.

2. The Necessity of Human Purpose

A. Why Human Existence Must Be Purposeful

If human life were purposeless, it would imply the following:

- Reality lacks relational intelligibility.
- The emergence of free, rational beings was accidental.
- The causal joint of divine action was indifferent to the unfolding of finite existence.

However, we have already established the following:

- Reality is not arbitrary but structured.
- The triadic nature of existence demands relational participation.
- Finite beings exist to allow structured participation in divine actuality.

Therefore, human life cannot be without purpose—it must serve a necessary function within divine self-expression.

B. The Fulfillment of Human Purpose

Since human life must have a necessary function, we must now ask what that function is. The logical answer is that the highest purpose of human existence is to align free will with the intelligibility of divine self-expression.

This means the following:

- Human beings must recognize their existence as participatory in divine actuality.
- The most meaningful use of free will is to align one's choices with the intelligibility of reality.
- The ultimate fulfillment of human life is to actively participate in the relational structure of divine expression.

Table 10.3. Alignment of Free Will with Divine Self-Expression
This table demonstrates how varying degrees of alignment with divine intelligibility result in corresponding levels of coherence, disintegration, or fulfillment within divinely structured reality.

Degree of Alignment with Divine Self-Expression	Consequence
Complete alignment with structured reality within finitude	Maximum coherence with the intelligible order of reality (optimal fulfillment within the structured differentiation of finitude)
Partial alignment	Limited fulfillment; tension between structured reality and disordered differentiation
Rejection of alignment	Diminished participation in reality; self-imposed cognitive and ontological dissonance leading to disintegration from intelligible order and separation from Truth

Thus, the final unification of divine action and human purpose is found in the full participation of free will in divine actuality.

3. The Resolution of Existence within Divine Potentiation

Having examined the necessary structure of divine action, we conclude the following:

- Divine action is not an external intervention—it is the sustaining foundation of all reality.
- Free will is not an independent force—it is a mode of participation in divine actuality.
- Human life is not arbitrary—it must serve a necessary function in the relational structure of Being itself.
- The highest purpose of human existence is to align free will with the intelligibility of divine self-expression.

Thus, existence is not arbitrary—it is an intelligible structure of divine potentiation wherein all rational beings are called to full participation in Being itself.

4. Moving Forward: The Alignment of Knowing and Willing

Chapter 10 concluded that human existence is neither accidental nor autonomous. Free will is not an isolated power but a structured mode of participation in divine self-expression. Human purpose is fulfilled not in arbitrary choice, but in aligning finite will with the intelligibility of Being itself.

Chapter 11 now turns to the faculties that make such alignment possible: *intellect* and *will*. It explores how finite knowledge must be ordered toward truth and how love and morality are not human inventions but reflections of divine actuality. Here, understanding moves inward toward the *soul's* structured engagement with Truth itself.

11

The Necessary Union of Intellect, Will, and Divine Truth

Introduction: The Problem of Human Understanding

In the previous chapters, we established that divine omniscience is not an attribute of God but the necessary actuality of Being per se. However, this raises two profound questions. First, since omniscience is the fullness of knowledge, how do finite beings, who experience knowledge in fragments, relate to it? And how does human *intellect* (the ability to know) and will (the ability to choose) interact with divine Truth?

These questions are crucial because they determine whether human reason is merely subjective or whether it participates in a higher, objective truth. They also reveal why knowledge alone is insufficient for understanding divine actuality—our will must also be properly oriented toward Truth itself for knowledge to be complete.

This chapter will explore the necessary relationship between *intellect*, *will*, and divine Truth and establish the following:

- *Intellect* is the faculty by which finite beings participate in Truth, but it does not create Truth.
- The *will* determines whether one aligns with Truth or rejects it, shaping one's capacity for participation in divine actuality.

- Love and morality are not human constructs but structured reflections of divine actuality.
- Divine illumination is necessary—without it, the finite *intellect* remains wanting.

This chapter is crucial for understanding the beatific vision, where *intellect* and *will* find their ultimate fulfillment in seeing divine actuality without distortion.[1]

1. *The Intellect as the Capacity for Truth*

Human *intellect* is not a generator of Truth, but a means of discovering and conforming to what is already true. This distinction is crucial because modern relativism falsely claims that truth is a human construct—a view that contradicts the very nature of Being per se.

A. The Relationship Between Divine Truth and Finite Knowledge

- God is Truth. Divine omniscience is not a collection of facts but the total, unified knowledge of all.
- Finite *intellect* does not create Truth. We do not invent Truth but participate in it by discovering what already is.
- Human knowledge is fragmented. Unlike divine knowledge, which is immediate and total, human knowledge is:
  - Sequential (acquired over time)
  - Limited (bound by perception and reasoning capacity)
  - Influenced by the *will* (our moral choices affect what we accept as true)

---

1. The term "beatific vision" was classically formulated by Aquinas in *Summa Theologiae* I, q 12, art. 1, to describe the soul's final union with God through intellectual vision. Though the result here is the same, the conclusion is reached independently by metaphysical deduction from the impossibility of nonexistence and the necessity of structured participation in Being.

This limitation means that learning, reasoning, and contemplation are not inventions of knowledge but a gradual participation in the reality that already exists.

B. Truth and the Limits of Human Perception

Many misunderstandings arise because finite perception is incomplete:

- A person in a dark room may perceive a rope as a snake, but their perception does not change reality.
- Human reasoning must align with what is true, not just what appears to be true.

This is why the *intellect* must be guided by something beyond its own finite operations.

Divine illumination—the non-coercive elevation of the *intellect* into structured alignment with infinite Truth—is not an added perception or mystical insight but the metaphysical condition that makes full participation in Truth possible. Without such illumination, the finite intellect remains bound to fragmented understanding; it cannot, by its own power, reach the fullness of actuality.

2. The Will as the Capacity for Participation in Truth

If intellect alone were sufficient for full participation in divine Truth, then knowledge would be automatic, and error would not exist. However, the will plays a crucial role here because Truth must be freely chosen, not merely known.

The Role of Will in Accepting or Rejecting Truth

- Divine Will is perfectly ordered. God does not waver in knowledge or action. His Will and Truth are unified.
- Finite will must be directed toward Truth. Unlike God, humans must align their will with Truth through conscious effort.
- Misalignment produces error. When the will rejects Truth, it creates disorder in both *intellect* and action, through the following:

- Neglect (passive ignorance)
- Distortion (intellectual dishonesty)
- Malice (active rejection of Truth)

This explains why Truth alone is insufficient for moral perfection—the will must be properly ordered to Truth for knowledge to have its full effect.

3. Love and Morality as Participation in Divine Truth

Since Truth is not created by the finite *intellect* but discovered, morality is not a human invention. Moral laws are not arbitrary social constructs; they are necessary reflections of divine Truth.

Relativism as the Rejection of Truth

- Relativism claims morality is subjective, but this is self-defeating.
    - If all moral claims are relative, then relativism has no claim to Truth.
    - If morality is purely subjective, then murder and kindness would be equally valid choices.
- True morality is participation in divine Truth.
    - Love is not mere emotion but the rational choice to seek the true good of another.
    - Relativism is not love—it is an imposter that seeks popularity over divine imitation.
- Love is meaningful only when it is directed toward the true *Good*.
    - Just as a doctor must tell a patient the truth about their illness, true love requires guiding others toward Truth, not approving all behaviors.

Thus, morality is not externally imposed rules, but the natural consequence of aligning with divine Truth.

4. The Beatific Vision as the Fulfillment of Intellect and Will

Since the *intellect* seeks knowledge and the will seeks Love, their logical fulfillment is direct participation in divine Truth—Communion.

THE BEATIFIC VISION AS THE COMPLETION OF HUMAN RATIONALITY

- The *intellect* seeks to know fully. The only final satisfaction for knowledge is Truth without distortion.
- The *will* seeks to love fully. The only final satisfaction for Love is Goodness itself.
- Both are fulfilled in the beatific vision, where the barriers of time, perception, and error are removed, allowing for the following:
  - Complete finite knowledge (the *soul* receives all that can be known according to its nature, without distortion, but not in the infinite mode of divine self-knowing, which cannot be possessed by the finite)
  - Perfect love (the will rests fully in the *Good* by sharing in it—Love is the structured act of self-gift)
  - Total participation in divine Truth (the *intellect* is united without error to the actuality of Being, according to its structured capacity; to exceed that capacity would be a collapse into actuality, which is contrary to the purpose of creation—essentially God changing his mind—an act that is metaphysically impossible)

This fulfillment does not make the finite infinite, but it allows for unrestricted access to infinite Truth and Love.

5. The Logical Necessity of Divine Illumination

Since finite beings are incapable of reaching such complete knowledge by their own power, divine illumination is necessary.

Why Divine Illumination Is Not Optional

- The finite cannot reach the infinite by itself. Reason alone is insufficient for perfect knowledge.
- Divine illumination allows finite beings to access truth beyond their natural limitations. Otherwise, the mind remains lacking.
- Without divine illumination, *intellect* remains forever fragmented. Learning remains sequential, never reaching unity.

This means that divine self-revelation is not a mere religious claim, but a metaphysical necessity.

6. Participation as Alignment with Truth

- Truth is not something finite beings own, alter, or redefine; rather, they enter it by aligning with the fullness of reality as structured by divine actuality.
- Will must align with Truth for understanding to be complete.
- The beatific vision is the ultimate fulfillment of *intellect* and *will*.
- Divine illumination is necessary for finite *intellect* to progressively participate in Truth, culminating in its fullest apprehension in the beatific vision.
- Love is not passive approval of all choices but the active alignment of one's will with divine Truth, which is Love itself.

7. Moving Forward: From the Structure of Truth to the Fulfillment of Rational Participation

Because *intellect* and *will* are the faculties by which the finite *soul* participates in divine actuality, human beings are not mere observers of reality—we are active participants in its unfolding. Truth is not only to be known but to be lived and will is not fulfilled merely by choosing but by choosing in accordance with divine intelligibility. This alignment between *intellect, will,* and structured reality is the foundation for understanding the proper place of the human person within creation. In the next chapter, we explore how this alignment gives rise to the ordered development of creation—not as a sequence of historical events, but as the metaphysical unfolding of rational participation in divine Truth, culminating in the full intelligibility of human existence.

12

Divine Action and the Structure of Reality

Introduction: The Problem of Divine Action

ONE OF THE MOST enduring challenges in philosophy and theology is how God acts within creation.

If, as has been shown, God is absolute, infinite, and unchanging, then how can he interact with a finite, dynamic universe?

Many theological and philosophical frameworks struggle with this problem, offering three primary models:

1. Interventionist Models—God acts from outside reality as an external force
2. Deistic Models—God creates but does not act within creation
3. Process Theology—God evolves alongside creation

Each of these models fails because they do one of the following:

- Compromise divine immutability (implying that God undergoes change)
- Make God distant or uninvolved in reality
- Introduce contradiction by making divine action dependent on time and space

Divine Action and the Structure of Reality

This chapter presents a coherent alternative to these models. Divine action is not a temporal intervention but the very ground of reality. We will explore the following:

- The causal joint—the necessary metaphysical principle by which finite reality emerges from infinite actuality
- Why divine action does not change God but sustains all things without alteration
- Why all divine action is unified, dissolving the false distinction between natural and miraculous

1. The Causal Joint: How God Acts Without Changing

The causal joint is the necessary metaphysical principle by which finite reality emerges from infinite actuality, without implying change or division within divine actuality.

Infinite actuality (God) potentiates finite reality (creation) without undergoing change or division. This solves the apparent contradiction between divine immutability and God's involvement in creation.

Key Metaphysical Principles of the Causal Joint

- God is pure act (*actus purus*)—there is no unrealized potential in God, so his action must be:
  - Entirely present
  - Complete and unchanging
  - Not dependent on external conditions
- Deceleration of IRM is the creative act.
  - Finite existence does not arise by addition to or subtraction from God.
  - Finite existence is not a transformation within God.
  - Instead, creation emerges as a structured deceleration of IRM, allowing contingent beings to exist.[1]

---

1. Creation is not outside God—there is no "outside" to infinite Being. Yet God does not make room for creation within himself by division or change. Rather, he potentiates structured reality through self-limitation, allowing finite participation in Being without modifying divine actuality.

The Infinite Reservoir

- The Causal Joint is sustaining, not intervening.
  - Divine action is not an external force that steps into creation.
  - God is not reacting to events. Rather, his action is the reason anything exists at all moments.
  - Time exists because divine action sustains motion and change.

Thus, divine action is not a moment in time but the continuous reason time exists.

2. General and Special Divine Action: A False Dichotomy

The traditional distinction between general and special divine action is a human perception bias, not an actual division in divine causality.

Table 12.1. Revising the Concepts of General and Special Divine Action
This table dismantles the false dichotomy between general and special divine action by showing that all divine action is unified and structurally foreknown within infinite actuality.

Traditional View	Reality in the Metaphysical Framework
General divine action—God sustains the universe through natural laws.	All divine action is unified—God does not sustain some things naturally and others miraculously.
Special divine action—God takes exception to the natural order with miracles, responses to prayer, and other timely interventions.	Miracles are not exceptions to divine action but moments where divine action is more perceptibly evident.

A. Miracles as Perceptual, Not Ontological Exceptions

- Many assume that miracles are exceptions to natural law, but this misunderstands divine action.
- God is the sustainer of natural law, meaning that any perceived violation is not a breakage but an intentional act within the same unified reality.

- What are singled out as miracles occur within divine order, not as disruptions of it.

B. Prayer and Divine Action

A common question is this: How can divine action be immutable? Doesn't God change his mind in response to prayer?

The answer is no—prayer does not change God but aligns finite will with divine actuality.

- God hears prayers before the person praying really exists (since God knows all things all at once).
- Prayers are not causes of divine action but part of the logical structure of reality—God creates a universe in which prayers and their responses are foreknown and integrated.
- Prayer does not convince God to act; rather, it allows creatures to align themselves with his will.
- Your prayer is not only foreknown—it is preselected as part of the very reason you were born.

What appears as divine response is, in fact, selected participation within the eternal act of divine order.[2]

3. *The Universe as a Relational Expression of Divine Action*

Because divine action is not interventionist but sustaining, the universe is a relational manifestation of divine will.

---

2. What is often called "unanswered prayer" is not divine absence but the perfection of unchanging Love resisting distortion. God does not fulfill requests that would deepen misalignment but instead sustains the soul toward right participation—even through silence. True prayer is not a means of enlisting God in finite desire but an act of reorienting the will toward divine actuality. It participates in the logic of Love by seeking union, not control, and opens the soul to structured alignment with the Truth it did not create. To will what God wills is never a disappointment, for such prayer is already a form of communion.

Table 12.2. Reality's Relationship with Divine Action

This table demonstrates how all aspects of finite reality—time, energy, and consciousness—exist only through continuous divine sustenance, not occasional intervention.

Aspect of Reality	Relationship to Divine Action
Time	Exists because divine action sustains motion and change
Energy	Exists because divine action differentiates power into finite expressions
Consciousness	Exists because divine action sustains knowledge as a participatory reality

Thus, the entire universe is a structured relationship between the finite and the infinite.

4. Divine Action and Free Will: Reconciling Foreknowledge and Choice

A common objection to divine omnipotence and omniscience is: If God already knows the future, how can human free will exist?

The Solution: Foreknowledge Does Not Equal Determinism

- God does not foresee as if he looks ahead. He knows all events as part of a single, eternal act.
- Human free choices exist within a structured reality. Divine omniscience includes knowledge of all possible choices, which means the following:
  - Every contingent decision is foreknown but not determined.
  - Free will is a foreknown factor in structured creation.
  - The structure of reality was chosen to allow rational beings to participate in divine order.

Thus, foreknowledge does not negate freedom. It ensures that all choices unfold within divine order.

5. Divine Action as the Unity of Reality

By understanding divine action as necessarily sustaining of all existence, we resolve the false dilemmas of the following:

- Intervention vs. Non-Intervention—God does not step in to creation; he is its continuous ground
- General vs. Special Action—all divine action is unified; miracles are perceptual distinctions, not ontological ones
- Foreknowledge vs. Free Will—divine action allows for real choice within a structured order
- Natural vs. Miraculous—all divine action is miraculous in its sustaining nature

Divine action is not separate from the structure of reality—it is the act by which all reality is sustained and made receivable.

The next chapter will explore how this framework aligns with scientific inquiry, metaphysics, and theological doctrine, demonstrating the full coherence between divine action and the structure of reality.

6. Moving Forward: The Unity of Knowing and Being

Chapter 12 concluded that divine action is not reactive or episodic, but the continuous structuring of all actuality. Prayer, causality, and perception are not interruptions of divine will—they are participations within it. What appears as response is, in truth, selected alignment within an always-actual, always-sustaining act.

Chapter 13 now turns to the nature of knowledge. It dismantles the artificial separation between science, metaphysics, and theology, showing that each is a mode of participation in Truth, not by observation alone but through structured relation to Being. If reality is structured, then knowing must also be structured, and the causal joint is the key that makes knowledge possible at all.

13

Science, Theology, and the Convergence on Truth

Introduction: The Shift from Divided Knowledge to Participatory Knowing

MANY ASSUME THAT SCIENCE, metaphysics, and theology exist in conflict—each seeking different truths in incompatible ways. Science is often seen as based on observation and experimentation, while theology is considered a matter of faith, and metaphysics is treated as abstract speculation. This division creates the false impression that these fields are separate or even opposed.

However, the metaphysics developed in this book demands a radical shift in how we understand knowledge. Science, metaphysics, and theology are not distinct and independent disciplines competing for truth. Instead, they represent diverse ways in which finite minds participate in the structured intelligibility of reality. They are not just methods of inquiry but modes of aligning with Truth itself.

This chapter will demonstrate the following:

- Knowledge is not just about observing reality, it is about participating in it.
- Science, metaphysics, and theology are not rivals but complementary ways of aligning with the intelligibility of Being.

- A new epistemology is necessary, one based on participation rather than mere observation or deduction.
- The causal joint of divine action is the key to understanding how knowledge is possible at all.

By the end of this chapter, it will be clear that the future of science, metaphysics, and theology lies in their unified role as participatory ways of knowing.

1. Science: Understanding the Physical Structure of Reality

Science is the study of the material universe through observation, measurement, and experimentation. It excels at describing patterns, mechanisms, and relationships within physical reality. However, science is often mistaken as the only valid way to know something. This mistake arises because science is highly effective at explaining how things work—but not why they exist in the first place.

Science, by itself, cannot do the following:

- Explain why there is something rather than nothing.
- Establish why physical laws exist at all.
- Account for the very intelligibility and order that allows scientific inquiry to function.

Thus, while science is a powerful tool for describing contingent reality, it does not provide the deeper foundation necessary to explain why reality is structured in the first place.

2. Metaphysics: Establishing the Necessary Foundation of Knowledge

Metaphysics is traditionally understood as the study of being, causality, and first principles. But considering the framework developed in this book, metaphysics is more than just abstract reasoning—it is the means by which reason aligns with the necessary structure of Being itself.

Metaphysics demonstrates the following:

- All contingent things require a necessary foundation.
- Reality must be sustained by something beyond it, but actuality does not.

- Causality, order, and intelligibility are not arbitrary—they must be grounded in infinite actuality.

Unlike science, which studies the material order, metaphysics establishes the very conditions that make science possible. It does not merely analyze what we observe but explains why there must be something to observe in the first place.

3. Theology: The Fulfillment of Rational Inquiry

Theology, as understood in this framework, is not separate from metaphysics but is its completion.

While metaphysics proves the necessity of infinite actuality, theology reveals the nature of that actuality and the purpose of creation. It extends beyond what reason alone can establish by integrating divine revelation—the self-expression of Being itself.

- Science describes how reality behaves.
- Metaphysics establishes why reality must exist.
- Theology reveals the deeper nature of triune actuality, completing rational inquiry by illuminating the purpose of creation as divine self-expression.

This integration resolves the long-standing artificial separation between faith and reason.

Thus theology, when understood in light of this metaphysics, is not irrational belief. It is the culmination of rational inquiry into the nature of existence.

4. The Causal Joint: The Key to Unified Knowledge

The causal joint is where the triune actuality potentiates finite reality through structured differentiation. This is not merely a philosophical idea. It is the reason knowledge is possible at all.

- Science investigates the structured differentiation within reality.
- Metaphysics explains why differentiation must exist within a sustained order.

- Theology reveals that this differentiation is the self-expression of perfect, relational Being.

Thus, the causal joint is not about sustaining divine actuality—God does not require sustenance—but about potentiating reality. Knowledge is a form of participation in structured reality, rather than just an act of detached observation.

5. The New Epistemology: Knowing as Participating

With this foundation, we can now redefine how we think about knowledge.

- Science is not just observation; it is structured exploration of divine differentiation.
- Metaphysics is not just deduction; it is alignment with the necessary intelligibility of Being.
- Theology is not just doctrine; it is a fuller participation in divine self-revelation.

This means that knowledge is not about accumulating facts but about aligning with actuality per se.

Traditional epistemology assumes knowledge is something we acquire. This book shows that Truth is something in which we participate. This restructured ontology demands a restructured epistemology—one where knowledge is not an external possession but a relational mode of being.

6. The Future of Knowledge

By understanding science, metaphysics, and theology as complementary ways of participating in triune actuality, we overcome the false conflicts between the following:

- Faith and reason
- Empirical and metaphysical inquiry
- Observation and revelation

This chapter has focused on the internal realignment of science, theology, and metaphysics as ways of knowing. In a later chapter we will see that this realignment is not merely theoretical. Scientific discovery—especially in physics and cosmology—has already begun to reflect this metaphysical unity empirically.

7. *Moving Forward: From Knowing Truth to Participating in It*

The previous chapter established that science, metaphysics, and theology are not rival disciplines but complementary ways of participating in the structured intelligibility of Being. Knowledge, properly understood, is not external acquisition but relational alignment with the actuality of divine self-expression. But since knowledge is participation, then knowing is not enough. The knower must become the participant.

This leads to the next necessary step in the metaphysical argument: the perfection of participation. Chapter 14 explores how finite beings—whose participation in Being per se is limited, sequential, and imperfect—must be gradually elevated into fuller communion with divine actuality. Through a structured, non-coercive ascent, intellect and will are drawn toward their fulfillment. Knowledge gives way to transformation, and the logic of participation demands its completion, not merely in understanding but in becoming what the soul was always meant to be.

14

Participation in Divine Action

PART ONE: THE STRUCTURE OF PARTICIPATION

The Necessity of Participation

IN PREVIOUS CHAPTERS, WE established that all finite reality emerges from Being per se and that divine action is the sustaining cause of all things. However, this raises a crucial question: How does finite creation participate in divine action without compromising divine immutability?

Participation is the central concept that bridges the gap between the infinite and the finite. Finite beings do not possess existence intrinsically but only as a continuous act of being sustained by divine actuality. However, mere existence is not fulfillment. True fulfillment requires active, structured participation in divine actuality.

This chapter will explore the following:

- The relational nature of finite existence
- The structured hierarchy of participation in Being per se
- The necessity of ordered participation in divine Truth and action
- The limitations of finite participation and why fulfillment is not automatic
- The logical requirement of a means for perfecting participation beyond the natural capacity of finite beings

Understanding the distinction between participation in divine actuality and participation in reality is crucial because it clarifies why finite beings cannot reach perfection independently and why fulfillment must be more than mere existence. It must be the progressive realization of participation in divine actuality sustained by Being per se.

1. The Relational Nature of Finite Existence

Unlike infinite actuality, which is self-sustaining existence necessarily, finite beings are defined by contingency. This means the following:

- They do not possess being absolutely; they exist by participation in Being per se.
- They do not possess knowledge intrinsically; Truth is not generated but discovered.
- They do not possess perfect will alignment; their will is not self-justifying but must be directed toward Truth.

Since finite beings are not self-existent, their existence, knowledge, and moral order are necessarily dependent upon their participation in structured reality, which is potentiated through the causal joint of divine action. Participation is, therefore, not an abstract concept but the very principle that defines how the finite relates to the infinite. The difference between a rock, a plant, an animal, and a human being is not merely a matter of physical complexity but of increasing levels of participation in actuality.

2. The Hierarchy of Participation in Being

Because all things exist as far as they participate in Being per se, participation is not uniform. There is a structured order—a hierarchy—of how different beings engage in Existence, Truth, and Divine Action.

Table 14.1 Hierarchy of Participation in Being

This table illustrates how different levels of finite being—ranging from inanimate matter to rational beings—participate in Being per se through progressively structured relations to divine actuality.

Level of Being	Mode of Participation	Relation to Divine Action
Inanimate matter	Passive participation in existence	Exists but does not actively relate to divine Truth
Living beings (plants, animals)	Active but unconscious participation	Engage with reality but do not rationally discern Truth
Rational Beings (humans, angels)	Conscious participation through intellect and will	Capable of aligning themselves with divine Truth
Perfected beings (the beatific vision)	Full and unrestricted participation	Direct, unmediated knowledge of God

The higher the form of being, the more active and voluntary its participation in divine actuality. This explains why moral and rational agency are unique to higher beings and why human free will plays a pivotal role in structured participation.

3. Ordered Participation in Divine Truth and Action

Since as rational beings we can recognize and align ourselves with divine actuality, our optimal degree of participation is not automatic. It requires intellect and will.

- The human *intellect* seeks Truth, but since finite beings do not possess absolute knowledge, our *intellect* must be oriented toward divine Truth to avoid error.
- The human *will* seeks the *Good*, but since finite *will* lacks intrinsic perfection, it must be ordered toward divine actuality to reach fulfillment.

This necessity of ordered participation explains why alignment with Truth is not optional—it is the logical requirement for any rational being to function properly. Any deviation from this order leads to deficiency, falsehood, and disorder, not because of external imposition but because participation in Truth is the ontological structure of finite existence.

A misalignment between human intellect, will, and divine Truth results in the following:

- Intellectual error—the mind is disconnected from divine actuality, leading to false beliefs and a stronger connection to finite reality
- Moral disorder—the will seeks goods in a disordered manner, leading to suffering
- Existential fragmentation—the soul becomes separated from its own fulfillment

Thus, free will is not about choosing arbitrarily, but about freely conforming to divine Truth.

The more aligned the will is to Truth, the greater its freedom and participation in divine actuality.

4. The Problem of Imperfect Participation

While all things participate in Being per se to some degree, imperfect beings cannot fully participate in divine actuality by their own power. This leads to two key problems: a deficiency in knowledge and a deficiency in will.

A. Deficiency in Knowledge

Human beings cannot access Truth directly. We must seek understanding through reason, revelation, and structured engagement with reality as the medium potentiated by the causal joint—the only mediator between God and Man—through which we may approach divine actuality. This means the following:

- Human knowledge is fragmented (acquired in bits and pieces over time).
- Human reasoning is sequential (we must infer Truth step by step).
- Human access to Truth is limited (we must overcome ignorance and error).

Thus, no finite being, no matter how intelligent, can possess perfect knowledge on its own.

B. Deficiency in Will

Since the finite will is not inherently perfect, it requires a process of alignment with divine Truth to avoid moral and existential disorder. This means the following:

- The will is subject to misalignment (it can pursue false goods).
- It is affected by self-centered inclinations (it can act irrationally).
- It requires formation and discipline (virtue is not automatic).

This imperfection creates a structural limitation on how finite beings relate to divine actuality. It also leads to the necessity of an external means by which participation in Being per se can be perfected, a means that does not rely on finite power alone but bridges the gap between finite and infinite reality. Such a means must preserve the integrity of free will while providing the necessary elevation that finite beings cannot achieve independently.

The nature of this external means—whether through divine illumination, the structured potentiation of the soul, or what theology calls grace—must be explored to understand how imperfect participation is ultimately perfected. Properly understood, grace is not a supernatural supplement added to nature, but the theological name for the metaphysical elevation by which finite will is drawn—without coercion—into deeper alignment with divine actuality.

5. *The Logical Need for Fulfillment*

If finite beings are to reach their fullest participation in divine actuality, there must be a logical path toward fulfillment—one that overcomes the limitations imposed by imperfect participation. This necessity leads to some crucial questions with logical answers:

- Is fulfillment possible through finite effort alone?
  - No, because finite reality is necessarily contingent and imperfect.
- Must fulfillment come through direct divine action?
  - Yes, but without compromising divine immutability or human nature.

- What kind of divine action is necessary?
  - One that perfects participation in Being per se without violating the logical separation between finite and infinite.

The answers to these questions naturally lead to the next stage of the argument: how finite participation in divine actuality reaches its necessary fulfillment through a metaphysical process that allows for elevation into perfect participation.

In part one, "The Structure of Participation," we have demonstrated the following:

- Finite beings do not possess existence, truth, or goodness intrinsically but only by participation in Being per se.
- This participation is structured hierarchically, with rational beings capable of conscious alignment with divine actuality.
- Ordered participation in divine Truth is a necessity, not a choice; misalignment leads to disorder by nature.
- Imperfect participation creates a gap between finite and infinite, which must be bridged if fulfillment is to occur.
- A logical means of fulfillment must exist, one that elevates finite participation without contradicting divine perfection.

6. Moving Forward: The Limits of Imperfect Participation

Having established that all finite beings participate in Being per se through a structured hierarchy of intellect, will, and existence, we now turn to the inevitable consequence—imperfect participation, by its nature, cannot complete itself. The next section will show why divine action is required to elevate finite beings beyond their intrinsic limitations—without coercion, absorption, or contradiction of their structure.

PART TWO: IMPERFECT PARTICIPATION CANNOT FULFILL ITSELF

Why Fulfillment Requires More Than Existence

In part one, we established that finite beings participate in Being per se at different levels, with rational beings uniquely capable of aligning their intellect and will with divine actuality.

However, because finite participation is necessarily limited and imperfect, it requires a structured means of fulfillment—one that allows rational beings to reach their proper end in perfect participation without violating divine immutability.

Here we will explore the following:

- Why imperfect participation must be elevated toward perfection
- The necessity of divine action in perfecting participation
- The metaphysical principles that allow human beings to be elevated without violating their nature
- The role of divine illumination in overcoming the limitations of human intellect and will.
- Why fulfillment requires more than moral striving; it requires a real participation in divine actuality

Understanding the perfection of participation is crucial because it clarifies why finite existence is not static and why divine action is necessary to complete the process that began at the causal joint.

1. *Why Imperfect Participation Must Be Elevated Toward Perfection*

A. The Fundamental Incompleteness of Imperfect Participation

Finite beings, by their very nature, experience fragmented existence, incomplete knowledge, and imperfect moral alignment. This is not an accidental limitation or an evil but an inherent consequence of finitude. The imperfections of finite participation include:

- Partial knowledge—finite intellects can grasp aspects of Truth but not the whole

- Flawed will—the will can choose false goods or act in ignorance
- Temporal limitation—every action occurs sequentially, making direct knowledge of divine actuality impossible in the present state

This inherent incompleteness means that no finite being, by its own power, can attain the fullness of Truth, Good, or Being. The final cause of rational existence cannot be mere partial participation; it must be the fullest participation in divine actuality possible to a finite nature.

B. The Teleology of Rational Beings Requires Fulfillment

Teleology, or final causality, dictates that every being has an ultimate purpose toward which it is directed. For rational creatures, that purpose must be the highest possible form of participation in Truth and Good, a participation that finite effort alone cannot achieve.

- Since finite beings are oriented toward Truth, their ultimate end must be the most complete knowledge of divine actuality possible.
- Since finite beings are oriented toward the Good, their ultimate end must be the most perfect alignment with divine will possible.
- Since finite beings are relational, their ultimate end must be the fullest possible communion with the divine.

If no such fulfillment were possible, rational creatures would be permanently unfulfilled, contradicting the very structure of reason and will. Thus, the perfection of participation—that is, the fullest possible participation in Truth, Good, and Communion—is not an optional benefit or external reward; it is the necessary *telos* of relational participation in *existence itself*.

2. The Necessity of Divine Action in Perfecting Participation

Since imperfect participation cannot perfect itself, then an external source is required to elevate the finite toward its completion. However, this source cannot be another finite entity since all finite things share the same limitations. Instead, the only possible means of perfecting finite participation is direct divine action.

Table 14.2. Why Imperfect Beings Cannot Perfect Themselves
This table demonstrates the inherent limitations of finite intellect, will, and temporality, showing why divine action is necessary to elevate finite beings toward perfect participation in divine actuality.

Problem	Why Finite Beings Cannot Solve It	Why Divine Action is Necessary
Partial knowledge	No finite intellect can attain comprehensive Truth independently.	Only divine illumination can grant unrestricted access to Truth.
Flawed will	The finite will is free but not infallible; it requires external guidance.	Only direct participation in divine goodness can ensure perfect moral alignment.
Temporal limitation	The finite perceives sequentially, never fully grasping reality at once.	Only divine actuality exists outside time, allowing for complete and simultaneous knowledge.

Since the finite order cannot reach its own fulfillment, divine action must intervene to provide a structured, non-coercive, and elevating means of participation in divine actuality.

3. How Finite Beings Can Be Elevated Without Violation of Their Nature

A key objection to divine elevation is the concern that if finite beings were granted perfect participation, they would cease to be finite—that they would somehow lose their individuality and dissolve into infinite actuality. However, this is not what perfect participation entails.

The Principle of Participation Without Absorption

Participation does not mean absorption. Just as a mirror can reflect light without becoming the light, so too can finite beings participate in divine actuality without being erased. This follows from four principles:

- Infinite Being can share without diminution.
- God is not a finite resource that must be divided among participants.
- Infinite actuality remains infinite even while elevating the finite.
- The divine nature is fully shared without depletion or fragmentation.

The Infinite Reservoir

4. Finite Beings Retain Their Structure

- Finite minds do not cease to exist; they are perfected in knowledge.
- Finite wills do not disappear; they are perfectly aligned with Truth.
- Finite persons do not merge into one; they retain individuality while experiencing direct communion with the divine.

5. The Perfection of Form Without Change in Essence

- A cup does not cease to be a cup when it is filled with water; it simply reaches its proper function.
- Similarly, rational beings do not cease to be rational beings when they are granted perfect participation; they fulfill their ultimate nature.

Thus, perfect participation does not destroy finitude. It fulfills it.

Why These Analogies Work—Reality Is Structured for Participation

The analogies in this chapter—light illuminating objects without destroying them, melodies being perfected in harmony, and finite beings being elevated rather than absorbed—are not mere illustrations. They work precisely because they reflect the actual structure of reality.

1. Light and Illumination
   - Light does not erase what it touches; it allows it to be seen as it truly is.
   - Divine actuality perfects rational creatures not by negating their uniqueness but by revealing and elevating their true nature.
2. The Finite and the Infinite
   - The finite is structured to receive from the infinite without ceasing to be finite.

- Just as a cup is filled without ceasing to be a cup, finite beings participate in divine actuality without losing their distinctiveness.

3. Unity and Distinction

    - A melody is not lost when played in harmony; it is completed.
    - Similarly, participation in divine actuality does not erase individuality but brings it to its highest fulfillment.

These analogies hold because they describe a fundamental truth: reality is structured for participation. The finite does not oppose the infinite but depends on it, and divine actuality does not erase created uniqueness but sustains, fulfills, and perfects it.

6. *The Role of Divine Illumination in Perfecting Participation*

Because finite intellects cannot attain access to perfect knowledge by their own power, divine illumination must provide the means of participation in omniscience.

A. The Nature of Divine Illumination

Divine illumination does not operate like finite learning, where information is gained sequentially. Instead, it does the following:

- Removes barriers to Truth rather than adding new facts
- Allows direct perception of divine actuality rather than mediated knowledge.
- Unites intellect with divine actuality so that Truth is no longer fragmented

This does not mean finite beings become omniscient in the same way as God but that their participation in Truth becomes unrestricted. They see divine actuality as it is, rather than through partial and flawed perception.

B. Why This Requires a Direct Divine Act

The limitations of finite cognition are not self-correcting. Even the most advanced intellect cannot break through its own sequential nature without external elevation. This is why divine action is necessary—not to override reason but to bring it to its completion.

C. The Logical Need for a Means of Fulfillment

In part two, "Imperfect Participation Cannot Fulfill Itself," we have demonstrated the following:

- Imperfect participation is not self-perfecting; it must be elevated.
- Divine action is necessary to perfect finite intellect and will.
- Participation does not mean dissolution; finitude is retained and perfected.
- Divine illumination is required to overcome the barriers of fragmented knowledge.
- Moral striving alone is insufficient; real participation in divine actuality is required.

This naturally leads to the question of how divine action manifests in history and provides a structured path toward perfected participation, which will be explored in part three.

7. Moving Forward: The Necessity of a Structured Means

If finite beings cannot attain perfect participation by their own power, then divine action must provide the structure by which such fulfillment becomes possible, not through coercion but through the sustaining potentiation of a path that respects rational freedom. In the next part, we examine how grace, free will, and revelation operate together—not as competing forces but as interdependent modes—by which finite beings may ascend toward perfected participation in divine actuality.

PART THREE: THE MEANS OF PARTICIPATION

How Divine Action Perfects Finite Nature Without Overriding It

Having established that finite participation in Being per se must be perfected, the question remains: How does this elevation occur?

Because finite beings cannot elevate themselves, there must exist a structured, non-coercive means by which they are drawn into full participation in divine actuality. This means the following:

- Participation must be gradual; the finite cannot instantaneously transition into full participation in divine actuality without violating its nature.
- Divine action must be structured; it must provide a means of ascent that respects free will and rational development.
- The process must integrate finite understanding; it cannot bypass rational engagement but must elevate it.

The next section will explore the following:

- The necessity of structured participation in divine actuality
- The nature of progressive elevation through divine action
- The teleological process by which finite beings are drawn toward fulfillment
- How free will and grace interact in the perfection of participation
- The role of divine revelation in guiding finite beings toward their ultimate participation

Understanding this structured process of elevation clarifies why participation in divine actuality does not eliminate the need for free engagement but instead requires it as part of the ascent toward fulfillment.

1. *The Necessity of Structured Participation in Divine Actuality*

Since finite beings do not possess immediate access to divine actuality, they require a structured mode of participation that allows for gradual ascent toward fulfillment.

A. Why Participation Cannot Be Instantaneous

A common misconception is that participation in divine actuality must occur instantaneously, as though finite beings could simply be absorbed into infinite actuality without transition. However, this is metaphysically incoherent for several reasons:

- Finite beings are temporal—their experience of reality unfolds in sequence.
- Knowledge must be integrated—intellects cannot comprehend infinite actuality all at once.
- Freedom must be preserved—the will must participate voluntarily rather than by coercion.

Just as a child cannot instantly possess the knowledge of an adult, so, too, can finite intellects not immediately grasp divine actuality in its fullness. Instead, participation must occur through a structured ascent that aligns with the nature of finite rationality.

B. The Hierarchy of Structured Participation

Because participation in Being per se is hierarchical, the process of ascending toward full participation follows a structured pattern.

Table 14.3. Structured Hierarchy of Ascent Toward Participation
This table presents the progressive stages by which finite beings are gradually elevated into deeper participation in divine actuality, integrating rational inquiry, moral alignment, spiritual illumination, and final union.

Level of Participation	Mode of Ascent	Relation to Divine Action
Basic rational inquiry	Engaging in reason and seeking Truth	Indirect participation through intellect
Moral alignment	Aligning will with divine Truth	Participation through ethical order
Spiritual illumination	Receiving divine knowledge	Direct participation in revealed truth
Perfected participation (beatific vision)	Unmediated union with divine actuality	Full participation in Being per se

This structure ensures that finite beings are not overwhelmed but are gradually drawn into full participation in a way that respects their rational nature and free will. Because finite beings require structured participation, divine action must provide a progressive means of ascent rather than an instantaneous transformation.

C. The Stages of Ascent Toward Divine Participation

Since the finite must be gradually elevated, divine action operates through three key stages of participation:

- Illumination—the finite intellect is progressively freed from ignorance, allowing for deeper engagement with divine Truth.
- Purification—the will is gradually aligned with divine goodness, removing barriers to participation.
- Union—the intellect and will achieve perfect alignment with divine actuality, leading to full participatory communion.

Each stage builds upon the previous in the following ways:

- Illumination without purification leads to intellectual arrogance (knowing truth but not living it).
- Purification without illumination leads to blind obedience (acting correctly but without understanding).
- Purification and illumination together lead to union, where intellect and will are perfectly harmonized with divine actuality.

2. Free Will and Grace in the Perfection of Participation

A key tension in discussions of human participation in divine actuality is the relationship between free will and divine grace.

- If the perfection of participation were purely a result of grace, then human freedom would seem unnecessary.
- If the perfection of participation were purely a result of human effort, then grace would seem unnecessary.
- But human freedom and divine grace must be properly integrated to preserve the non-coercive structure of participatory ascent.

A. Free Will as the Capacity for Participation

Free will is not about arbitrary choice. It is the faculty by which rational beings align themselves with divine actuality.

- The will must be freely oriented toward Truth for participation to be authentic.
- Compelled participation would violate rational freedom, making it meaningless.
- Thus, the process of divine elevation is structured so that communion remains a choice rather than a compulsion.

B. Divine Grace as the Means of Participation

Since human beings cannot bring themselves into perfect communion by their own power, divine grace is the structured act through which such elevation becomes possible.

- Grace is not an external force that overrides freedom, but the sustaining act by which the soul is potentiated in its ascent toward divine actuality.
- Human beings cannot approach fulfillment without grace; yet without free will, grace could not be received as participation.

Thus, divine action provides the structure within which free will remains intact while still drawing the human person toward greater participation. This dynamic ensures that the perfection of communion is neither automatic nor impossible. It is sustained by grace and freely consented to by the will.

3. The Role of Divine Revelation in Guiding Finite Beings

Since participation in divine actuality must be structured, revelation serves as a necessary guide to lead finite beings toward full participation.

A. Why Revelation Is Necessary

Because finite intellects are limited, they cannot fully grasp divine actuality without some form of guidance.

- Science and philosophy can lead toward partial truths but cannot reveal ultimate reality.
- If divine actuality were unknowable, communion would be impossible.
- Revelation provides the necessary knowledge that finite beings could not otherwise attain.

B. The Integration of Revelation with Rational Inquiry

- Revelation does not contradict reason; it extends and fulfills it.
- Truth must be received intellectually; participation in divine actuality does not bypass rational engagement.
- Revelation aligns with structured participation, ensuring that finite beings can integrate divine Truth without coercion.

Thus, divine revelation is not an imposition upon reason but rather the fulfillment of rational inquiry within the structured ascent toward divine actuality.

4. Moving Forward: The Fulfillment of Participation

In part three, "The Means of Participation," we have demonstrated the following:

- Finite beings require structured participation in divine actuality.
- Participation cannot be instantaneous; it must be gradual and progressive.
- Divine action provides a structured ascent, ensuring that finite intellects and wills are properly formed.
- Free will and grace interact harmoniously, making full communion both possible and non-coercive.

- Revelation serves as the guiding principle, ensuring that finite beings can engage divine actuality without contradiction.

We have now seen that participation in divine actuality must unfold through an ordered ascent, guided by grace, revealed in structure, and fulfilled in freedom. But this ascent leads somewhere. It reaches a terminus, not in dissolution but in the full realization of rational nature. The next part of this chapter explores the necessary fulfillment of participation in the beatific vision: the unmediated, eternal communion of the finite soul with divine actuality.

PART FOUR: THE LOGIC OF THE BEATIFIC VISION

From Temporal Structure to Eternal Communion

Having established that finite beings must be progressively elevated toward divine actuality through structured participation, we now reach the necessary conclusion of this process: the beatific vision—the state of full and direct participation in Being per se.

Here we will consider the following:

- Why the beatific vision is the only logically necessary fulfillment of participation
- How it differs from mere intellectual enlightenment or moral virtue
- Why participation in divine actuality does not erase individual identity but perfects it
- How time and sequence are overcome in the final state of participation
- The logical necessity of the beatific vision for the completion of divine action

By clarifying the nature of this ultimate participation, we will see that the purpose of creation is not merely to exist but to be fulfilled in unmediated communion with divine actuality.

1. Why the Beatific Vision Is the Necessary Fulfillment of Participation

A. The Problem of Partial Participation

If finite beings never reach full communion, then the following results:

- Their intellects remain incomplete, always seeking but never attaining the whole of Truth.
- Their wills remain imperfect, always struggling toward the good but never perfectly aligned.
- Their existence remains fragmented, always in process but never reaching fulfillment.

This would render finite rationality a contradiction—a faculty designed to seek Truth yet incapable of fully attaining it. Thus, there must exist a state of full, unrestricted participation in divine actuality, or else rationality would be futile.

B. The Beatific Vision as the Necessary Solution

The beatific vision—the direct, unmediated knowledge of divine actuality—solves this problem in the following ways:

- Eliminating fragmented knowledge—intellect no longer perceives in parts but grasps Truth as a unified whole
- Perfecting the will—there is no longer struggle, only full alignment with divine goodness
- Fulfilling existence—finite beings reach the intended culmination of their participation, which is communion with their creator

Thus, the beatific vision is not a reward for good behavior but the necessary final cause of rational existence.

2. The Beatific Vision vs. Intellectual Enlightenment or Moral Virtue

A common misconception is that the beatific vision is simply a greater form of knowledge or moral perfection. However, this misunderstands the nature of ultimate participation.

Table 14.4. The Beatific Vision and the Nature of Ultimate Participation
This table contrasts partial, finite participation with the unmediated fullness of the beatific vision, showing why only direct participation in divine actuality fulfills the structure of rational existence.

Lesser Participation	The Beatific Vision
Philosophical knowledge—partial truths are attained through reason, but ultimate Truth remains beyond reach	Total knowledge—Truth is no longer sought; it is fully known in direct divine presence
Moral perfection—the will strives to align with goodness but remains susceptible to weakness	Perfected will—there is no more struggle; the will is fully and freely united with the divine good
Temporal awareness—consciousness experiences reality in sequence	Eternal knowledge—Truth is perceived in totality, without the limitations of time

Thus, the beatific vision is not an extension of ordinary knowledge or virtue. It is an entirely different mode of participation in divine actuality.

3. Why Individuality Is Not Erased in the Beatific Vision

A common objection is that direct participation in divine actuality would mean the loss of individual identity—that the self would be *absorbed* into God and cease to exist. This is a misunderstanding of what it means to participate in infinite actuality.

Participation Without Absorption

Participation does not mean merging into God; it means attaining the fullest possible relation to divine actuality while remaining distinct.

- God is infinite; he does not need to consume finite beings to elevate them.
- Each being retains its uniqueness; just as light shines on many surfaces without making them identical, divine actuality is fully shared without erasing individuality.
- The self is perfected, not dissolved; participation does not destroy the finite but brings it to its highest potential.

Thus, each being fully retains its individuality while also experiencing perfect communion with divine actuality. The soul reaches its final consummation, not by expansion into infinitude but by receiving—without resistance or remainder—the actuality of God in the full measure of its own structure.

Teleology, or final causality, dictates that every being has an ultimate purpose toward which it is directed. For rational creatures, that purpose is not self-determined but arises from the very structure of their being, which is ordered toward Truth, Good, and Communion. This final cause cannot be mere partial participation; it must be the fullest participation in divine actuality possible to a finite nature. To have eternal life, then, is not to become infinite but to be eternally sustained by the infinite, to participate in divine actuality to the fullest extent possible for a finite being, without confusion, collapse, or loss of distinction.

4. *The Overcoming of Time and Sequence in the Beatific Vision*

A key distinction between ordinary knowledge and divine Truth is that finite consciousness perceives in sequence—one moment after another. However, this limitation must be overcome in the beatific vision.

A. The Problem of Sequential Perception

- Finite intellects process Truth bit by bit, never grasping the whole at once.
- This creates gaps in knowledge—the mind is always moving toward understanding rather than fully possessing it.
- The will makes decisions over time, rather than immediately aligning with absolute Good.

Thus, in the beatific vision, time-bound perception must be transcended so that knowledge is fully actual rather than sequentially experienced.

B. The Transition to Eternal Knowledge

Time exists because finite minds process knowledge sequentially—one moment at a time. The transition to eternal knowledge is not a loss of awareness but the removal of fragmentation.

In divine actuality, knowledge is not received in parts but grasped as a unified whole, much like seeing an entire landscape at once instead of piecing it together step by step.

To participate in divine actuality is not to stop learning in the human sense but to reach a state where Truth is fully apprehended in a single, perfect act rather than gradually acquired.

Thus, in the beatific vision, time as a limitation is overcome, and rational beings experience divine Truth in a singular, perfect act of knowledge.

5. The Logical Necessity of the Beatific Vision for Divine Action to Be Complete

Because divine action is the sustaining principle of all things, the final goal of divine action must be the full participation of rational beings in divine actuality.

A. Why Divine Action Requires a Fulfillment

If creation were never fulfilled, then divine action would be:

- Perpetually incomplete—always sustaining beings without ever perfecting them
- Lacking *teleology*—without an ultimate purpose or fulfillment
- Inconsistent with divine omniscience—a purposeless creation contradicts divine wisdom

Thus, divine action must bring rational beings to a necessary fulfillment, or else divine creation would lack a final cause.

B. Why the Beatific Vision Is the Only Possible Completion

- The intellect seeks full knowledge; only the beatific vision satisfies this pursuit.
- The will seeks full goodness; only the beatific vision perfects it.
- Existence seeks its highest form; only direct participation in divine actuality fulfills it.

Thus, any alternative to the beatific vision would leave rational existence inherently unfulfilled, making the beatific vision a logical necessity for the completion of divine action.

6. The Beatific Vision as the Completion of Divine Participation

In part four, we have demonstrated the following:

- The beatific vision is the necessary fulfillment of rational existence; without it, participation remains incomplete.
- It is not mere intellectual enlightenment or moral virtue; it is a different mode of being beyond time and sequence.
- Individuality is perfected, not erased; finite beings retain their uniqueness while fully participating in divine actuality.
- Time and sequence are overcome; Truth is fully known at once, rather than processed gradually.
- Divine action is incomplete without it since all rational existence is ordered toward full communion in divine actuality.

7. Moving Forward: The Final Ascent

Part five now turns to the fulfillment of human participation. It examines why rational beings, structured by intellect and will, cannot rest in partial knowledge or moral striving alone but are necessarily ordered toward full communion with the divine. This final ascent—the beatific vision—is not a theological embellishment but the metaphysical consequence of the structure of Being itself. It is where the logic of Being reaches its *telos*, and the soul at last sees, loves, and rests in the actuality from which it was always sustained.

PART FIVE: THE TRANSITION TO PERFECTED PARTICIPATION—THE PROCESS OF ELEVATION

In Part four, we established that the beatific vision is the only possible fulfillment of rational existence—the logical culmination of divine action. However, this raises a crucial question: How does finite participation transition from imperfection to perfection?

Since finite beings cannot elevate themselves, the process of fulfillment must be structured by divine action. In part five, we ask the following questions:

- Why must elevation be gradual rather than instantaneous?
- Why is the structured transition from partial to perfect participation a metaphysical necessity?
- How does divine action provide the means of elevation without coercion?
- Why does free will remain essential even in perfected participation?
- What is the role of grace in the mechanism of divine elevation?

By understanding the process of participation, we can clarify how finite beings attain their final fulfillment in the beatific vision.

1. Why the Transition Must Be Gradual Rather Than Instantaneous

A common question regarding divine fulfillment is this: Since divine action sustains all things at every moment, why must the soul's participation in perfection unfold through process rather than occur all at once?

The answer lies in the nature of finite existence and the following principle: divine action does not bypass or override created reality but elevates participation according to its inherent structure. It does not replace free will but brings it to its fullest expression.

If finite beings were immediately perfected in participation, this would:

- Eliminate the voluntary nature of alignment with divine Truth, turning participation into compulsion rather than free assent.
- Remove the relational process of knowledge, which is necessary for Truth to be fully internalized rather than imposed.
- Disrupt the ordered ascent toward divine actuality, which ensures that participation is fully integrated rather than externally granted.

Thus, divine action must respect the structure of rational existence, guiding participation toward perfection without bypassing its natural capacities.

2. The Necessity of Gradual Elevation

The process of perfected participation must be gradual because of the following:

- Finite intellects must move from partial to full knowledge in an ordered way.
- Finite wills must be progressively aligned with divine Truth through relational experience.
- Divine action is relational, not coercive—it elevates beings through their own capacities rather than forcing change upon them.

Thus, the transition to perfected participation must be a structured ascent, not an imposed transformation.

3. The Metaphysical Necessity of a Structured Transition

If participation in divine actuality is not instantaneous, then there must be a structured means by which it is achieved. This structured transition is necessary because:

- Truth is relational—knowledge must be internalized, not merely possessed.
- Virtue is formed—the will must become fully disposed to divine goodness.
- Existence is teleological—all things must reach their fulfillment in the proper order.

4. Participation as a Continuum

Rather than a sudden shift, participation in divine actuality follows a structured path, moving gradually in a stage-like progression.

Table 14.5. Graduated Participation in Divine Actuality
This table maps the structured process of elevation from imperfect to perfect participation, illustrating the continuity of divine action as it leads rational beings to fulfillment without coercion.

Stage	Mode of Participation	Relation to Divine Fulfillment
Partial knowledge	Finite beings grasp Truth in limited ways.	Rational creatures begin aligning with divine Truth.
Growth in understanding	The intellect deepens its awareness of divine reality.	Knowledge moves from fragmented to integrated perception.
Moral alignment	The will becomes more attuned to divine goodness.	The struggle between self-will and divine order is resolved.
Unrestricted participation	The soul is in full communion with divine actuality.	Rational beings reach their highest fulfillment.

Since participation is relational, finite beings must progress through these stages in alignment with their own nature, rather than being forcibly changed.

5. How Divine Action Provides the Means of Elevation

Since finite beings cannot elevate themselves, divine action must provide the means by which they do the following:

- Receive knowledge beyond their natural limits
- Align their will with divine goodness
- Overcome the barriers imposed by time and limitation

6. Divine Action as an Invitation, Not a Coercion

A crucial distinction must be made.

- Divine action is not forceful; it does not compel participation.
- Divine action is elevative; it provides the means for participation while preserving freedom.
- Divine action is relational; it unfolds through the natural structure of rational existence.

Thus, divine action operates as an invitation to fulfillment, not a subversion of free participation.

7. Why Free Will Remains Essential in Perfected Participation

Since divine fulfillment is the necessary end of rational beings, does free will cease to exist in perfected participation?

The answer is no. Free will remains, but it is no longer conflicted; it is fulfilled and freely aligned with the Good.

8. The Problem of Free Will in Fulfillment

In imperfect participation, the will struggles because of the following:

- It is divided, choosing between true goods and lesser, apparent goods.
- It is subject to error; it does not always align with absolute goodness.
- It experiences tension between self-direction and divine order.

If perfected participation required coercion, then freedom would be abolished. However, in the beatific vision, the will remains free, but its freedom is no longer bound by ignorance or the attraction of lesser goods. Instead of struggling toward the good, it now chooses with full knowledge of it, operating in complete alignment with divine actuality.

There is no loss of choice, but all choices are made within the full knowledge of divine goodness without confusion or contradiction.

Freedom reaches its highest form—the unrestricted ability to choose what is truly and perfectly good.

Thus, perfected participation does not mean the loss of freedom but its highest realization, where choice is no longer divided by uncertainty but fully oriented toward divine actuality.

9. The Role of Grace as the Mechanism of Divine Elevation

Since the finite cannot self-elevate, the mechanism by which divine action brings participation to fulfillment is grace.

What is Grace?

Grace is not mere divine favor but the active presence of divine actuality sustaining and elevating participation.

- Grace perfects knowledge. It allows the intellect to perceive divine Truth more clearly.
- Grace perfects the will. It strengthens the will's alignment with divine goodness.
- Grace removes barriers. It elevates finite participation beyond its natural limits.

Grace is the structured means by which divine action, through the causal joint, elevates finite beings, bridging the gap between imperfect and perfect participation without violating free will.

10. The Process of Elevation as the Final Unfolding of Divine Action

In part five we have demonstrated the following:

- The transition to perfected participation must be gradual to respect the nature of rational existence.
- A structured ascent is necessary; participation follows a logical order toward fulfillment.
- Divine action provides the means of elevation; it invites rather than forces participation.
- Free will is not abolished but perfected; it becomes fully aligned with divine Truth.
- Grace is the mechanism of elevation; it bridges the gap between imperfect and perfect participation.

This leads into chapter 15, where we will explore the following:

- The metaphysical final moment of transition into the beatific vision
- The completion of divine action as the perfecting of all rational beings
- The full realization of participation in Being per se

In doing so, we will bring the discussion of finite participation in divine actuality to its logical conclusion: the perfect fulfillment of all things in divine actuality.

11. Closing the Arc: From Deceleration to Return

The logic of participation does not end with the soul. Creation is structured by the same metaphysical arc: energy, mass, time, and extension are not external to divine action but are its slowed expression—its deceleration into receptivity.

The body, like the soul, is sustained by the causal joint. But unlike the soul, it is fully bound to decelerated structure—matter, entropy, and temporality. At death, the soul accelerates, not symbolically but ontologically. It returns toward the causal joint, seeking the beatific fulfillment for which it was structured. The body, however, must wait.

Why?

Because the cosmos has not yet caught up. The return of the body requires not escape from matter but its transfiguration—a cosmic acceleration that collapses mass into energy, time into act, and extension into communion. The resurrection of the body is not the reversal of physics; it is its fulfillment.

Thus, the beatific vision is not merely the soul's rest. It is the metaphysical precondition for the resurrection of matter, the reconstitution of the world, and the consummation of divine action.

Moving Forward: The Soul's Ascent and the Cosmos's Delay

Since the soul, through divine elevation, attains perfect participation in actuality, we must ask: Why does the body not return with it? Why does the resurrection not occur at once?

This is not a matter of psychological waiting or temporal delay because neither the soul nor the body exists, at that point, in a mode where "waiting" applies. The body, as matter, does not persist in a conscious state. The soul, having been drawn beyond sequence, no longer abides in time as it once did. What appears as delay belongs not to the person, but to the cosmos—to the still-decelerated order of creation.

Physics is the expression of divine action in decelerated form. Energy becomes mass. Motion becomes time. Relation becomes space. These are not merely empirical features. They are modes of metaphysical slowing, structures by which finite reality is sustained in its differentiation from infinite actuality. The body, as an expression of this decelerated order, cannot yet be drawn into the fullness of participation until creation is consummated.

The resurrection is not the reunion of the soul with some preexisting material remnant, but the transfiguration of all matter—the acceleration of the entire physical order into a form adequate to divine actuality. Until then, the cosmos remains incomplete, and so, too, does embodied fulfillment.

Chapter 15 now turns to this logic: why the body cannot yet return, why the physical universe must await its transfiguration, and how the eschaton marks not an end but the completion of divine action in the return of all creation to the actuality from which it was structured.

15

The Waiting Soul
Structure, Time, and the Logic of Return

Introduction: The Metaphysical Structure of Deferred Resurrection

THE SOUL, PERFECTED IN participation, no longer moves through temporal sequence. Its relation to Truth is no longer partial, nor is its reception of Love strained by resistance. It abides now in the divine actuality from which it was always sustained. But the body does not yet return. Death, though overcome for the soul, still reigns in matter. The cosmos persists in its structure. Creation remains unfinished.

Why?

This chapter follows that question through to its metaphysical ground. The delay is not punishment. It is not neglect. It is structure. The body, unlike the soul, is constituted by the decelerated logic of time, space, and mass—forms of divine action expressed as constraint. The soul, having passed through death, is no longer bound by them. But the body, and all matter with it, remains suspended within a world not yet transfigured.

Resurrection, then, is not the return of a waiting form. It is the fulfillment of the cosmos. The return of the body requires, not escape from matter but its elevation—the reconstitution of physical form in full alignment with divine actuality. This is not metaphor. It is the physics of the end, the metaphysical completion of the universe.

1. Why the Body Cannot Yet Return

Since the soul, in death, is sustained directly in divine actuality—no longer mediated by material structure, temporal sequence, or deficient knowledge—then we must ask: Why does the body remain absent from this perfection?

The answer is not symbolic or devotional but structural: the body is not merely slow in relation to the soul; it is constituted by slowness. Its very form is a decelerated expression of divine action—space, mass, and energy congealed into coherent limitation. Its identity, persistence, and meaningful distinction all arise from this deceleration.

But deceleration is not degradation. It is the condition by which matter becomes form and structure emerges in time. In the logic of creation, the deceleration of infinite actuality into space-time-energy is not an accident but a necessity. Without it, there is no universe, no differentiation, no embodiment, no relationality. The soul is not trapped by the body but initiated through it. And yet, once the soul has returned to direct participation in divine actuality, the body cannot follow because the field from which it draws its coherence is still unfolding.

The body belongs to a cosmos that remains in process. The logic of physical structure—sequential actualization, reciprocal causality, gravitational inertia, and entropic decay—is not a punishment for finitude. It is the very texture of a creation still in motion. To bring back the body—to raise it not merely to life but to eternal life—would require, not the reversal of time but its consummation, not the escape from physicality but its transfiguration.

This is why the soul and the body are not "separated" in the ordinary sense. The soul is not waiting. The body is not lost. Rather, the cosmos is unfinished. What we call "death" is not the disruption of nature but its very structure metaphysically expressed. The soul, having fulfilled its ascent, participates now in that which sustains the whole; the body cannot yet be drawn up until the whole is fulfilled.

The resurrection of the body, then, is not a future event placed along a timeline. It is the consequence of cosmic fulfillment. The body does not come back because the soul desires it or because history demands it, but because the logic of creation requires that nothing remain incomplete. Every aspect of form, every quanta of energy, every cell and sequence will be drawn into alignment, not simply repeated or rebuilt but accelerated, elevated, and made able to participate in divine actuality without ceasing to be what it was.

Until then, the body is not "waiting." It is being fulfilled.

2. Acceleration and the Transfiguration of Matter

Acceleration of the soul, in this metaphysical framework, is not movement through space. It is not a change in velocity in the physical sense. It is the elevation of a mode of participation—from lower to higher actuality, from fragmented structure to integrated fullness. In the case of the soul, this elevation occurs at death: freed from the temporal sequence that structures bodily life, the soul no longer receives Truth incrementally but is drawn into direct relation with divine actuality. This is not omniscience, but unmediated participation according to the soul's capacity.

The body, however, cannot be elevated in the same way, not because it is unworthy but because its structure is constituted by the very limitations that the soul transcends. Mass is not a container for energy; it is energy slowed. Space is not a void between things; it is extension structured by relational difference. Time is not merely the passing of events; it is the sequence of potentiation—decelerated Being expressed through motion. These forms are not illusions to be escaped. They are the foundation of all physical structure.

It is not a division of nature or worth but of rhythm, akin to the distinction between dance partners moving at different speeds to the music that brought them together. The soul participates immediately; the body, still bound to cosmic time, cannot yet follow. For matter to be transfigured—truly elevated into participation in divine actuality—it must undergo, not annihilation but acceleration, not a return to chaos or nothingness but an integration into the higher logic from which it came. This means not discarding mass but resolving it into the energy it already is, not dissolving space but collapsing extension into communion, not escaping time but completing it such that sequence no longer mediates actuality but becomes the form of a total act.

This process cannot occur arbitrarily. The cosmos is not a shell to be shed but a structure to be fulfilled. To resurrect the body is not to override physics but to reveal that physics was always, at its root, the structured expression of metaphysical logic. The transformation of the body will come when the structure of the cosmos is transfigured, when all that has been slowed, stretched, and spaced out is drawn back, not by reversal but by consummation. Acceleration is the ontological condition of resurrection.

And this is why only God can do it. To accelerate any body—every atom, every bond—into perfect participation without collapse, distortion, or loss of identity would require more than omnipotence. It would require omniscience—the total knowledge of every form, every relation, every history, and every becoming, integrated perfectly into a new act of structure. This is not a technical feat but an act of infinite sustaining. The resurrection of the body is not the restoration of what was but the divine transfiguration of what still is, drawn up, not backward but into the Omega of all Becoming.

3. The Resurrection as the Completion of Cosmic Form

Since the soul's return to divine actuality is immediate, and the body's is not, the reason lies, not in disparity of worth but in difference of structure. The soul is not more important than the body; it is simply less delayed. The body is structured through time, space, and extension. It is not outside the logic of Being. It is the slowest and widest expression of that logic. And because divine action does not bypass structure but fulfills it, the resurrection of the body can only occur when the cosmos is brought to its proper completion.

The cosmos is not an inert container. It is the field of relational potentiation—every act of matter and motion held in tension by the divine will. To transfigure the body is to bring the field of its constitution into alignment with divine actuality. This cannot happen to one alone but to all. The resurrection is not an isolated miracle; it is the consummation of creation.

The eschaton is therefore not a disruption of physics but the realization of its purpose. The very laws by which we measure change—entropy, inertia, decay—are not mistakes but modes of delay that give structure to the history of fulfillment. What decays is not lost. What slows is not abandoned. The logic of Being sustains even the dispersal of form, not to dissolve it but to hold it open for transfiguration.

This is why the resurrection is universal, not universal in the sense that all are saved but in the sense that no act of divine formation is meaningless. The transfiguration of the body is not a private event. It is the moment when the decelerated forms of space, time, and energy are drawn up into the relational fullness from which they descend. It is the moment when the created order becomes what it was always meant to be: not the background of salvation but its medium.

And in this final act, the soul is not simply reunited with a body. It is fulfilled as a person in full communion with the whole of creation. For what is personhood if not the structured relation of intellect, will, and form in communion with the Good? And what is the Good if not the infinite act of Being in whom all structure is sustained?

To speak of resurrection is to speak, not only of bodies but of relational order, of the Good that draws all creation toward itself. It is to affirm that no created thing, rightly formed, will be lost; that the logic of Being cannot be defeated by entropy; that what God has called into structured participation will not end in fragmentation but in unity.

4. Moving Forward: From Cosmic Transfiguration to Personal Fulfillment in the Logos

The resurrection of the body is not a theological accessory. It is the culmination of creation's metaphysical structure. The logic of Being does not discard the physical; it fulfills it. In this light, the body's return is not an interruption of physics but its transfiguration, an acceleration into the very act that sustains it. This fulfillment, however, is not merely cosmic; it is personal. The soul, already drawn into divine actuality, does not await the body in time. Rather, the whole person is ordered toward union through a logic that sustains both soul and cosmos without contradiction.

This transition—from individual soul to embodied person, from decelerated cosmos to accelerated fulfillment—cannot be understood apart from the *Logos*. For it is through the *Logos* that creation came to be, and through the *Logos* that all things return. Divine action is not only the origin but the path and the end. And since this is so, then the structure of fulfillment must be intelligible, personal, and ordered because the *Logos* is all three.

As Pope Leo XIV observes, when Jesus asks, "Who do you say that I am?" and Peter replies, "You are the Christ, the Son of the Living God," Peter names both "the gift of God and the path to follow in order to allow himself to be changed by that gift." These are, in Pope Leo's words, "two inseparable aspects of salvation entrusted to the Church to be proclaimed for the good of the human race."[1] The *Logos* is not only the origin of creation but also the very structure of its return, the gift through which all being is sustained, and the way by which it is fulfilled.

5. Moving Forward: From Cosmic Fulfillment to Personal Participation in the Logos

The resurrection of the body reveals that even the slowest form of created being is destined for elevation, not by erasure but by fulfillment. Yet this fulfillment is not mechanical, impersonal, or abstract. It is ordered by and into the *Logos*, the fully actual self-expression of divine Being. What the cosmos achieves in structure, the person must receive in communion. The *Logos* is not only the origin and logic of creation, but the form and end of all participation. To understand how divine action is fulfilled, we must now turn to the *Logos* himself—where metaphysical necessity and personal destiny converge.

---

1. Leo XIV, "Homily at Inaugural Mass."

16

The Fulfillment of Divine Action in the Logos

Introduction: The Fulfilled Self-Expression of Divine Action

THE PREVIOUS CHAPTER BROUGHT the metaphysical structure of divine action to its eschatological horizon: the resurrection of the body, the transfiguration of matter, and the consummation of cosmic time. Yet even this does not exhaust the logic of divine action. For since creation begins through the structured self-gift of infinite actuality, and because that gift moves toward fulfillment, not by reversal but by elevation, we must now ask: What is the final form of divine self-expression by which such fulfillment is made personal, intelligible, and complete?

This chapter turns from the structure of eschatology to the principle by which that structure is ordered: the *Logos*. Not a symbol and not merely a theological concept, the Logos is the fully actual, eternally begotten self-expression of divine Being—the principle through whom all things were made, are sustained, and are drawn back into communion.

We now ask: What does it mean for divine action to be fulfilled? How does the Logos complete the arc of creation and return? Why must rational beings be fulfilled—not only structurally but personally—through participation in the Logos?

These questions do not arise from the doctrinal assumptions with which they so closely correspond but from the metaphysical trajectory already established. If divine action is the sustaining logic of all being, then its culmination must be both structural and personal. In the Logos, we find both—the principle of creation and the person of fulfillment.

By the end of this chapter, it will be clear that the Logos is not an optional feature of Christian theology but the necessary metaphysical ground of all rational participation in divine actuality.

1. *The Logos as the Necessary Self-Expression of Being per se*

The term Logos, traditionally translated as "word" or "reason," carries profound ontological and metaphysical significance. It does not denote a temporal or linguistic utterance but the fully actual self-expression of Being per se—the perfect act by which infinite actuality knows and expresses itself eternally and without *privation*. Through the Logos, creation gains structured access to Truth, enabling rational beings to apprehend divine reality through the faculty of reason.

This means the following:

- If God is infinite actuality, then self-expression is not an optional attribute—it is necessary.
- This self-expression cannot be separate from God, nor can it be imperfect—it must be fully actual.
- Because God is omniscient, his self-knowledge must be infinitely complete, eternal, and perfect.

Thus, the Logos—the Divine Word—is not created but eternally begotten as the full self- expression of Being per se.

- There is no division in God, yet there is a perfect relational actuality in his self- expression.
- This *infinite reciprocal information* exchange within divine actuality is what theology describes as the procession of the Son from the Father—a necessity of divine self-knowledge, Love eternally reciprocated.

The Fulfillment of Divine Action in the Logos 165

This is why the Logos is not a contingent reality but a metaphysical necessity—God must fully express himself, and this expression is the Logos.

2. The Causal Joint and the Relationship Between Infinite and Finite Expression

At the causal joint, divine self-expression does not undergo intrinsic change but relates to the finite order through the deceleration of infinite reciprocal motion. This Deceleration structures the emergence of relational differentiation, potentiality, and contingent existence, enabling the following:

- Relational differentiation—the structured emergence of distinct beings, governed by logic, ensuring that creation is intelligible, ordered, and coherent rather than chaotic
- Potentiality—the possibility for finite beings to develop over time, progressing toward greater participation in divine actuality
- Contingent existence—finite reality is not self-sustaining; it is continuously potentiated empowered through divine actuality

  It is crucial here to distinguish two modes of information exchange:

- *Infinite reciprocal information exchange* (Triune Exchange)
    - This occurs within divine actuality.
    - It is perfect, necessary, and simultaneous.
    - There is no fragmentation, limitation, or sequence—Truth is whole.
- *Finite Reciprocal Information Exchange* (Triadic Exchange)
    - This occurs within created reality.
    - It is structured through Deceleration, introducing sequence, limitation, and progression.
    - It necessarily involves imperfect knowledge, requiring structured participation to approach divine Truth.

These two species of exchange highlight a key truth: all creation is a relational expression of divine actuality but in a limited, structured form.

If God's omniscience entails perfect knowledge of all possible realities, then the following must be true:

- The final cause of creation is its participation in divine perfection.
- This participation is only possible through the Logos who is both the causal joint of creation and its fulfillment.

3. The Logos as the Bridge Between Infinite and Finite

Now that we have established that the Logos is the perfect self-expression of Being per se, we must show why the Logos is also the necessary bridge between the infinite and the finite. The transition from infinite actuality to finite reality is structured through the Logos as the causal joint.

This transition occurs through deceleration of IRM that structures the emergence of finite reality, ensuring that divine actuality can be engaged without overwhelming contingent existence. However, just as Deceleration potentiates structured differentiation and contingency, acceleration potentiates the structured ascent of participation.

Participation in divine actuality is not a static state but an ordered movement, an elevation structured through the potentiated acceleration of *finite reciprocal motion*. This ensures that finite beings, while remaining contingent, are progressively drawn toward divine actuality in a manner that preserves freedom, rational integrity, and structured participation.

The Logos, as the causal joint, not only structures the emergence of creation but also sustains the very path of return, ensuring that structured participation finds its fulfillment in divine actuality. Just as the deceleration of infinite reciprocal motion reveals triune relationality within finite structure, the acceleration of that same motion potentiates the return of the finite to the infinite, not by dissolving distinction but by perfecting it.

Structured acceleration does not erase the finite. It elevates it. This completes the relational arc of divine action, moving from structured differentiation to perfected communion. Finite beings do not lose themselves in this process; rather, they are drawn into deeper participation within the infinite without ceasing to be finite.

To clarify the key dimensions of divine action:

- Structured differentiation—creation is not an undifferentiated blur, but a field of ordered distinctions, each sustained by divine intentionality
- Relational participation—finite beings cannot directly apprehend infinite actuality, but they ascend into it through the Logos by structured, potentiated participation.

Thus, the Logos is not only the source of creation but also its path and goal, the principle by which all contingent reality is drawn toward its fulfillment in the infinite.

This means the following:

- The intelligibility of reality depends entirely on the Logos. Without the Logos, there is no coherence, no order, and no rational access to truth.
- Finite beings can only reach fulfillment through structured ascent into the Logos because participation in divine actuality requires alignment with the Logos' rational order.
- Without the Logos, there would be no structured intelligibility, no relational participation, and no teleological fulfillment because all contingent reality exists by potentiation through divine self-expression.

4. *The Logos as the Rational Order of Reality*

Since God is infinite actuality, then creation must necessarily reflect divine Truth as the rational structure of Being itself. The Logos is not an externally imposed framework but the very principle that makes intelligibility possible—the necessary articulation of divine actuality into structured reality. This means that Logos is not merely a rational principle or organizing force but the fully actual, fully real, and necessarily relational self-expression of Being per se. As such, the Logos is not only the source of all distinction and order but also the means of structured participation, the bridge through which finite minds ascend toward divine actuality while retaining their own distinct mode of being.

Because the Logos is fully actual and fully real, it does the following:

- Structures the intelligibility of all things—finite reality is not self-sufficient; its order derives from the Logos
- Sustains rationality—the very coherence of logic and reason is possible only because the Logos is both Truth and the eternal rational order of Being per se
- Ensures that reality is not arbitrary—the finite does not merely exist but is ordered toward a *telos*, which is participation in divine actuality

Key Principle: the rational order of the universe is not imposed externally—it is the necessary manifestation of divine self-expression.

5. *The Logos as the Origin and Sustainer of Reality*

The Gospel of John declares, "All things were made through Him, and without Him was not anything made that was made" (John 1:3).

This reveals what metaphysical reasoning has now confirmed: the Logos is the necessary self-expression of Being per se. Divine actuality, being perfect, must fully express itself, and this perfect self-expression is the Logos.

- The Logos is not an imposed structure but the very reason intelligibility exists at all.
- It is not merely a principle but the active rational order by which all distinctions, relations, and participations occur in reality.

This means the following:

- Finite beings do not generate truth; they engage with Truth through structured knowledge.
- The universe does not exist independently but is continuously upheld by the rational order of the Logos.
- Reality is not mechanistic but relational, reflecting the triune nature of divine being.
- Finite beings are not self-sustaining; they participate in existence through the divine Logos.

The Logos, then, is not only the cause of creation but also the principle of its sustained intelligibility and rational structure.

6. The Logos as the Fulfillment of Divine Action

In this chapter, we have demonstrated the following:

- The Logos is the necessary self-expression of Being per se; divine actuality must fully express itself.
- The Logos is the causal joint between infinite and finite reality, making structured participation possible.
- The Logos is the rational order of reality, ensuring that all things are intelligible and coherent.
- The Logos is the necessary fulfillment of divine action, ensuring that finite being is ordered toward communion with the infinite.

Thus, the entire structure of existence—from Being per se to finite reality—is a coherent, relational expression of divine action. The Logos is not only the origin of structured participation but also its sustaining principle and teleological fulfillment.

This raises the next unavoidable questions:

- Since the Logos structures both the emergence and the return of creation, how is this structured participation perfected?
- Since participation in divine actuality is not imposed but potentiated, what is the necessary mode of elevation?
- Since contingent beings are to be drawn into full communion without annihilation, how does divine self-expression provide the perfect means of fulfillment?

These questions lead directly to the next chapter.

7. Moving Forward: From the Logos to the Hypostatic Fulfillment

Having established the Logos as the eternal self-expression of divine actuality—the causal joint through which all finite being is structured, sustained, and drawn toward fulfillment—we now encounter a further necessity: this divine self-expression must not only make creation intelligible, but render participation in it possible. The rational structure of reality is not merely abstract; it is personal, relational, and incarnational. It is not enough for the Logos to structure the world; the Logos must enter it.

Thus, we turn to the incarnation, not as a symbolic descent but as the metaphysical fulfillment of divine action within finite nature. In Christ, divine actuality assumes human form, engaging the soul's ascent toward Truth through the very structures it created. The hypostatic union reveals not only who God is but how the soul is drawn into communion: through relation, through time, through structured participation; not bypassed but fulfilled.

In what follows, we will see why the incarnation is not optional to salvation but necessary to the logic of divine action. The Logos does not merely speak; he listens. And in listening, he lifts humanity toward its end.

17

The Hypostatic Union and the Rational Necessity of Decelerated Knowledge

Introduction: The Hypostatic Union as the Fulfillment of Divine Action

IN PREVIOUS CHAPTERS, WE established that divine action is not a temporal intervention but the sustaining principle of all existence. We demonstrated how infinite actuality (God) gives rise to finite reality through Deceleration, allowing for time, space, energy, and relational differentiation.

Now, we arrive at a crucial question: If divine action structures all reality through potentiation, then must it not also structure finite participation in divine actuality?

Because divine actuality is necessarily relational, it does not merely sustain contingent reality but must also provide the means for its full participation. The incarnation is not an event separate from this structure but its necessary fulfillment, the completion of the causal joint where divine actuality engages finite cognition without overwhelming or bypassing its structured ascent. Understanding the hypostatic union within this framework reveals why divine action must extend into finite relational participation rather than remain merely sustaining.

To advance our understanding, we must examine the hypostatic union—the union of divine and human natures in the Logos (Christ).

This chapter will demonstrate the following:

- The hypostatic union is not an arbitrary theological claim but the metaphysically necessary fulfillment of divine action at the causal joint.
- Decelerated information exchange—the process by which finite beings approach Truth sequentially rather than instantaneously—is a prerequisite of finite participation in divine actuality.
- The incarnation is the perfect bridge between infinite actuality and finite cognition, allowing humanity to be elevated into divine actuality.

In this analysis, we will see that Christ's human nature does not diminish divine omniscience but demonstrates how finite participation in infinite Truth must occur through structured, relational engagement—what we call prayer and revelation.

1. The Incarnation as the Extension of the Causal Joint

The causal joint—where infinite actuality allows for finite differentiation without diminishing divine perfection—finds its fulfillment in the hypostatic union.

Just as:

- Infinite actuality potentiates finite reality through Deceleration (creating space, time, and change).
- So, also, the incarnation potentiates finite beings' access to divine knowledge.

WHY THE INCARNATION IS NECESSARY FOR DIVINE PARTICIPATION

- If divine action is the sustaining cause of all things, then creation is already in relation to divine actuality.

- However, because finite beings experience knowledge sequentially, they do not immediately grasp divine Truth in its fullness.
- The incarnation provides the necessary bridge; God enters finite cognition without abandoning divine omniscience.

Thus, the Logos assuming a human nature ensures that finite beings can freely participate in divine Truth without contradiction or force. And this is why the Son of Man must pray.

2. The Son of Man Must Pray: The Necessity of Decelerated Knowledge

One of the most misunderstood aspects of Christ's earthly life is his need to pray. If the Logos possesses divine knowledge, why must he engage in prayer? The answer lies in the necessity of decelerated knowledge.

Because finite cognition necessarily engages Truth sequentially—through relational participation, experience, and structured ascent—the perfect assumption of human nature requires engagement with this same structure. The Logos does not merely simulate human cognition; he fully assumes it, ensuring that finite knowledge is not bypassed but fulfilled through structured ascent.

Christ does not pray due to limitation, but because in assuming human nature, he consents to access what he is—Truth itself—through the very structure of human participation he came to redeem. The Logos assumes human nature completely, including its structured ascent toward knowledge—not as a concession but as a metaphysical necessity of relational participation in divine actuality. This assumption does not compromise divine omniscience but fulfills the necessary mode of finite cognition that is fully and truly human.

Decelerated Knowledge as the Condition of Finite Participation

As we established in previous chapters, finite knowledge differs from divine knowledge as follows:

- God's knowledge is instantaneous and total—nothing is learned; all is known.

- Finite knowledge is sequential and relational—humans learn through experience, language, and time.

For the Logos to truly assume human nature, he must do the following

- Experience knowledge relationally, as humans do
- Engage in prayer, not because of deficiency but because human knowledge requires structured engagement with divine Truth

Thus, Christ prays not because he is not Truth but because his human nature participates in knowledge through finite means.

3. The Decelerated Access to Divine Knowledge: The Key to the Incarnation

Why does Christ learn and grow if divine Truth is complete?

The answer lies in the necessity of structured ascent. Finite cognition does not receive knowledge as an undivided whole; it processes information through relational participation, sequence, and experience. Therefore, the Logos, in assuming human nature fully, does not circumvent this structure but fully engages it. As Scripture affirms, "And Jesus grew in wisdom and stature" (Luke 2:52).

This does not imply a deficiency in divine omniscience but rather the perfect adherence to the nature of finite cognition, wherein knowledge is received progressively rather than possessed in totality from the outset. This reveals why prayer and relational knowledge are not optional but fundamental to human participation in divine actuality. The incarnation thus perfects participation rather than bypassing it, demonstrating that human elevation to divine Truth must occur through engagement rather than imposition.

- This does not mean his divine intellect was incomplete, but that his human intellect followed the necessary process of finite cognition.
- By undergoing the full experience of human learning, the incarnate Logos demonstrates the following:
  - How finite beings engage with divine Truth (step-by-step)
  - Why prayer and relational knowledge are necessary for human participation in divine actuality

The Hypostatic Union and the Rational Necessity of Decelerated Knowledge 175

- That full participation in divine actuality does not bypass the nature of finite existence; it elevates it

Thus, the incarnation is the rational fulfillment of divine action, not a mere historical event.

4. The Hypostatic Union is the Rational Fulfillment of Divine Action

Thus, the structure of divine action remains internally consistent, showing the following

- Infinite actuality sustains finite existence.
- Deceleration structures finite cognition.
- The incarnation is not merely a historical moment but the necessary completion of divine self-expression within structured participation.

The fulfillment of divine action in the hypostatic union ensures that finite beings do not remain distant observers of divine actuality but become active participants through structured ascent.

This reinforces the internal consistency of divine action—from infinite actuality to structured differentiation, from Deceleration to relational engagement, and from finite cognition to perfected participation. The incarnation does not impose divine Truth upon creation; it provides the necessary means for finite minds to be drawn into Truth without contradiction, preserving both divine perfection and finite integrity.

Having established that divine action is not only possible but necessary, it remains to be seen whether traditional arguments for God's existence converge upon this truth. Classical arguments—whether teleological, cosmological, moral, or ontological—are often framed as independent lines of reasoning. However, because Triune actuality is the infinite act by which all existence is structured, these arguments must ultimately point to the same metaphysical foundation.

5. Moving Forward: From Relational Participation to Metaphysical Foundation

If the incarnation reveals the necessary structure by which divine actuality engages finite cognition—through relational, decelerated participation—then it also demands that our very capacity to know, to pray, and to ascend toward truth must be grounded in a metaphysical reality greater than any one revelation. The hypostatic union is not an isolated miracle but the culmination of a logic already implicit in the structure of Being.

To follow this logic fully, we must now ask: What makes divine action not only possible but necessary? What lies beneath the claims of theology, beneath the rationality of the Logos, beneath the structure of creation?

The next chapter will show that every classical argument for God's existence ultimately converges upon a deeper truth: the alternative to divine actuality is not an empty void but a metaphysical impossibility. The argument from nonexistence now becomes the key by which all reasoned ascent to God is unified.

18

The Argument from Nonexistence as Unifying Classical Arguments for God

Introduction: Reframing Classical Arguments in Light of Divine Potentiation

Throughout history, arguments for God's existence—teleological, cosmological, moral, and ontological—have been presented as distinct and separate approaches, each addressing a particular aspect of reality. However, this fragmentation obscures the deeper unity underlying these arguments. Each of them, when examined within the framework of divine potentiation, is an expression of the same fundamental truth: the argument from nonexistence.

This argument posits that all being is potentiated by God through divine self-suppression (kenosis), wherein God, the perfectly actual potentiator, limits himself to allow for the structured emergence of creation. This self-giving act follows the logic of love, providing not only the foundation for finite existence but also for moral order and rationality.

Thus, rather than treating these classical arguments as distinct and competing, this chapter will demonstrate how they are unified under the fundamental reality of divine self-suppression, revealing a coherent vision of God's existence.

1. The Teleological Argument: The Intelligible Creation

The teleological argument asserts that the universe exhibits intelligible order, suggesting a purposeful designer. Traditionally, this has been framed as an appeal to fine-tuning—the precise balance of physical laws necessary for life.

However, within the framework of divine potentiation, the order we observe is not simply imposed externally but emerges from God's self-suppression of *infinite reciprocal information* exchange. The act of divine kenosis structures the potentiality of the cosmos, ensuring that creation unfolds in a way that reflects rational intelligibility.

Thus, the teleological argument is not merely an appeal to design but a demonstration of how reality is an ordered expression of divine self-giving. Fine-tuning is neither euphemistic nor accidental but the inevitable result of God's unequivocal potentiating act where creation, though finite, remains rationally structured in its participation in infinite actuality.

2. The Cosmological Argument (Including Kalam): Deceleration and the Necessity of Creation

Cosmological arguments demonstrate that the universe must have a necessary foundation because finite existence is not self-explanatory. The impossibility of an infinite regress highlights that contingent realities cannot explain themselves and must ultimately be grounded in a necessary source, one that does not merely cause existence but structures it through divine potentiation.

Within the framework of divine potentiation, this causal necessity is directly linked to divine self-limitation. Creation is a structured act of divine Deceleration where God, who exists outside of time and change, deliberately limits IRM to generate a structured, finite reality.

- The impossibility of infinite regress is resolved when we understand that existence is necessarily structured by divine self-suppression.
- God does not begin to create in time; rather, he potentiates reality as an expression of his eternal actuality.
- Divine foreknowledge ensures a particular creation, unfolding precisely as willed, for God knows the full structure of reality before he potentiates it.

Thus, the cosmological argument—especially the Kalam argument's emphasis on a finite past—finds its deepest grounding in the necessity of divine potentiation. Reality is not merely caused but structured by the self-giving act of Being per se.

3. The Moral Argument: Love as the Ground of Moral Order

The moral argument suggests that objective moral values require a transcendent foundation. However, morality is not simply an externally imposed law; it must be intrinsic to the very structure of existence.

Within the framework of divine potentiation, morality is understood as a direct consequence of divine self-giving.

- Justice is ordered love, not an arbitrary legal construct.
- Moral action is a participation in divine potentiation, where creatures reflect the self-giving nature of God.
- Goodness is not merely commanded but potentiated, meaning ethical life is structured within reality.

Thus, the moral argument is not merely about an external moral lawgiver but about the very logic of creation. Human existence is structured by divine kenosis. Therefore, moral life is an expression of participation in divine self-giving.

4. The Ontological Argument: The Necessity of the Perfectly Actual Potentiator

The ontological argument, as formulated by Anselm, asserts that a maximally great being must exist necessarily, but it does so by relying on a conceptual definition rather than an unavoidable ontological reality. However, if we begin instead with two irrefutable facts—that something exists and that nonexistence is impossible—then necessity is not an abstract property assigned to God but the unavoidable foundation of all being. In this framework, God is not merely postulated as a necessary being but recognized as the perfectly actual potentiator whose self-suppression structures contingent reality.

Within the framework of divine potentiation, this argument takes on a new and deeper significance.

- God is not merely a conceptually necessary being but a metaphysically inevitable one.
- The very structure of being requires a perfectly actual potentiator whose self-suppression makes the contingent possible.
- Without divine self-giving, no contingent being could exist, for nothing could sustain itself apart from the act of potentiation.

Thus, the ontological argument finds its fullest expression in the necessity of divine self-suppression—the only possible ground of reality is a being who is perfectly actual yet potentiates without loss.

5. The Argument from Nonexistence as the Unifying Principle

The following classical arguments are not separate but integrated expressions of a single reality:

- Teleological argument—grounded in the ordered nature of divine potentiation
- Cosmological arguments—coherent through the necessity of divine Deceleration
- Moral arguments—reinforced by the logic of love; grounded in kenotic self-giving
- Ontological arguments—resolved in the inevitability of the perfectly actual potentiator

When viewed in isolation, these arguments provide partial insights into God's nature. But when unified through the argument from nonexistence, they reveal a single, cohesive vision of divine action.

6. Resolving Objections and Counterarguments to the Argument from Nonexistence

This unified framework resolves common objections raised against traditional theistic arguments.

- Infinite regress in cosmology: divine potentiation eliminates the need for an external cause while resolving the paradoxes of infinite regress by showing that existence is structured by God's necessary self-giving.

- Fine-tuning as mere chance: the teleological argument gains metaphysical grounding by showing that order is intrinsic to divine self-suppression, not an arbitrary imposition.
- Moral subjectivity: by grounding morality in the structure of *existence itself*, this framework overcomes critiques that morality is either arbitrary or socially constructed.
- Kant's critique of the ontological argument: the necessity of God is not merely conceptual but structurally unavoidable within the argument from nonexistence.[1]

These responses do not merely defend the classical arguments. They strengthen them by placing them within a coherent and necessary metaphysical framework.

7. Practical Implications: Morality as Participation in Divine Action

This framework is not merely theoretical. It has direct implications for how we understand moral life.

- Freedom and responsibility: human freedom mirrors divine potentiation—just as God potentiates rather than determines, moral responsibility is a response to divine self-giving.
- Justice as ordered love: justice is not retributive but an act of right ordering, mirroring divine kenosis.
- Ethics as participation: goodness is realized through alignment with divine potentiation, making moral action an extension of God's creative act.

Thus, the argument from nonexistence does not merely unify classical proofs, it extends into lived reality, showing that morality is a mode of participation in divine self-giving.

---

1. Kant, *Critique of Pure Reason*, A592/B620:563–69.

8. The Necessity of Divine Potentiation

Rather than treating arguments for God's existence as isolated, we now see them as cohesive expressions of a single truth. Existence, order, morality, and necessity all point toward a perfectly actual potentiator whose self-suppression structures reality.

This unified approach not only clarifies traditional theistic proofs but reveals the full depth of divine action where God is not merely an abstract conclusion but the necessary ground of all being, all order, and all moral life.

9. Moving Forward: From Unity of Proofs to the Demands of Participation

Having established that the classical arguments for God's existence—teleological, cosmological, moral, and ontological—converge not merely by rhetorical harmony but by metaphysical necessity upon the argument from nonexistence, we are left with a crucial task: to clarify how this unified vision compels a deeper understanding of our place within it. Because all existence is structured by divine potentiation—by the self-suppression of the perfectly actual—finite reality does not merely point to God; it is sustained moment by moment in participatory relation to Him.

In the next chapter we follow this logic to its inevitable next step: the demand that every instance of finite misalignment be understood not as a mere philosophical error but as a metaphysical deviation from the structured act of finite participation in divine actuality. It is to this task that we now turn.

19

The Logical Necessity of Divine Participation

Introduction: The Problem of Finite Misalignment

THROUGHOUT THIS WORK, WE have demonstrated that all finite existence emerges from Being per se through Deceleration. This process introduces the following:

- Individuation—the distinction between beings
- Potentiality—the ability for change and growth
- Limitation—the structured constraints necessary for relational differentiation

While these conditions allow for finite existence, they also impose barriers to a finite being's ability to fully participate in divine actuality.

The problem that arises is finite misalignment, the fact that finite beings are the following:

- Structurally incapable of full self-realignment with infinite actuality
- Bound by Deceleration, making direct knowledge of perfect Truth impossible through natural means
- Subject to fragmentation, meaning their intellect and will do not automatically align with divine perfection

This chapter will demonstrate the following:

- Finite beings require structured participation in Being per se to attain fulfillment.
- The necessary correction must come from the very causal joint that allowed for finite emergence without contradicting divine immutability.
- The causal joint—the Divine Word—must enter into the finite order, experiencing limitation in order to provide the means of realignment.

Thus, what is traditionally called redemption is not merely a theological construct but a metaphysical necessity arising from the very structure of existence. The hypostatic union follows as the only rational solution to restore full participation in Being per se.

1. *The Finite's Inability to Restore Participation on its Own*

As previously discussed, Deceleration introduces the conditions necessary for finite existence, but it also imposes barriers to perfect participation in Being per se.

The Three Fundamental Limitations of Finite Beings

- Fragmented Knowledge
  - Finite intellects process Truth sequentially rather than as a unified whole.
  - Divine knowledge is total and instantaneous while finite knowledge is discursive and mediated.
  - This means finite beings can never, by their own power, reach perfect Truth; they can only approach it.
- Independent Will
  - The finite will, though rational, does not automatically align with absolute actuality.
  - Free will introduces the potential for misalignment, requiring external guidance to conform to Truth.

- Without participation in divine actuality, the finite will remains subject to error, fragmentation, and self-restriction.
- Temporal and Material Constraints
  - Unlike Being per se, which is fully actual, finite beings exist in a state of becoming.
  - Their existence is mediated through materiality and temporality, preventing direct participation in divine actuality.
  - As long as they remain bound by time and change, their participation in divine Truth remains limited.

Given these limitations, no finite being can fully realign itself with infinite actuality by its own power. There must be a means of correction, not an external cause imposing itself on reality but the very structure of reality making possible its own restoration.

Only the causal joint—the infinite potentiator—can be this bridge, for it is both the carrier at the beginning and the carrier at the end, the Alpha and the Omega. From within, God potentiates all being; as Redeemer, he is not an external force but the very means by which the finite is drawn into participation with infinite actuality without contradiction.

2. The Necessary Solution: The Divine Word as the Causal Joint

Since the finite order is created and sustained by the causal joint of divine action, it follows that any realignment must occur through this same causal joint.

However, the solution must meet three logical conditions:

- It cannot violate divine immutability.
  - The infinite cannot change into the finite, as that would imply a contradiction in Being per se.
- It must allow finite beings to retain their nature.
  - If realignment destroyed individuality, it would contradict the purpose of Deceleration in the first place.
- It must provide a direct participatory mechanism.
  - Finite beings must be able to freely engage in the process of realignment, not merely be externally altered.

The only rational solution that satisfies all three conditions is the following:

- The causal joint—the Divine Word—must enter into the finite order.
- The Logos must assume finite constraints while remaining fully actual.
- Through this participation, finite beings are elevated into divine actuality.

This is what traditional theology calls the hypostatic union, but here it is established as a logical necessity rather than a religious doctrine.

3. The Logical Role of the Hypostatic Union

If the infinite were to impose participation externally, the following would occur to finite beings:

- They would not retain their distinct nature; instead, they would be absorbed into infinity.
- They would lose their freedom, making rational participation in Truth impossible.

Instead, the infinite must enter into the finite in the following ways:

- Without ceasing to be infinite
- Without violating divine omniscience, omnipotence, or omnibenevolence
- In a way that allows finite beings to choose rational participation rather than being forcibly altered

This means the following:

- The Divine Word must experience finite limitation to make participation accessible.
- The Son of Man must pray, not because the Logos lacks knowledge but because human participation in divine actuality must involve relational engagement rather than instantaneous absorption.
- Redemption must occur within the finite order, ensuring that finite beings can logically engage with the process of realignment.

Thus, the incarnation (in theological terms), or the embodied participation of the divine Word in finite experience (in metaphysical terms), is not optional. It is the only possible means by which finite beings can be restored to full participation in Being per se.

4. The Fulfillment of Divine Participation in the Beatific Vision

Since participation in divine actuality is the only rational means by which finite beings can be elevated into infinite actuality, then this participation must reach its culmination in direct knowledge of God.

This final state of participation is what theology calls the beatific vision, and it is logically necessary because of the following:

- Finite intellects must eventually overcome fragmentation.
    - As long as knowledge remains partial and sequential, participation is incomplete.
    - The beatific vision ensures that knowledge is no longer mediated by time or limitation.
- The will must be fully aligned with the Good.
    - Free will, though real, must be perfected through voluntary participation in divine Truth.
    - The beatific vision is the state where rational will reaches its full perfection without coercion.
- Participation must be total, not partial.
    - Since divine action is sustaining all things, then the only final fulfillment is unrestricted participation in divine actuality.
    - The beatific vision ensures that participation is no longer fragmented but complete.

Thus, participation in divine actuality is not an arbitrary reward; it is the logical fulfillment of rational participation in Being per se.

5. The Rationality of Divine Participation

This chapter has demonstrated the following:

- Finite beings, due to the structural limitations of Deceleration, cannot fully participate in Being per se on their own.
- The solution must come through the causal joint, the very means by which finite existence emerged.
- The Divine Word must enter into finite experience to provide the means of realignment without violating divine immutability.
- The beatific vision is the necessary fulfillment of rational participation, not an arbitrary theological hope but the logical culmination of divine action.

Thus, what is traditionally called redemption is not a theological assumption; it is a metaphysical necessity.

6. Moving Forward: From Realignment to Fulfillment

If the incarnation is the rational necessity by which the finite is drawn into infinite actuality without contradiction, then the beatific vision is its fulfillment—the elevation of rational participation into the unmediated reception of Truth. What has been structurally potentiated through divine action must also reach its end, not in dissolution but in perfected alignment.

The previous chapter demonstrated why redemption is not an external rescue but an internal fulfillment of metaphysical logic. Now we turn to the final question: What does it mean for rational beings to be completed?

Since divine action is both the origin and the path, the Logos must also be the end, not as terminus but as fullness. The next chapter will examine how structured participation becomes direct, how limitation is overcome without loss of identity, and why the beatific vision is not only possible but necessary.

20

The Fulfillment of Rational Participation in Divine Truth

Introduction: The Final Stage of Participation

HAVING ESTABLISHED THAT FINITE beings require structured participation in divine actuality and that the Logos serves as the causal joint through which this participation is made possible, we must now examine the completion of this process.

The question that arises is this: What is the final state of rational beings in relation to divine actuality?

This chapter will explore the following:

- The necessity of a final participation that removes all barriers between finite reason and infinite actuality.

- The transition from structured participation to direct participation in divine knowledge.

- The resolution of all rational and moral deficiencies within the beatific vision.

The conclusion of this process is not a dissolution of the finite into the infinite but the perfected state in which finite rational beings attain unrestricted access to divine Truth without contradiction.

The Infinite Reservoir

1. *The Logical Necessity of a Final Participation*

A. The Problem of Limited Knowledge in Finite Beings

Throughout this book, we have demonstrated that finite beings experience reality sequentially, processing Truth itself in fragmented portions rather than as a whole. This limitation is intrinsic to Deceleration from *infinite reciprocal information* exchange and is manifested in reality by the following:

- Cognition in time—finite knowledge is acquired step by step, constrained by time
- Imperfect will alignment—rational beings must continually reorient their will toward truth
- Knowledge gaps—no finite intellect, unaided, accesses Truth in its entirety.

If the purpose of rational participation is alignment with divine actuality, then it follows that this alignment must eventually culminate in a state where fragmentation is overcome. Otherwise, participation remains incomplete and rational beings would always exist in a state of partial ignorance.

B. The Teleology of Rational Beings

A fundamental principle of metaphysics is that all things tend toward their fulfillment.

- The intellect seeks Truth; it cannot be satisfied with incomplete knowledge.
- The will seeks the Good; it cannot be satisfied with imperfect participation.
- Both are only fully realized in unrestricted participation in divine actuality.

This means the following:

- The ultimate end of rational beings must be direct, unmediated knowledge of divine actuality.
- Partial knowledge is a state of becoming, not a state of fulfillment.

- Since the causal joint is not merely what makes participation possible but is the very structure by which it is sustained and elevated, it must also serve as the means by which participation is perfected.

Therefore, the culmination of rational participation is logically necessary, not as an arbitrary gift but as the completion logically entailed by the structure of rational existence.

2. Transition from Structured to Direct Participation

A. The Purpose of Structured Participation

In earlier chapters, we established that structured participation allows finite beings to engage in reciprocal information exchange with divine actuality within their limitations.

This structure is necessary for the following:

- Moral development—the alignment of the will with truth
- Intellectual formation—the progressive uncovering of knowledge
- Freedom within constraints—the exercise of reasoned choice

However, the limitations of *finite reciprocal information* exchange point toward a fuller state of participation, not one in which structure is discarded but in which it is transfigured. In the beatific vision, the soul no longer relies on finite relational knowing but receives Truth directly, without distortion or delay. What was once mediated through time and becoming is now conformed to the triune form of divine actuality where structure is no longer a scaffold but a shared act.

B. The Elimination of Knowledge Barriers

The primary barrier to full participation is the fragmentation of knowledge. Structured participation compensates for this through the following:

- Logical reasoning—the gradual deductive approach to Truth
- Experience-based learning—the interpretation of events over time
- The guidance of previously acquired knowledge—the use of memory, understanding and tradition.

But once rational beings reach the final state of participation, these compensatory mechanisms are no longer required.

The Logos serves as the bridge between structured knowledge and direct knowledge, removing the following:

- The temporal constraints on understanding
- The need for discursive reasoning
- The separation between the knowing self and absolute Truth

In this perfected state, rational beings no longer acquire knowledge as a sequential process but instead exist in immediate relation to Truth itself.

This does not mean that structure disappears. Rather, it is transfigured. The limitations of *finite reciprocal information* exchange give way to a fuller state of participation, not by the loss of structure but by its elevation. In the beatific vision, the soul no longer relies on mediated knowing but receives, all at once, all that God shares. What was once processed through time and partiality is now received as a unified act of triune participation. Structure is no longer a scaffold for becoming but the very form of eternal communion.

3. The Beatific Vision as the Fulfillment of Rational Participation

A. The Resolution of All Deficiencies

Earlier, we demonstrated that finite beings experience knowledge in bits, constrained by time. The beatific vision is the final state where this limitation is removed, fulfilling the following:

- The intellect's pursuit of complete knowledge
- The will's perfect alignment with the Good
- The full relational participation in divine actuality

In the beatific vision, rational beings do not merge into the infinite but retain individuality while participating without quantitative limits.

B. The Necessity of Direct Knowledge

If divine actuality is omniscient and relational, then full participation in divine actuality requires direct, unmediated knowledge.

The beatific vision is not an abstraction. It is the logical consequence of *infinite reciprocal information* exchange extended to its fullest possible participation.

This means the following:

- Consciousness is no longer sequential; it perceives Truth immediately.
- The will is fully realized; it no longer wavers or hesitates.
- Participation is total; the intellect is no longer hindered by limitations.

The beatific vision is thus the final reality in which rational participation achieves its fullest expression.

It is not the annihilation of the finite but the elevation of the finite into unrestricted knowledge and love of divine actuality.

4. *The Logical Completion of the Metaphysical Framework*

This chapter has demonstrated the following:

- Rational participation in divine actuality requires an ultimate fulfillment.
- Structured participation serves as a necessary preparation for direct participation.
- The causal joint (Logos) is both the means of initial participation (Creator) and the bridge to perfected participation (Redeemer).
- The beatific vision is not a theological assumption but a metaphysical necessity; the completion of what rational beings are meant to become.

Thus, divine actuality does not impose fulfillment arbitrarily, nor does it force participation. Rather, it provides the logical conditions for rational beings to freely ascend into full participation in *infinite reciprocal information* exchange.

This process, structured by deceleration from infinite reciprocal motion, is now seen in its entirety, from its first movement at the causal joint where divine actuality gave rise to finite form, to its final realization in the unrestricted participation of rational beings in Truth itself.

Though we can discern that the structuring of reality required such deceleration, only divine omniscience contains the full rhythm and form by which this chosen cosmos came to be. What to us appears as the unfolding of space, time, and energy—explored in part by the physical sciences—is, in God, a single act of structured self-gift, measured, sustained, and fulfilled according to the eternal beat of triune love.

5. Moving Forward: From Fulfillment to Elevation

Chapter 20 established that the final *telos* of rational beings is direct participation in divine actuality—what theology calls the beatific vision—as the necessary fulfillment of their structured ascent. This fulfillment is not merely a theological hope but the metaphysical consequence of beings formed to participate in Truth, Goodness, and Being through the Logos.

Yet such fulfillment presupposes an even more fundamental reality: that the finite, in all its contingency, cannot reach the infinite by its own power. The logic of participation requires more than ascent. It requires elevation. Chapter 21 therefore shifts from the inner *teleology* of rational beings to the absolute metaphysical condition that sustains it—that the finite can only reach its end through divine initiative. This initiative is not imposed from without but fulfilled from within through the hypostatic union, where the eternal Logos enters finite limitation to raise it beyond itself. Only thus can the final act of divine self-gift be completed, and structured existence find its elevation into the fullness of triune love.

21

The Metaphysical Necessity of Divine Elevation

Introduction: The Absolute Separation of the Finite from the Infinite

In previous chapters, we established that finite reality is structured through divine action brought into existence through Deceleration at the causal joint (Logos) and sustained by the continuous participation of finite beings in divine actuality. However, a fundamental metaphysical truth must be emphasized: the separation of the finite from the infinite is absolute.

- The finite cannot elevate itself to the infinite by its own power.
- The infinite is not separate from the finite but rather sustains it at every moment.
- From the finite perspective, however, there is an unbridgeable abyss between the finite and the infinite, a separation that can only be resolved by divine action.

This chapter will explore the following:

- The necessity of divine elevation; why the finite cannot return to the infinite on its own

- The role of the Logos as the necessary bridge, fulfilling divine action in both creation and restoration
- The beatific vision as the final state of rational beings, ensuring ultimate participation in divine actuality without negating the distinction between Creator and creation

The fulfillment of creation is not the finite reascending to the infinite by its own efforts but rather the infinite elevating the finite to participate in divine actuality. This distinction is crucial. It clarifies why redemption is necessary and why it must be an act of divine initiative rather than human achievement.

1. The Necessary Fulfillment of All Creation

A. The Finite Cannot Return to the Infinite on Its Own

Since the finite emerges through Deceleration, it is entirely contingent upon divine action for its existence. It lacks any power to transcend its own limitations.

- The finite does not contain the infinite; it cannot generate infinite actuality from within itself.
- The finite is bound by time, space, and change; it has no access to eternity unless the divine action elevates it beyond those constraints.
- The finite is structured by relational differentiation; its participation in being is mediated, never direct.

Therefore, any return to unity with the infinite cannot originate from the finite. It must be an act of infinite actuality, not a process of finite ascension.

B. The Infinite Remains All in All

While the finite cannot return to the infinite on its own, the infinite does not cease to sustain the finite. This means the following:

- God does not abandon creation; his presence sustains all things at every moment.

The Metaphysical Necessity of Divine Elevation

- Omnipresence ensures that no part of reality is external to God, even though the finite exists in distinction from him.
- Participatory access to divine actuality is made possible, not merely by the sustaining presence of the infinite but by a distinct act of divine elevation that draws the finite beyond its natural limits.

This distinction helps clarify why creation, while always dependent on the infinite, does not automatically enjoy the fullness of participation in divine actuality. Fulfillment requires more than existence; it requires divine elevation.

2. The Logic of Divine Elevation

Since the finite cannot return to the infinite by itself, then the only logical resolution is that the infinite must act to elevate the finite. This follows necessarily from the metaphysical structure we have established, which is as follows:

- Since the finite is absolutely separated, then only infinite power can bridge the gap.
- Since the infinite is all in all, then it can act within the finite without contradiction.
- Since creation exists with a final cause, that cause must be its fulfillment in divine actuality.

Thus, divine elevation is not an arbitrary divine choice; it is a metaphysical necessity. Because God wills creation, he necessarily wills its fulfillment, not as a return initiated by the finite but as an elevation initiated by the infinite.

3. The Hypostatic Union: The Fulfillment of Divine Elevation

At the causal joint, the infinite expresses itself in creation without diminishing its perfection. However, to elevate the finite, there must be a means by which divine actuality enters into finite existence without ceasing to be infinite. This is precisely what is fulfilled in the hypostatic union.

A. The Hypostatic Union as the Perfect Bridge

The hypostatic union—the divine and human natures united in the Logos—is the only possible means of elevation because of the following:

- It is the infinite, remaining fully itself, that descends into the finite, thereby making participation in divine actuality truly possible.
- The hypostatic union establishes a real participation of finite nature in divine actuality without contradiction.
- It provides the only means by which the finite can be elevated without violating the absolute immutability of the infinite.

Thus, the Logos unites infinite and finite in a way that allows the finite to participate in the infinite without abolishing its own nature.

B. The Necessity of Divine Action in Fulfillment

Since divine action alone can elevate the finite, the work of the Logos is not a contingent possibility; it is a necessary fulfillment of the metaphysical structure we have established.

- The Logos does not intervene in history in a contingent way; his presence as the bridge between infinite and finite is logically required.
- The incarnation is not an event merely within time; it is the metaphysical solution to the problem of finite separation.
- Redemption is not simply a response to sin; it is the necessary means by which the finite is elevated to its fulfillment.

Thus, the fulfillment of all things is not the finite reascending to the infinite in the sense of dissolution but an elevation to participation in divine actuality.

4. *The Completion of the Finite in the Beatific Vision*

Since fulfillment is the elevation of the finite, then the final state of all rational beings must be full participation in divine Truth—what is traditionally called the beatific vision. This follows logically:

- Finite consciousness cannot fully know the infinite on its own.

- Divine omniscience requires that ultimate knowledge must be unified in divine actuality.
- The only possible resolution is that the finite is elevated into direct participation in divine knowledge.

Thus, as we expressed earlier, the beatific vision is not simply a reward. It is the logical fulfillment of finite consciousness. The finite, which cannot bridge the gap to the infinite, must be elevated into divine Truth by divine action.

5. The Absolute Necessity of Divine Elevation

This chapter has demonstrated the following:

- The separation of the finite from the infinite is absolute; the finite cannot return by its own power.
- The infinite remains all in all, but participatory access to divine actuality requires a distinct divine act.
- Divine elevation is necessary because the finite cannot bridge the gap to the infinite.
- The hypostatic union is the only possible bridge, allowing finite participation in infinite actuality.
- The beatific vision is the completion of this process, ensuring that finite beings achieve their ultimate fulfillment in divine knowledge.

Thus, the completion of all things is not a return of the finite to the infinite by its own power, but a divinely initiated elevation that perfects finite existence in divine actuality.

With this established, the next chapter will explore how this understanding integrates with the broader framework of divine action, ensuring that the logical structure remains internally consistent and complete.

6. Moving Forward: From Separation to Structure

Chapter 21 clarified that the separation between finite and infinite is absolute from the side of the creature, and only divine action, not human striving, can span this abyss. Yet it also revealed that divine elevation is not arbitrary or extrinsic. It is the necessary fulfillment of the very logic by which finite beings were created. This prepares us for a deeper metaphysical realization in Chapter 22—that the Logos is not only the origin of creation but its completion. The same causal joint through which Being is decelerated for creation is now revealed as the point of reascent, not a return to undifferentiated infinity but an elevation into perfect participation through the structure of divine-human union. Fulfillment, then, is not escape from the finite but its transfiguration through the Logos.

22

The Logos as the Bridge of Fulfillment

Introduction: The Necessity of the Infinite Bridge

IN THE FRAMEWORK ESTABLISHED thus far, the finite is necessarily and absolutely separated from the infinite. It cannot, by its own power, bridge this gap, nor can it elevate itself to participation in divine actuality. However, the infinite is not separated from the finite. The sustaining presence of the infinite ensures that finite existence continues, but sustaining presence alone does not confer participatory access to divine actuality. Such access requires an act of elevation, which can only be initiated by the infinite.

This chapter will explore how the Logos, the metaphysically begotten of Being per se, is not subject to the limitations of the finitude but, in the hypostatic union, assumes finite nature while remaining fully divine. Through the hypostatic union, the Logos reconciles the created order to its source, not by negating its finitude but by elevating it toward fulfillment in the divine.

1. The Hypostatic Union as the Causal Joint of Fulfillment

In previous chapters, we established that creation is the result of divine self-suppression, a metaphysical deceleration of triunity that generates finite existence while preserving the infinite's unchanging actuality. The hypostatic union of the divine and human in Christ mirrors this metaphysical process in the following ways:

- Since deceleration of the infinite loving exchange at the causal joint makes room for finite creation, the Logos, in assuming human nature, makes room within finitude for the infinite to be present without negating the finite.
- Since the causal joint is the necessary point of interaction between infinite actuality and finite potentiality, so, too, is the hypostatic union the necessary means by which the finite is elevated forward into participation with the infinite without annihilation.

Why Is This Necessary?

The finite, by its very nature, cannot traverse the gap. The infinite must take on finitude in order to draw it back into participation.

Thus, the Logos does not intervene as an external force. Rather, he becomes the bridge between finite and infinite, not by diminishing the infinite, nor by negating the finite, but by perfecting the relationship between them.

2. *The Logos in Time: Praying and Knowing Simultaneously*

A unique aspect of the hypostatic union is the interaction between the divine Truth that is Logos and the finite cognitive processes of the assumed human nature. Because the Logos assumes a finite nature, he must engage with reality as a finite being does—experiencing sequential moments, learning, growing, and even praying.

- The Logos, as infinite, is not subject to time. In the divine essence, all knowledge is immediate and total.
- Yet in assuming human nature, the Logos consents to operate within the limitations of finite cognition—processing truths in time, through a physical structure that mediates metaphysical actuality.
- Thus, using theological terms, the Son of Man prays, not because he lacks knowledge as the Logos but because the human nature he assumes necessitates engagement with the Father from within finitude.

What seems like a paradox—that the one who prays is also the one who hears the prayer—is not a contradiction but a revelation of the very structure that makes finite participation in divine actuality possible. This is only paradoxical to those unaware of the continuous act of structured potentiation at the causal joint. If the Logos were only divine and never assumed finitude, there would be no bridge. If the Logos were merely finite and not divine, he could not elevate creation. Only as both can the Logos reconcile finitude with infinity.

3. The Teleology of Creation: Elevation, Not Absorption

A common misunderstanding of divine fulfillment is the idea that all things must be absorbed into the infinite, losing their distinctiveness. However, the logic we have followed dictates that fulfillment does not mean annihilation.

- The finite does not cease to be finite, but it is drawn into participation with the infinite.
- The Logos does not eliminate finitude but preserves it, fulfilling its purpose by uniting it with divine actuality.
- This fulfillment is achieved, not through a dissolution of identity but through an elevation that completes what was always intended.

Thus, the final elevation does not erase the distinction between Creator and creation. Rather, it secures that distinction while perfecting the relationship between them. The hypostatic union is the template through which all finite beings, by grace, are invited into participation with the infinite.

4. The Logos as the Final Elevation of Rational Beings

If rational beings were made for participation in divine actuality, then the Logos must be both the origin and the fulfillment of that participation. This follows necessarily for the following reasons:

- Creation was initiated through the causal joint—the Logos as the divine self-expression through which all things were made.

- The finite cannot return unaided to the infinite; rational creatures, once separated from divine actuality, cannot return by their own power.
- The only solution is divine elevation; the Logos must enter the finite order to provide the necessary means for rational beings to be drawn back into participation in divine actuality.

This elevation is not imposed but freely given, ensuring that participation remains an act of free will rather than compulsion. The Logos, in assuming finite nature, provides the perfect means by which the finite may be elevated while retaining its rational distinctiveness.

5. The Necessary Fulfillment of All Things

The trajectory of creation is not an endless cycle of separation and return, nor is it an inevitable dissolution into infinity. Instead, it is a structured process whereby:

- Finite beings are sustained by the infinite, given the opportunity to choose rational participation, and ultimately elevated through the Logos.
- All souls are necessarily completed as intended, not by absorption but fulfillment in perfect unity without loss of distinction.

Thus, the Logos bridges the infinite gap, not by diminishing the infinite, nor by negating the finite, but by bringing both into a singular, perfect union.

This is the final elevation, the true meaning of divine fulfillment, and the logical completion of all creation.

6. Moving Forward: From the Bridge to the Cross

Chapter 22 established the Logos as the perfect bridge, uniting finite and infinite, not by absorbing distinction but by fulfilling it in structured relation. The hypostatic union is shown to be the metaphysical hinge upon which all elevation turns; it is through this union that rational beings are drawn into divine actuality without annihilation. But how, precisely, is this elevation accomplished within a fallen world? The next chapter turns to the cross, not as a contradiction of divine justice or a concession to mercy but as their perfect intersection. What the hypostatic union makes ontologically real, the cross makes historically real; justice is satisfied, mercy is extended, and the way is opened for the finite to enter divine Truth without violation.

23

The Cross as the Intersection of Justice and Mercy

Introduction: The Apparent Contradiction of Justice and Mercy

ONE OF THE MOST perplexing aspects of divine action is the relationship between justice and mercy. At the human level, these concepts often seem to be in tension.

- Justice demands that order be maintained, that actions have consequences, and that each being receives what is due.
- Mercy, on the other hand, offers forgiveness, restoration, and elevation beyond what is strictly deserved.

But, if divine justice is perfect, then how can God show mercy without violating justice? If divine mercy is infinite, then how can God still uphold justice?

The cross provides the resolution to this apparent contradiction. At the cross, justice is not overridden by mercy; justice is fulfilled through mercy. Divine justice is not compromised; rather, it is brought to its highest fulfillment in the self-giving act of the Logos. This chapter explores why the cross is not merely an act of redemption but the metaphysical intersection where divine justice and mercy are reconciled.

1. The Metaphysical Nature of Divine Justice and Mercy

To understand why the cross is necessary, we must first establish what divine justice and mercy truly are.

A. What Is Divine Justice?

- Justice, in its purest form, is the principle by which all things receive what is due according to their nature and actions.
- It ensures that truth is upheld, order is maintained, and violations of divine reality are rectified.
- Justice is not merely punitive; it is the guarantee that reality remains coherent and structured.

In divine terms, justice means that God, as Being per se, cannot contradict his nature. Sin is a *privation* of the good, a deviation from divine actuality. If God were to ignore sin, Truth itself would be compromised.

B. What Is Divine Mercy?

- Mercy is not the suspension of justice but its completion in a higher order.
- While justice ensures that all things receive their due, mercy allows for the restoration of beings who, by their own actions, have severed themselves from participation in the divine.
- Divine mercy does not ignore justice but rather fulfills it by making restoration possible.

Thus, justice ensures truth, while mercy ensures that Truth is accessible even to those who have fallen away from it.

2. Why Mercy Must Operate Within Justice

At the human level, justice and mercy seem irreconcilable. We typically think of them in opposition.

- A just judge enforces the law without exception.

- A merciful judge grants leniency, reducing punishment.

But God's justice and mercy are not in competition. They are two expressions of the same divine reality.

A. A World of Pure Justice Would Be Uninhabitable

If justice existed without mercy, then every violation of divine order would result in immediate separation from God, meaning no opportunity for redemption.

- Sin would result in instant exclusion from participation in divine actuality.
- No human being could be saved, as all have fallen short (Rom 3:23).
- This would be a world where justice is inflexible but incomplete.

B. A World of Pure Mercy Would Be Meaningless

If only mercy existed, then justice would be abandoned, making all actions ultimately irrelevant.

- There would be no real consequences for evil or good, as all would be forgiven regardless of choice.
- There would be no moral order because participation in divine reality would be granted arbitrarily.
- This would be a world where mercy is limitless but meaningless.

For divine action to maintain order while allowing restoration, justice and mercy must be harmonized rather than opposed. The cross is where this happens.

3. The Cross as the Fulfillment of Both Justice and Mercy

The crucifixion of Christ is not merely a theological concept. It is the metaphysical resolution of the problem of justice and mercy.

A. Justice Fulfilled, Not Overridden

- Sin is a real disorder, a deviation from divine actuality; justice demands that disorder be rectified.
- If left unaddressed, sin would result in permanent separation from God, as disorder cannot coexist with divine perfection.
- The Logos assumes human nature and experiences the full consequence of sin, not because he is guilty but because he enters into the condition of fallen creation.
- In doing so, Christ does not cancel justice but satisfies it in himself, absorbing the consequences of sin without violating divine order.

B. Mercy Extended, Not Arbitrary

- By taking on the full consequence of sin, Christ makes mercy possible without negating justice.
- Mercy is now accessible, not as an unjust suspension of consequence but as a path to restoration.
- Those who unite themselves with Christ share in his elevation. This means the following:
  - Sin does not go unaddressed.
  - Mercy is not an unconditional pardon but a restorative participation in divine actuality.
- Free will remains intact; participation in mercy is a choice, not an automatic process.

Thus, the cross does not negate justice. It fulfills it in a way that allows for mercy to be realized.

4. The Cross as the Logical Resolution of Divine Action

The necessity of the cross can now be seen as a logical conclusion of divine action rather than a mere historical event.

- Justice and mercy must be united; otherwise, divine action would be either tyrannical or meaningless.
- The Logos, as the causal joint, must enter the finite order; only he can restore the broken relationship between finite beings and infinite actuality.
- The cross is the necessary mechanism through which the finite is elevated.
- Resurrection is the proof that mercy is not merely forgiveness but restoration to participation in divine actuality.

The cross, then, is the only possible resolution to the seeming paradox of justice and mercy.

5. Human Participation in the Justice and Mercy of the Cross

The metaphysical structure of justice and mercy extends beyond the divine realm. It applies to human morality and social order.

A. Why Human Justice Must Reflect Divine Justice

- Human justice systems that focus only on punishment fail because they do not allow for redemption.
- Human justice systems that focus only on forgiveness fail because they do not uphold truth.
- True justice must be ordered love, ensuring that mercy perfects justice rather than negating it.

B. Why Human Mercy Must Reflect Divine Mercy

- Mercy is not the abandonment of justice but its highest expression.
- To be merciful does not mean removing consequences but rather offering restoration.
- This applies to all relationships—social, personal, and moral.

In short, to live justly is to uphold truth, and to be merciful is to offer participation in that truth.

6. *The Cross as the Center of Reality*

The cross is not just a theological claim. It is the necessary fulfillment of divine justice and mercy.

- Justice ensures truth is maintained.
- Mercy ensures that Truth is made accessible.
- The cross is where these two principles become one.

This is why the cross is not just an event in history but the central metaphysical reality upon which all divine action is structured.

7. *Moving Forward: From Fulfilled Action to Rational Hope*

The previous chapter revealed that the cross is not a paradox to be endured, but a metaphysical necessity where divine justice and divine mercy are not merely reconciled but fulfilled in a single act of infinite self-gift. At the cross, we see the final coherence of divine action—justice is not set aside but perfected; mercy is not indulgence but ordered elevation. This resolution is not a suspension of law but the triumph of Love that fulfills the law in its deepest purpose.

What, then, follows such an act? Because the cross is the perfect intersection of Truth and Love, what remains is hope, not a vague optimism but a rational certainty grounded in the structure of Being itself. Chapter 24 explores this hope as the necessary expectation that what was begun at the causal joint and fulfilled on the cross will reach its consummation in the beatific vision. This is not sentimental theology. It is metaphysical *teleology*. Hope in Christ is not a feeling but the certitude that divine justice and mercy, having intersected in time, will bring all things to their proper end in eternity.

24

The Hope of the Christ
Justice and Mercy as the Foundation of Redemption

Introduction: The Christ as the Embodiment of Hope

THE HOPE OF CHRIST is not merely a subjective optimism or a psychological crutch. It is the necessary expectation that divine justice and mercy will be fully realized in the fulfillment of all things. Since justice ensures that divine order is maintained and mercy ensures that finite beings are not irredeemably lost, then the very structure of reality must lead to an ultimate resolution where both are perfectly enacted.

This chapter will demonstrate the following:

- The hope of Christ is grounded in the perfect unity of justice and mercy.
- Justice alone would leave creation in despair, while mercy alone would render divine order meaningless.
- The Christ is the necessary fulfillment of divine action, ensuring that justice and mercy are realized in history and eternity.
- Redemption is not an arbitrary act of divine will but the rational completion of God's creative and sustaining action.

- The hope of Christ, therefore, is not merely personal salvation but the assurance that divine Love structures all reality, ensuring that all who freely participate in it will be elevated into the fullness of being.

1. The Christ as the Bridge Between Justice and Mercy

Christ is not merely a religious figure or a moral teacher. He is the incarnate Logos, the causal joint through which divine actuality is expressed in creation. This means that Christ is the following:

- The fulfillment of divine justice, ensuring that the structure of reality remains intact and that every moral action has its necessary consequence.
- The embodiment of divine mercy, ensuring that justice does not become mere retribution but remains oriented toward restoration and participation in divine actuality.

    Without Christ, justice alone would leave no room for redemption.

- If justice operated without mercy, all beings would fall permanently from participation in divine actuality at the first moment of failure.
- If mercy operated without justice, participation in divine actuality would have no meaning, as there would be no distinction between good and evil, truth and falsehood, order and disorder.

Thus, Christ is the only rational resolution to the necessity of justice and mercy, ensuring that justice does not crush creation and that mercy does not nullify moral reality.

2. The Hope of Christ in the Face of Despair

The world, as it exists in time, is filled with suffering, injustice, and moral failure. From a purely materialist perspective, history appears to be an unending cycle of decay and renewal, without ultimate resolution. But the hope of Christ provides a rational certainty:

- Evil and suffering are not the final realities; they are *privations* of the good, which will ultimately be resolved in divine justice.

- Redemption is not a possibility but a certainty since the very structure of creation is designed for finite beings to be elevated.
- Despair is ultimately irrational because it assumes that justice and mercy can be severed, which contradicts the unity of divine actuality.

Hope in Christ, therefore, is not mere optimism. It is the logical recognition of the following:

- God's justice will right every wrong.
- God's mercy ensures that beings who err are not irredeemably lost.
- The fulfillment of all things is an inevitable consequence of divine action.

This is why hope is an act of rational participation in divine reality, not a passive wish.

3. The Cross as the Manifestation of the Hope of Christ

The cross is not an event of historical tragedy but the manifestation of the absolute unity of justice and mercy. On the cross the following occurs:

- Justice is fulfilled; sin, as a *privation* of the good, is accounted for, ensuring that moral disorder is rectified.
- Mercy is enacted; justice is not carried out through destruction but through an act of self-giving love that makes participation in divine reality possible.

Thus, the cross is the singular moment in history where the unity of justice and mercy is revealed in its fullness. This means the following:

- The cross is not merely an atonement; it is the metaphysical resolution of creation's redeemable fall.
- Redemption is not merely a gift; it is a structural necessity within divine action.
- Hope in Christ is not abstract; it is grounded in the certainty that the same divine order that sustains existence will also complete it.

This is why Christ's death is not merely a sacrifice. It is the act by which divine order reaches its fulfillment.

4. The Resurrection as the Triumph of Justice and Mercy

If the cross is the fulfillment of divine justice and mercy, then the resurrection is the revelation that divine order is ultimately victorious over disorder. The resurrection proves the following:

- The consequences of sin (death) are not ultimate.
- Justice and mercy do not compete but work toward the same end—the elevation of finite being.
- The promise of redemption is not theoretical; it is embodied in the resurrected Christ.

Thus, the hope of Christ is not merely a future expectation but a present reality, demonstrated in the historical fact of the resurrection.

Through the resurrection, the following results:

- Justice ensures that sin does not reign.
- Mercy ensures that those who repent are not lost.
- Hope is made visible, not only because the future fulfillment of all things has begun in time but because, in divine actuality, "It is finished" (John 19:30).

The Resurrection is not merely a historical signal. It is the temporal manifestation of a metaphysical certainty. What unfolds in time is the revealing of what is already fulfilled in the eternal act of divine love. The Resurrection is not only Christ's victory over death. It is the assurance that all creation may be elevated into participation in divine actuality, if they so choose.

5. The Beatific Vision as the Fulfillment of the Hope of Christ

If divine action necessarily leads to fulfillment, then hope is ultimately fulfilled in the beatific vision—the direct participation of rational beings in divine actuality.

This means the following:

- Justice is fulfilled; all that is false, evil, and imperfect is removed, ensuring that divine order is fully realized.
- Mercy is fulfilled; all who freely participate in divine love are elevated into full knowledge and union with God.

- The hope of Christ is fully realized, not as a distant dream but as the necessary completion of rational existence.

Thus, hope is not a passive waiting. It is an active participation in the reality of divine fulfillment made eternal by the Logos.

6. *The Rational Certainty of the Hope of Christ*

This chapter has demonstrated the following:

- Hope is not an emotional response but a rational necessity grounded in the unity of justice and mercy.
- Without Christ, justice would lead to despair, and mercy would become meaningless.
- The cross is the point where justice and mercy are fully enacted, ensuring that redemption is not an arbitrary act but the necessary completion of divine action.
- The resurrection proves that the hope of Christ is not theoretical but real—the final elevation of creation has already begun.
- The beatific vision is the fulfillment of this hope, where all who participate in divine actuality are perfected in Love and Truth.

Thus, the hope of Christ is the hope of reality—the certainty that divine action will complete what it has begun.

7. *Moving Forward: From Fulfilled Hope to the Problem of Evil*

Having shown that the hope of Christ is not an abstraction but the metaphysical certainty that divine justice and mercy are fulfilled in the cross, resurrection, and beatific elevation, we are now positioned to face the objection most often raised against such hope: the reality of evil. How can a world structured by divine Love harbor such disorder? If Christ has already made fulfillment possible, why do suffering, injustice, and rebellion persist?

The next chapter does not shy away from this question. Instead, it reveals that the problem of evil is not a threat to divine action but its most compelling confirmation. Evil, far from undermining God's existence, proves the need for divine justice and the logic of redemptive mercy.

The structure of creation entails both the risk of misalignment and the possibility of restoration, but only if finite freedom remains real and the divine offer remains freely received. What follows, then, is not a defense of evil, but a diagnosis of its origin and a revelation of its resolution—that only the Logos, through the Spirit, can overcome the collapse of meaning caused by the refusal of relational truth.

25

The Problem of Evil and the Necessity of Divine Order

Introduction: The Misunderstanding of Evil

THE SO-CALLED PROBLEM OF evil has long been used as an argument against God's existence. However, this argument is based on a misunderstanding. Evil is not a flaw in creation but a necessary companion to it. It is not an independent force but what happens when there are creatures.

This chapter will demonstrate the following:

- Evil is an inevitable consequence of creation because only God is purely and infinitely good.
- It is logically impossible for God to create what is all-good because that would be God.
- The true problem of evil is not its existence but the rejection of its solution.
- God's justice and mercy ensure that evil is neither ultimate nor unresolved.

Thus, rather than disproving God, the existence of evil confirms the necessity of divine justice and redemption.

The Problem of Evil and the Necessity of Divine Order

1. *Evil as the Necessary Companion to Creation*

A common assumption is that if God were all-powerful and all-good, he would create a world without evil. But this assumption contains a fundamental contradiction.

A. Only God Is All-Good

- Goodness is not a property that God possesses; God is Goodness itself.
- For God to create something all-good, he would have to create another God, which is impossible.
- Any created thing, by definition, lacks the fullness of divine perfection and is therefore limited.

Thus, imperfection is an unavoidable reality of creation. This is not a defect but a necessary distinction between Creator and creature.

B. Free Will and the Certainty of Evil

- Free will is the ability to choose between real alternatives.
- If creatures were only able to choose good, they would not be free.
- Without the ability to choose evil, goodness would have no meaning.

Thus, the existence of free creatures not only permits but guarantees the emergence of evil. This is not a flaw in divine design but a metaphysical necessity of rational creation.

C. Evil Is Not a Created Thing

- Evil does not exist as a thing in itself; it is a *privation*, or a lack of good.
  - Cold does not exist, it is simply the absence of heat; similarly, evil does not exist, it is the absence of good.
- God creates only what is good, but creatures can reject good; this rejection is what we call evil.

Thus, evil is not something God causes, but something creatures bring about through their choices.

2. Evil Is Not the Problem—The Rejection of its Solution Is

A. The True Problem of Evil

If evil is inevitable where creatures exist, then the real question is not why evil exists but how it is overcome.

- The real problem of evil is not its existence, but humanity's rejection of the solution to evil.
- God does not leave creation in its fallen state; he provides a means of redemption.
- The real tragedy is not that suffering exists, but that people refuse the very thing that saves them from it.

B. The Cross as the Answer to Evil

- The incarnation is not a divine reaction to evil; it is the completion of divine action.
- The cross does not just fix evil; it transforms it into the path toward participation in divine actuality.
- Christ does not remove suffering; he enters into it, showing that suffering can become redemptive.

Thus, the cross is not merely a response to evil but the very structure of divine Love at work in creation.

3. Divine Justice and Mercy Ensure That Evil Is Not Ultimate

If justice alone existed, all creatures would fall at the first error. But if mercy alone existed, evil would go uncorrected, and moral order would be meaningless.

A. Justice Ensures That Evil Is Accounted For

- No act of evil is ignored or erased; every action has its consequences.
- Justice ensures that free will is meaningful; evil choices lead to disorder, while good choices lead to fulfillment.
- Hell is not an arbitrary punishment; it is the logical result of rejecting divine order.

B. Mercy Ensures That Evil Can Be Overcome

- If justice were the only reality, creation would be doomed.
- Mercy makes redemption possible but does not override justice; it fulfills it.

Christ, by assuming the burden of sin, ensures justice's demand for order is satisfied without the total destruction of creation.

Justice ensures that evil is addressed as real disorder, and mercy ensures that disorder is not the final word.

The Unforgivable Sin as Metaphysical Refusal of Being

The true "problem of evil" is not its existence but the rejection of its solution.

The so-called "unforgivable sin"—blasphemy against the Spirit—is not unforgivable because God refuses to forgive but because the sinner refuses the only structure through which forgiveness is offered.

In this metaphysical system:

- Being per se is infinite, triune actuality—Knower, Known, and the Spirit.
- Finite beings are structured participations in this relational triune order.
- Creation is made possible through the deceleration of infinite reciprocal motion at the causal joint.

- Redemption occurs through the same structure—the Logos assumes limitation to reconcile it.
- The Spirit is the medium of return—relational reunion within Being.
  - To reject the Spirit is to reject relationality, to reject reconciliation and communion.
  - To reject relationality is to reject the Logos.
  - To reject the Logos is to choose non-participation in Truth.

4. Suffering as the Path to Perfection

A. Why Does God Allow So Much Suffering?

Even if we accept that some evil must exist, why does there seem to be so much?

- Suffering reveals the limits of the created order and calls creatures to seek the infinite.
- Moral suffering (caused by sin) teaches the reality of moral law.
- Physical suffering (disease, natural disasters) invites humility and dependence on God.

B. Suffering Is Transformed by the Cross

- Without the cross, suffering is meaningless.
- With the cross, suffering is redemptive.
- Jesus does not merely suffer for us; he suffers with us.

Thus, suffering is not pointless pain. It is part of the journey toward fuller participation in divine actuality.

5. Evil as Confirmation of the Metaphysical Structure of Divine Action

When rightly understood, evil does not disprove God's existence but confirms the metaphysical necessity of divine action. Evil is not a created substance but the *privation* of the Good, a disorder that can only exist where the Good is first present. Its very recognizability presupposes a standard of order, justice, and truth grounded in something greater than finite being.

- The recognition of moral evil presupposes the existence of objective moral order.
- Moral order must be grounded in the actuality of divine Goodness, not in finite consensus or subjective feeling.

Without the actuality of the Good, evil would not be recognizable as disorder, nor would justice or mercy have any rational foundation.

Thus, rather than undermining the metaphysics of participation in divine actuality, the existence of evil highlights its necessity. Justice is required to restore order; mercy is required to restore participation. Both reveal that the solution to evil is not found in denial or despair, but in the structure of divine action that alone makes restoration possible.

6. The Logical Resolution of Evil Through the Spirit

As we have shown, the true problem of evil is not its existence but the rejection of its solution. Evil, as a privation of good, manifests most acutely when the offer of reconciliation through the Logos is rejected. This rejection is not merely a moral error. It is metaphysically traceable to a refusal of Being per se.

Just as the medium of all divine knowing—the Spirit—proceeds from the Father and the Son, it is this same Spirit that communicates the structure of Good to the conscience of every finite rational being. To reject the offeror (the Known) who offers reconciliation is to reject the Spirit of Love (the medium of Knowing), and thus to reject the Knower (the Father) himself. This is not mere metaphor. The metaphysical structure of divine knowing—Knower, Known, and the act of Knowing—is the very foundation of all reality. To reject the Logos and blaspheme the

Spirit is to misalign with this structure completely, severing oneself from the source of Being.

The most horrific evils do not emerge from arbitrary darkness but from the willful rejection of the structure of Goodness. This rejection blinds the soul to the Good itself, for to turn away from the Spirit is to silence the voice of conscience. Misalignment with the Good is thus not only a moral failure but a failure of recognition—evil becomes unrecognizable. In its place remains only the tyranny of disordered appetites and the collapse of all relational meaning.

This is why the logic of divine action predicts both the reality of evil and its only resolution. It is not that evil disproves God but that only if God is can this logic be anticipated at all. The rejection of this solution, then, is not merely tragic. It is the unforgivable sin, for it rejects the very structure of reconciliation.

7. Evil: An Argument for the Necessity of Divine Action

This chapter has demonstrated the following:

- Evil is what happens when there are creatures.
- God cannot create a world without evil unless he does not create at all.
- The real problem is not evil but the rejection of its solution.
- Justice ensures that evil is accounted for, and mercy ensures that it is overcome.
- The cross is not just an answer to suffering; it is the reason suffering can lead to redemption.

Thus, evil is not an argument against God. It is an argument for the necessity of divine action, justice, and mercy.

8. Moving Forward: From Evil to Final Fulfillment

Chapter 25 revealed that evil, while real as privation, exists only because creation participates imperfectly in the Good. It is not a flaw in Being but a metaphysical consequence of finite freedom. What remains, then, is not to deny or suppress evil but to trace how divine action completes what creation alone cannot: the restoration of order, participation, and fulfillment. In the next chapter, we move from the logic of divine redemption to the logic of divine completion where justice and mercy are not merely reconciled but fulfilled in the elevation of all creation into its proper share in infinite actuality. Fulfillment is not escape from finitude, but its perfection.

26

From the Logic of Divine Redemption to the Logic of Divine Completion

Introduction: The Ultimate Destiny of Creation

HAVING RESOLVED THE PROBLEM of evil, we now turn to the final destiny of all things. Since creation was brought forth through divine action, sustained by omnipotence, and ordered toward a purposeful end, then we ask: What is the fulfillment of this process?

The answer is found in the necessary participation of the finite in the infinite. This chapter will demonstrate that the ultimate fulfillment of creation is not annihilation, dissolution, or stagnation but a structured, elevated participation in divine actuality. The beatific vision, long discussed in theological and philosophical traditions, is the necessary final state of rational beings who, through divine order, are brought into full communion with God.

We will explore the following:

- Why the finite must ultimately participate in the infinite
- The logical necessity of the beatific vision
- How divine justice and mercy culminate in this participation
- Why this fulfillment does not negate individuality but perfects it

From the Logic of Divine Redemption to the Logic of Divine Completion 227

1. The Finite Must Ultimately Participate in the Infinite

As established in previous chapters, God is Being per se, the necessary ground of all existence. Finite beings, by contrast, are contingent—they exist by participation in what is actual. Since all existence flows from infinite actuality, then the proper end of rational beings must be a return to participation in that actuality.

- Finite existence is not self-sufficient; it requires continuous sustenance from infinite being.
- Rational creatures are ordered toward truth; the intellect naturally seeks to know what is ultimate and complete.
- The will is ordered toward the good; the human desire for justice, beauty, and fulfillment reflects an inherent orientation toward divine perfection.

This means that the proper and final state of rational creatures is not separation from God but union with him. However, this union does not mean a loss of personal identity. It means the perfection of each individual in the fullest participation of divine Truth, Love, and Actuality.

2. The Logical Necessity of the Beatific Vision

The beatific vision is often described in religious terms, but its foundation is metaphysical. It is not a mere reward for virtue; it is the necessary consequence of creation.

- God is omniscience—to know him fully is to possess total knowledge.
- God is omnipotence—to participate in him is to participate in the fullness of power per se.
- God is Love—to be united to him is to be in perfect relational fulfillment.

Since rational creatures are capable of knowledge, love, and participation, the only logical end for them is an unrestricted participation in these attributes. This is what is traditionally called the beatific vision.

- Participation in divine knowledge—the intellect is perfected by direct and unmediated knowledge of God

- Participation in divine love—the will is perfected by full unity with the Goodness of God
- Participation in divine presence—the finite is no longer constrained by limitations but experiences divine actuality as their reality

Thus, the beatific vision is not an arbitrary theological construct. It is the necessary final state of rational creatures who have been elevated by divine action.

3. The Culmination of Divine Justice and Mercy

The resolution of all things in divine actuality is not merely an abstract necessity. It is also the fulfillment of justice and mercy. Throughout history, thinkers have struggled with the question of how ultimate justice is achieved.

If moral evil exists, how is it reconciled? The answer is this: divine justice is not merely retributive—it is elevative.

- Justice ensures that no evil remains unresolved; every moral action has its necessary consequences.
- Mercy ensures that participation in divine life is made possible; the cross provides the means by which rational creatures are restored and elevated.
- Redemption is not mere forgiveness, it is transformation; the soul does not merely avoid punishment, it is reshaped into the fullness of its original purpose.

The fulfillment of divine justice and mercy is therefore not just a matter of reward and punishment. It is the restoration of all things to their intended participation in divine actuality.

This means that all rational creatures who accept divine order are not merely forgiven but perfected.

4. The Perfection of Individuality in Divine Participation

A common misconception is that participation in God means the loss of individuality. Many people mistakenly believe that if finite creatures are fully united with divine actuality, they must be absorbed into God and cease to exist as distinct beings. However, this is an error that arises

From the Logic of Divine Redemption to the Logic of Divine Completion

from thinking of God as one thing among other things, rather than as Being Itself.

The truth is that participation in divine actuality perfects individuality rather than erasing it. This follows necessarily from the nature of God and creation.

- God does not compete with creation. The infinite is not diminished by sharing itself with the finite. Unlike material things, which deplete when shared, divine actuality is unlimited. Just as a teacher does not lose knowledge by teaching students but instead elevates them to understanding, so, too, does participation in divine actuality elevate rather than absorb.

- Individual souls are perfected, not dissolved. Just as light illuminates without destroying the object it shines upon, divine actuality perfects rational creatures without erasing their uniqueness. The more an object reflects light, the more clearly it appears. Likewise, the more a soul participates in divine reality, the more fully it becomes what it was meant to be.

- True unity enhances distinction. Such a relation only appears paradoxical from the standpoint of finite intuition, which assumes that unity must come at the cost of individuality. But this assumption collapses under the logic of divine actuality, where unity perfects rather than erases distinction. The beatific vision does not eliminate individuality, it completes it. This is why the saints, rather than being indistinguishable, are strikingly different from one another. Each soul, in perfect participation, is fully itself in the most realized way possible.

These distinctions are crucial because they prevent a common misunderstanding. In truth, union with God does not involve the loss of oneself, but the becoming of one's fullest self.

The perfection of individuality is a logical necessity because God's act of creation was never about producing sameness but about structuring participation in the richness of divine Truth.

Thus, the beatific vision is not absorption but fulfillment, the elevation of rational beings into their most perfect, most actualized selves, made possible through divine love.

5. The Perfection of Individual Souls in Divine Actuality

We have demonstrated that the fulfillment of rational beings in divine actuality is not a process of dissolution but of perfection. The distinction between the Creator and the created remains, even as finite beings are elevated into full participation in the infinite. Just as light does not annihilate the object it illuminates, divine actuality does not erase individuality but brings it to its fullest realization.

Thus, the beatific vision does not mean the loss of self but the fulfillment of self.

- Every rational soul retains its unique identity while being perfected in the fullness of truth.
- The infinite does not consume the finite; it elevates it.
- The final state of participation is not a return to indistinct oneness but a perfected unity in which each soul, in its distinctive personhood, is brought into full knowledge and love.

This is the completion of the rational will, the intellect, and the purpose of creation.

6. Moving Forward: From Metaphysical Fulfillment to Empirical Revelation

Chapter 26 has demonstrated that the perfection of the rational soul does not result in its dissolution, but in its full participation in divine actuality. This is the beatific vision—the elevation of finite beings into perfect knowledge, perfect love, and perfect communion. But if this metaphysical fulfillment is the final state of the soul, what are the implications for the rest of reality?

Chapter 27 will expand the scope of inquiry from metaphysical completion to the revelation of metaphysical structure through creation. Scientific discovery, often treated as a competitor to theology, will now be shown to be an unwitting confirmation of the logic of divine action. The structure of the cosmos, from its inception to its fine-tuned coherence, discloses the metaphysical order upon which it depends. The next step, then, is not an abandonment of science but its transfiguration, to see in creation the logic of its Creator.

27

From Metaphysical Fulfillment to Empirical Revelation

Introduction: The Convergence of Philosophy, Theology, and Science

THROUGHOUT THIS WORK, WE have followed the logic of creation from its metaphysical origin to its necessary fulfillment in divine actuality. We have shown that divine action is not a series of intermittent interventions in the world but the continuous structure of reality—the act by which Being per se structures limitation, making itself receivable within finitude, not by change but by ordered self-suppression that sustains and elevates creation toward union without confusion or collapse.

What remains is to demonstrate how the empirical universe—the universe observed by science—reveals, even if dimly, the metaphysical order by which it was always structured. The point is not that science verifies metaphysics from some external stance but that empirical discovery functions as a delayed recognition of what metaphysics has already disclosed: the rational, participatory architecture of reality.

This chapter will demonstrate the following:

- Philosophy, theology, and science do not ultimately compete but converge when grounded in the logic of divine action.

- Scientific investigation, when honest about its assumptions, presupposes intelligibility, order, and relational structure, all of which are metaphysically grounded in divine self-gift.
- The most fundamental discoveries of modern science—cosmic expansion, quantum phenomena, fine-tuned constants—do not undermine metaphysics but rather express it imperfectly.
- The human mind, as participant in divine actuality, discovers not arbitrary mechanisms, but the echo of an eternal act—the empirical reverberation of metaphysical fulfillment.

What science glimpses as discovery is, in reality, the empirical unveiling of a structure already completed in divine omniscience. The fulfillment precedes the revelation. What unfolds in the laboratory is not the origin of meaning but the echo of a Logos already spoken.

1. The False Dichotomy Between Science and Divine Action

Modern discourse often presents science and theology as opposing forces with one grounded in empirical data and the other in faith. This is a false dichotomy for the following three reasons:

- Science presupposes order; the intelligibility of the universe is a prerequisite for scientific inquiry, and intelligibility requires a rational structure.
- Scientific laws describe but do not explain; physics identifies patterns in nature, but it does not provide an account of why those patterns exist in the first place.
- Divine action is not a competing force; God does not act instead of natural laws, rather, natural laws exist because of divine action.

A universe intelligible to science is possible only because divine action has structured limitation into being. Without this act, there would be no order to observe, no relations to measure, and no universe at all.

2. How Scientific Discovery Confirms the Metaphysical Structure of Reality

Though scientific inquiry is limited to the domain of measurable phenomena, it continually encounters the structured consequences of metaphysical truth. Properly interpreted, scientific observation discloses neither randomness nor emergence from non-being but the ordered manifestation of limitation structured by the actuality that cannot not be. What science registers as empirical discovery is often the measurable expression of the same metaphysical acts by which finite reality is potentiated through divine self-suppression.

From the expanding fabric of the cosmos to the constrained outcomes measured in quantum phenomena, from the exact values of physical constants to the coherence of living form, every domain reveals the same metaphysical truth: what exists does so by structured limitation, not chance. Here are just a few examples.

A. Cosmic Expansion as the Manifestation of Decelerated Actuality

The expansion of the universe is not evidence of a temporal beginning from nonexistence but the measurable effect of structured limitation. What appears to scientific measurement as a singular origin is not the origin of being but the first ontological threshold at which finite potential becomes intelligible and receivable as physical structure through the conditions of finitude established by divine limitation.[1]

This expansion is not driven by external force but is the physical manifestation of metaphysical deceleration, the act by which IRM is restrained, not by opposition but by divine self-limitation. Space, time, and motion emerge through this act, not as arbitrary constructs but as necessary conditions for relational participation. The expansion persists through negative pressure—the intrinsic metaphysical tension that

---

1. While this metaphysics affirms that the universe had a beginning, it does not identify that beginning with the Big Bang. Scientific models assign the origin of the universe to the Big Bang, but this framework holds that what science observes as the *beginning* is a structured phase within a greater act of divine deceleration, not the metaphysical beginning itself. The Big Bang may represent an inflection point in finite expansion, but it does not mark the origin of all reality. This metaphysics anticipates the observations but not the conclusions commonly drawn from them.

prevents collapse into undifferentiated unity and sustains the distinctness of finite structure.

Thus, what cosmology perceives as dynamic growth is the observable trace of the ordered limitation by which Being per se gives rise to and maintains the structured participation of the finite.

B. Quantum Indeterminacy and the Logic of Finite Limitation

Quantum phenomena confirm, not that reality is incomplete or dependent on the human mind but that the structure of finitude is upheld by precise metaphysical restraint. The apparently unpredictable behavior of quantum entities arises, not from indeterminacy in Being but from the strict limitation placed on how relational outcomes are temporally received within finite participation.[2]

So-called "quantum phenomena"—represented by terms such as "quantum superposition," "quantum entanglement," "quantum noise," and "quantum non-locality"—do not represent openness or indeterminate being. They reflect the necessary structure of exclusion whereby mutually exclusive outcomes cannot be disclosed simultaneously without violating the logic of finite distinction. These phenomena arise, not from metaphysical ambiguity but from the ordered restraint by which the infinite rate of information exchange (motion) in perfect actuality is decelerated into relational limitation.

The so-called "observer effect" does not indicate that human consciousness alters reality but that finite observers, by nature, access only one outcome at a time within a reality already fully structured in divine knowledge. What appears as probability is not an index of chance or collapse but the temporal and sequential reception of pre-structured distinction, not the resolution of chaos but the manifestation of order through limitation.

---

2. While the structure of quantum phenomena aligns with this metaphysics, many popular scientific interpretations of quantum mechanics do not. Historically, scientists have often lacked the metaphysical framework needed to interpret what they observe, leading to inflated claims about *quantum vacuums, infinities, singularities,* or the universe emerging from random fluctuations. This metaphysical system anticipates the phenomena but rejects these speculative conclusions, which exceed what observation alone can justify.

The more deeply physics investigates the fine structure of reality, the more frequently it encounters mathematical infinities, not because it approaches the divine but because it approaches the gap introduced by structured limitation. These infinities are not revelations of ultimate reality but mathematical symptoms of where receivable form nears its limit. They arise where decelerated actuality approaches the boundary beyond which structure can no longer be resolved by finite instruments. The appearance of the infinite here is not a glimpse of God but a sign that the domain of empirical inquiry has reached the edge of what finite participation can sustain. The contradiction does not lie in Being but in the attempt to force measurement beyond what has been finitely structured. These infinities, singularities, and conditions that have been named but remain undefined are not mysteries of divine presence; they are indicators of the precision with which divine power has limited itself to potentiate structured finitude.

C. Fine-Tuning and the Misreading of Structured Limitation

Many physical constants function, not as expressions of known causality but as signs of epistemic limitation—quantities introduced to preserve empirical models where foundational understanding is incomplete. Like the so-called "paradoxes" of quantum mechanics, they point, not to randomness or chance but to the boundary where metaphysical structure remains unrecognized by physical explanation.

In this framework, fine-tuning is not the result of improbability or design imposed from without. It is the necessary consequence of divine self-suppression where Being per se decelerates into structured limitation, and negative pressure sustains the distinction between infinite actuality and finite emergence. Constants appear "fine-tuned," not because they were selected from an external set of possibilities but because they reflect the only possible relational structure through which finite motion, time, and energy may exist.

Thus, the precision of natural laws and constants is not an invitation to statistical speculation. It is the empirical shadow of metaphysical necessity. Science glimpses the effects of order but often misreads their cause. As with quantum phenomena, what appears probabilistic or arbitrary is, in truth, the structured self-giving of the infinite, a cosmos sustained, not by odds but by intelligibility so deep it is beyond human reach.

D. Science Reveals Metaphysical Principles

Science does not uncover metaphysical principles by intention, but it cannot avoid revealing them. The expansion of the universe, the constraint of quantum behavior, and the fine-tuning of physical law all testify to a reality not born of chance but sustained by structure. They point to *no* beginning from nonexistence, *no* randomness at the root of order, and *no* need for epistemic invention. They confirm what metaphysics has already shown: Being per se does not erupt but gives; it does not explain itself through force, but through ordered self-limitation, and that finitude is not a failure of power but its structured participation.

3. The Human Mind as a Participant in Divine Truth

Because science is the discovery of structured reality. Human reason is not merely an accidental byproduct of evolution, it is the necessary function of rational beings created for participation in divine actuality.

- Knowledge is not passive but participatory; we do not simply observe reality, we interact with it.
- Mathematical truths are discovered, not invented, indicating that the universe is structured according to principles that exist independently of human cognition.
- Consciousness is irreducible to material processes; rational beings are necessarily structured for intelligible participation in divine actuality, and their consciousness and reason are not biological byproducts but finite expressions of the metaphysical order of Being itself.

Thus, the human capacity for reason reflects the structured participation of the finite intellect in divine Truth.

4. The Theological Necessity of Scientific Discovery

If divine action structures reality, then the advancement of knowledge is not incidental. It is a necessary aspect of creation's fulfillment.

- Science is not a secular enterprise but a theological one, even if it is not recognized as such.
- The discovery of order is a participation in divine wisdom, an alignment of human intellect with the rational structure of creation.
- Technology and innovation are not merely practical advances but fulfillments of potentiality, demonstrating that creation is meant to be explored, understood, and elevated.[3]

This aligns with divine self-giving. Just as God potentiates creation, so, too, does human knowledge participate in the continued unfolding of that potentiality.

5. The Limits of Science and the Necessity of Metaphysics

While science provides an empirical description of reality, it cannot answer the fundamental metaphysical questions that precede and make science possible. For example, science offers no answers to questions such as the following: Why is there something rather than nonexistence? What grounds the very possibility of existence? Why do the laws of nature exist, and why are they intelligible? Science does not explain why rational order exists; it presupposes it.

Every act of scientific inquiry depends on the prior reality of intelligibility, coherence, and structure in the object of study.

- The principle of sufficient reason requires that all reality be intelligible, not merely observed but grounded in necessity.
- The existence of contingent beings demands a necessary source, one that is not itself contingent.
- The very structure of knowledge, which presumes truth, consistency, and participation in rational order, requires an ultimate rational ground beyond empirical observation.

Thus, science does not replace metaphysics or theology; it ultimately requires them.

Scientific methods depend on the structured limitation of Being already in place before any observation occurs. What science studies is not unexplained order but received order—the visible.

3. This is only possible if one does so with the proper metaphysical grounding in the Creator.

6. Deepening the Convergence: Unique Contributions of Contemporary Scientific Discourse

A. The Finite Past and the Misunderstood Beginning

Modern cosmology has confirmed that the universe had a temporal beginning, often assigned to the Big Bang. However, while this aligns with the metaphysical necessity that the universe is not eternal, it does not mean that the Big Bang is the metaphysical beginning. The beginning of the universe is not reducible to a physical singularity or quantum event. Rather, it is the structured result of divine self-suppression, the deceleration of IRM at the causal joint through which finite reality is potentiated.

Time is contingent, emerging only within this structured limitation. The notion of a time "before" the Big Bang is a category error in physics but not in metaphysics, where the true beginning is not the first tick of physical time but the intentional potentiation of structured relationality. God is not the first cause in time but the uncaused cause of time, the Causal Joint through which Being per se limits itself without change, division, or deficiency to give rise to finitude.[4]

B. Snapshot Metaphysics and the Observer Effect

Quantum mechanics is often misunderstood through the lens of probabilistic collapse. But what is really happening is that the flow of *finite reciprocal motion* is so quick that only a "snapshot"—a frozen limitation—is detectable. This is not the collapse of possibility into being but the technological boundary of our capacity to interact with the unfolding of structured reality. Scientists mistake this snapshot for the emergence of reality when it is only the smallest capturable part of a much larger structured process.

---

4. While classical cosmological arguments such as the Kalam argument have helped reintroduce the concept of a finite past into philosophical discourse, they typically frame divine causality in temporal terms, as a first cause preceding the universe in time. In contrast, the present metaphysical system denies the ontological neutrality of time itself. Time is not a preexisting arena into which the universe emerges but a structured limitation potentiated by divine self-suppression. Thus, God is not the first cause in time but the uncaused cause of time, operating not as a sequential agent but as the Causal Joint by which infinite actuality continuously potentiates structured finitude. This distinction marks a departure from temporal cosmology toward metaphysical necessity.

The so-called "observer" is not collapsing potential into reality but interacting with an already potentiated structure, revealing the boundary of observation, not the boundary of Being.

The Copenhagen and Bohmian Interpretations of Quantum Mechanics

The Copenhagen and Bohmian interpretations of quantum mechanics attempt to resolve quantum paradoxes without questioning the flawed assumptions of classical materialism. One embraces anti-realism (where measurement creates reality), the other appeals to hidden variables (which fail under relativity). Neither approach accounts for the participatory nature of existence revealed in quantum phenomena. These paradoxes are not flaws in physics but indicators of a metaphysically incomplete framework.

Truth is not merely an intellectual pursuit. It is the foundation of civilization. Without metaphysical coherence, science becomes fragmented, morality becomes arbitrary, and culture loses its direction. The restoration of knowledge must begin with the reintegration of metaphysics and reality.

C. Infinities and the Edge of Finitude

As physicists probe ever deeper into the fine structure of the universe, they increasingly encounter mathematical infinities. These are not flaws in nature but signs that finite models are approaching the threshold between structured reality and infinite actuality. Rather than acknowledge this metaphysical boundary, physicists attempt to suppress or renormalize these infinities through mathematical manipulations.

To speak of cosmic origins while refusing to acknowledge the metaphysical conditions that make explanation possible is not scientific humility; it is the expression of a prior philosophical bias. Scientific reasoning presupposes intelligibility, causality, and order, none of which can be sustained without a metaphysical source.

The Misuse and Suppression of Mathematical Infinities in Physics

Mathematical infinities—particularly in cosmology, quantum gravity, and singularity models—are not glitches but thresholds. They signal where finite mathematics nears its limit before infinite actuality.

Instead of accepting these boundaries as signs of metaphysical depth, physicists often cancel or renormalize them through ad hoc techniques. In doing so, they obscure the deeper question: Why is reality structured this way at all?

Physics without metaphysics cannot coherently speak about first causes. When physicists speculate about origins using quantum fluctuations or vacuum states, they make metaphysical claims while denying the need for metaphysical grounding. This is not explanatory rigor; it is philosophical evasion.

"Man of the Gaps": The Real Modern Problem

The critique of theology for invoking a "God of the gaps" is well known. But in modern physics, a reverse problem has emerged—the "man of the gaps."

Faced with undefined constants, mathematical infinities, and unexplainable fine-tuning, scientists increasingly use statistical manipulations and provisional models to patch their theories. These are scaffolds, not explanations.

Where divine action would provide metaphysical coherence, modern science introduces placeholders. Where structured potentiation explains intelligibility, secular theories invoke randomness or emergence.

This is not a triumph of knowledge but an avoidance of the necessary question: Why is there structure at all?

D. Philosophy and Theology as Integration, Not Alternatives

Philosophy ensures that theology remains coherent, guarding against both scientism and fideism. Truth is One. If apparent conflict arises between theology and science, either the theology or the science—or both—have misunderstood their domains. A metaphysics of divine potentiation reveals intelligibility, coherence, and divine order where materialism sees only chance.

Theology then stands as the rational culmination of inquiry, not a mystical detour. The Logos is not just an idea but the rational structure of all that is. Revelation, rightly understood, clarifies what reason alone cannot yet express fully but never contradicts it.

7. Moving Forward: From Scientific Disclosure to Doctrinal Coherence

The previous chapter demonstrated that science, when understood within its metaphysical structure, confirms rather than contradicts divine action. The cosmos is not an accident of matter, but the measured consequence of divine self-gift, a revelation in form and order of what metaphysics had already made known. Yet while empirical discovery affirms the intelligibility of creation, it cannot resolve the theological fragmentation that continues to divide Christianity. For that, we must turn from the empirical to the doctrinal. If Truth is One, and divine action is coherent, then the divisions within Christianity cannot rest on genuine contradiction but must reflect partiality, misinterpretation, or metaphysical confusion. The next chapter undertakes that task, exposing how theology, when cut off from first principles, produces conflict, not because the truths differ but because the logic that should unify them has been forgotten.

28

Theological Conflicts in the Absence of Metaphysical Clarity

Introduction: The Fragmentation of Christian Thought

CHRISTIANITY, DESPITE BEING GROUNDED in the reality of divine Truth, has historically suffered from doctrinal fragmentation. Disputes over authority, interpretation, and theological emphasis have led to divisions between Roman Catholicism, Protestantism, and Eastern Orthodoxy, as well as intra-denominational conflicts. These divisions often arise, not from genuine contradictions but from misunderstandings, misapplied reasoning, and a failure to integrate theology with metaphysical clarity.

This chapter will demonstrate the following:

- Theological conflicts often persist due to historical inertia rather than substantive theological disagreements.
- Many divisions arise from incomplete metaphysical understanding rather than genuine contradiction.
- The fragmentation of Christian thought can only be resolved through a return to first principles, ensuring that theological claims align with the fundamental structure of divine reality.

This is not an argument for relativism, nor for erasing doctrinal distinctions arbitrarily. Rather, it is a call to recognize that Truth is unified, that no valid theological position can contradict metaphysical necessity, and that no metaphysical clarity can ever affirm what theological truth necessarily denies.

1. The Misplaced Priority of Authority Over Truth

A central issue in Christian division is the question of authority: Who determines doctrine?

Some traditions elevate ecclesiastical authority, others insist upon Scripture alone (*sola scriptura*), and others privilege individual revelation. These approaches, however, often fail to address the deeper question concerning not who decides but what is true.

- Roman Catholic and Eastern Orthodox Emphasis on Tradition
    - Roman Catholicism and Eastern Orthodoxy maintain that tradition and ecclesiastical authority are necessary to safeguard doctrine.
    - However, without a clear metaphysical foundation, tradition can sometimes become historical inertia where doctrines are defended, not because they are necessarily true but because they have been held for centuries.
- Protestantism and the *Sola Scriptura* Dilemma
    - Many Protestants claim that Scripture alone determines doctrine. However, Scripture must be interpreted, and without an objective metaphysical framework, interpretations multiply, leading to thousands of contradictory denominations.
    - Without a unifying principle, *sola scriptura* becomes *sola interpretatio*—scripture according to personal or cultural biases.
- Revelation Without Metaphysical Structure
    - Some modern Christian movements emphasize personal revelation over doctrine. However, revelation without philosophical clarity often results in contradictory claims, undermining our appreciation of the unity of Truth.

Thus, the true issue is not simply one of authority but one of coherence. Does a given theological position align with the necessary structure of divine actuality?

2. The Absurdity of Doctrinal Disputes Without Metaphysical Grounding

Many theological conflicts arise because doctrines are treated as isolated propositions rather than as necessary conclusions grounded in the nature of God and the structure of existence. Consider some of the classic debates that have divided Christianity.

A. Faith vs. Works: A False Division

- Protestantism has traditionally asserted justification by faith alone (*sola fide*), while Roman Catholicism and Eastern Orthodoxy emphasize the integration of faith and works.
- Metaphysically, these are not contradictions but necessary complements.
  - Faith is the alignment of the intellect and will with divine actuality.
  - Works are the realization of that interior participation.
  - To separate faith from works is as incoherent as separating cause from effect—they are two aspects of the same process.

B. The Eucharist: Symbolic or Real?

- The rejection of the Roman Catholic doctrine of transubstantiation by many Protestant traditions is often based on empirical skepticism—the idea that since the Eucharist does not appear to change; it cannot be truly Christ's body.
- However, this presumes a materialist metaphysics, demanding empirical verification for a reality that, by nature, transcends sensory access; it mirrors the posture of the doubting apostle Thomas who

Theological Conflicts in the Absence of Metaphysical Clarity

required physical proof before believing in what was already metaphysically and relationally present.

- The Eucharist, like the incarnation, is a metaphysical reality that does not contradict reason but transcends sensory measurement.
- This same logic, if applied consistently, would have rejected the incarnation since Christ's body, in its visible form, did not appear as anyone might imagine God to be; yet divinity was fully present in that finite, unassuming form.
- So, too, in the Eucharist, the substance is transformed in a way that transcends sensory measurement, revealing not less reality but more.

C. Predestination vs. Free Will: A Misapplied Dilemma

- Calvinism asserts that divine predestination determines salvation, while other traditions emphasize the freedom of the human will.
- But divine omniscience does not override free will; it integrates it.
  - God's knowledge of all possible realities includes free choices, ensuring that those choices remain fully real while still belonging to divine providence.
  - Predestination, properly understood, is not coercion; it is the necessary form of foreknown participation in a structured reality.

In each of these cases, theological debate persists, not because the underlying truth is inaccessible but because doctrinal positions are often framed in metaphysically uninformed, either-or terms rather than understood as distinct yet necessary expressions of structured participation in divine actuality.

D. The Metaphysical Necessity of Trinitarian Theology

The principle stated in the chapter introduction—namely, that no valid theological position can contradict metaphysical necessity, and that metaphysical clarity can never affirm what theological truth necessarily denies—exposes not only doctrinal imbalances but entire theological systems that collapse under ontological scrutiny. Chief among these is the denial of divine relationality found in Unitarian theology. God is indeed One, as both Trinitarians and Unitarians affirm, but metaphysics reveals that divine unity is not solitary—it is structured. The triune relations of Truth, Love, and Communion (Father, Son, and Spirit) are not theological speculations but the necessary structure of Being per se. Only within this structure does unity remain coherent in the infinite context of Love itself. A God conceived as numerically solitary and devoid of eternal relation cannot sustain creation, communicate truth, or preserve distinction without collapse.

Scripture alone may be interpreted in competing ways, but metaphysics, the Trinitarian reading of revelation, and the living tradition of the Roman Catholic Church speak with one voice. The Trinity is not revealed as an option; it is the only ontologically coherent foundation for participation, creation, and communion with God.

3. The Metaphysical Unity of Divine Revelation

Since truth cannot contradict itself, it follows that theological disagreements that appear as contradictions are often misinterpretations of reality.

- God is Truth itself (Being per se), which means that all divine revelation must be coherent.
- Scripture must be read metaphysically, not as a collection of isolated doctrines but as a unified articulation of divine Truth.
- Historical arguments should not determine doctrine; truth is determined by what is metaphysically necessary, not merely by what was historically believed.

For example, Roman Catholic–Protestant divisions over justification are not a metaphysical problem; they are a terminological misunderstanding. Similarly, the rejection of the Trinity by some traditions is not an intellectual advance, but a failure to grasp the metaphysical necessity of relational being.

If theology is to be fully rational, it must be grounded in what necessarily follows from the nature of God and creation, not in denominational traditions alone.[1]

---

1. This sentence articulates a metaphysically grounded approach to ecumenism that avoids both relativism and sectarianism. By rooting theological unity in what necessarily follows from the nature of God and creation, it affirms that true doctrinal

4. The Consequences of Theological Fragmentation

The failure to integrate philosophy, theology, and divine metaphysics has led to profound consequences, such as the following:

- Roman Catholicism's emphasis on historical continuity has sometimes led to an over-reliance on tradition without sufficient explanation in terms of metaphysical necessity.
- Protestantism's rejection of philosophical theology has resulted in an ever-growing number of denominations, each interpreting Scripture in isolation.
- The division between Christianity and Judaism has persisted in part because neither tradition has fully recognized that Christ is not a break from the covenant but its logical fulfillment.

These divisions are not signs of separate truths; they are signs of fragmented understanding.

5. Toward a Rationally Ordered Christianity

If theology is to reflect the unity of divine Truth, then its foundation must be metaphysical coherence. This requires the following:

- Reevaluating theological positions in light of first principles, not merely considering historical debates.
- Abandoning polemical disputes in favor of philosophical rigor, ensuring that doctrinal disagreements are resolved by truth, not tribalism.
- Recognizing that Christian unity does not require uniformity, but it does require coherence.

Metaphysical clarity does not destroy doctrine. It strengthens it by ensuring that theological claims reflect reality rather than cultural, historical, or political influences.

---

coherence must conform to the structure of divine actuality. Catholic Trinitarian theology, understood metaphysically, is not one tradition among many but the ontological expression of relational Being itself, within which all theological truth must ultimately converge. Unity, then, is not imposed by authority alone but revealed through metaphysical necessity.

6. A Call to Theological and Rational Unity

This chapter has demonstrated the following:

- Many theological conflicts are not genuine contradictions, but misunderstandings caused by incomplete metaphysical grounding.
- The question of authority in Christianity must be resolved by truth, not tradition alone.
- Scripture, tradition, and theological reasoning must be unified within a coherent metaphysical structure.
- Divisions within Christianity and between Christianity and Judaism are not proof of multiple truths; they are evidence of partial understandings.

True unity does not come from theological compromise. It comes from philosophical clarity. Christianity must be understood, not as a set of conflicting doctrines but as the fully rational revelation of divine Truth.

7. Moving Forward: From Theological Coherence to the Restoration of Justice

Just as theology suffers from the consequences of misapplied reasoning and historical inertia, political philosophy is likewise plagued by distortions that sever justice from its metaphysical foundation. Law and governance, when detached from divine order, lose their integrity, leading to the confusion of rights, freedoms, and justice seen in modern political discourse. Having traced the divisions within Christianity to their philosophical root, we now turn to the political sphere where similar errors have reshaped the interpretation of law, especially the US Constitution. The next chapter returns to the metaphysical grounding of justice, showing that only when law participates in divine Truth can liberty be rightly understood and society rightly ordered.

29

Political Philosophy, Justice, and the Misunderstood US Constitution

Introduction: The Intersection of Politics and Metaphysical Truth

Political philosophy is often treated as a purely human endeavor, shaped by historical contingencies and social contracts. However, at its core, political order is an extension of metaphysical reality. The structure of governance must reflect the fundamental truths about human nature, justice, and the moral order that underpin reality.

In particular, the US Constitution, while often debated in terms of legal and historical interpretations, is fundamentally a product of a metaphysical framework that affirms certain inalienable truths. Unfortunately, modern discourse has increasingly severed political philosophy from metaphysical foundations in the name of separation of church and state, leading to distorted views of justice, freedom, and governance.

But this severance is based on a categorical mistake: God is not a religious institution, a cultural tradition, or a finite concept. God, as Being Itself, is not a member of any human-made religious group. Appeals to separation of church and state are often used, not to protect freedom of conscience but to exclude metaphysical foundations from public discourse—a move that undermines both law and liberty.

This chapter will demonstrate the following:

- Justice is not a human construct but a reflection of divine order.
- Political philosophy, when properly structured, must align with metaphysical truth.
- The US Constitution, while historically contextual, is grounded in principles that mirror divine action and human participation in Truth.
- Modern political distortions arise from rejecting or misunderstanding these fundamental metaphysical truths.

By restoring a proper metaphysical perspective, political philosophy can be understood as an extension of the structure of divine justice rather than a mere product of historical or cultural contingency.

1. *The Metaphysics of Justice: Ordered Love as the Foundation of Society*

Justice is not an arbitrary social construct but a necessary consequence of the structure of existence. If divine action potentiates reality, then political and legal structures must reflect this order rather than impose a competing one.

1. *Justice as Ordered Love*
    - Justice is not merely fairness; it is the proper ordering of relationships according to Truth.
    - Since divine action is structured by self-suppression (kenosis) and love, true justice reflects this principle, governing with the aim of human flourishing within divine order.
    - A political system that distorts justice by prioritizing power, relativism, or materialistic definitions of equality loses its alignment with divine actuality.

2. *Freedom and Responsibility*
    - Freedom is not absolute autonomy but the capacity to act in accordance with Truth.
    - A just political order must recognize freedom as participation in divine actuality, ensuring that rights and responsibilities are inseparable.

- The modern distortion of freedom as mere self-assertion or personal autonomy without responsibility is metaphysically incoherent.

Thus, justice, rightly understood, is the reflection of divine Truth in human governance. Political systems that ignore this reality inevitably lead to disorder and tyranny.

2. The Declaration of Independence as the Metaphysical Charter of the United States

While the Constitution of 1787 provides the governing structure of the United States, it is not the nation's foundational act. That role belongs to the Declaration of Independence of 1776, which remains the original and enduring articulation of the moral and metaphysical order upon which the United States was founded. The Declaration is not merely a historical document of rebellion, but a metaphysical claim about the nature of rights, government, and justice. It establishes, with ontological clarity, that human beings are endowed by their Creator with unalienable rights, and that government exists to secure those rights.

This metaphysical foundation precedes and grounds all subsequent legal documents. The Declaration defines the "why" of the nation: the purpose of political society, the source of human dignity, and the moral limits of government. It affirms that rights are not granted by governments but recognized by them; they are not negotiated into existence but are metaphysically real and precede political order. In this way, the Declaration functions as the United States's metaphysical charter—the originating logic of its national identity.

The Articles of Confederation, though historically the first governing framework, did not and could not replace the metaphysical foundation laid by the Declaration. The Constitution of 1787 rightly replaced the Articles but not the Declaration, which continues to stand as the source of the moral principles the Constitution is meant to instantiate. The Constitution provides the form and structure of government; the Declaration provides its metaphysical justification. One defines the machinery; the other the end to which it must be directed.

Logically, then, no interpretation of the Constitution can be valid if it violates the principles set forth in the Declaration. Because the Declaration affirms that the purpose of government is to secure the unalienable rights endowed by the Creator, any law or interpretation that contradicts this end violates the nation's foundational logic, and any history used to support such a contradiction has no standing. The Constitution must be read as subordinate to the Declaration's metaphysical commitments, not as its replacement but as its servant. To sever the Constitution from the Declaration is to collapse law into procedure without purpose and freedom into mere formalism without moral content.

This priority of the Declaration is not legalistic but ontological. It does not rest on whether courts cite the Declaration as binding precedent; it rests on the fact that without it, there is no coherent justification for the authority of the Constitution. The Declaration establishes, not only that a people may constitute a government but why they must do so in a way that respects the truth of human nature and the source of rights. The American founding, properly understood, is not a mere historical event; it is a metaphysical assertion: government derives its legitimacy from conformity to the structure of created reality and the divine order of justice.

Thus, in any metaphysically coherent account of the US Constitution, the Declaration must be regarded, not as an obsolete artifact but as the enduring standard by which the Constitution must be interpreted and against which all political claims must be measured. It is the unrevoked ground of American legitimacy.

No mechanism exists—nor could one logically exist—by which the Declaration may be repealed or amended. As the original and enduring constitutional act of the United States, the Declaration is not subject to legislative revision or historical override. Its authority is not procedural but metaphysical. The Constitution of 1787, though amendable by design, must be interpreted and applied in continuity with the natural law principles set forth in the Declaration. Any constitutional amendment or legal interpretation that violates those principles is not merely mistaken; it is invalid, for it contradicts the very foundation upon which constitutional authority depends. The Declaration is the United States's first and only irrevocable constitution of justice; the Constitution is its servant, not its replacement. Political legitimacy in America begins and ends with fidelity to the metaphysical structure of unalienable rights endowed by the Creator.

3. The Foundational Legal Error Behind Modern Jurisprudence

Modern Supreme Court decisions that restrict public acknowledgment of God are not merely legal misinterpretations; they rest on a more basic metaphysical category error: the confusion of God with religion.

God, as affirmed in the Declaration of Independence, is not a sectarian concept. God is Being Itself—the Creator, the metaphysical source of unalienable rights, and the ground of justice. Religion, by contrast, refers to systems of worship, doctrine, and institutional authority.

When courts treat references to God as if they were endorsements of religion, they commit a category mistake that severs the Constitution from its ontological source. They mistake the ground of all rights for a sectarian preference, and, in doing so, they render the nation's founding metaphysical principles inadmissible in public reason.

This foundational confusion gives rise to a series of cascading errors that now shape American political and educational institutions

1. *Misinterpretation of the Establishment Clause*

    It conflates acknowledgment of divine actuality with the establishment of sectarian religion, thereby excluding even universal metaphysical claims from public discourse.

2. *Neglect of Foundational Principles*

    It dismisses the Declaration of Independence as a merely historical or rhetorical document, rather than the enduring metaphysical charter of the republic.

3. *Overemphasis on Secularism*

    It treats state neutrality as an obligation to metaphysical silence, thereby replacing moral clarity with relativism and civic cohesion with moral pluralism.

4. *Expansion of Coercion*

    Recasting voluntary expressions of rational conviction—moral or religious, such as prayer, acknowledgment of God, or reference to moral absolutes—as inherently coercive imposes a false standard of neutrality; this redefinition disrespects the freedom of moral and religious choice and discourages the legitimate public formation of conscience, and, in doing so, deprives society of the shared moral reference points necessary for virtue and public justice.

5. *Collapse of Public Education into a Metaphysical Void*

Removing God from education does not produce neutrality, it severs the pursuit of knowledge from its source in Truth; education without metaphysical grounding reduces to information without purpose, freedom without formation, and intellect without orientation to the Good. In such a vacuum, law becomes technique, rights become preferences, and students are instructed in competence without character.

Until this categorical error is corrected, constitutional interpretation will remain cut off from its origin, and American law will continue to drift into proceduralism without truth, liberty without purpose, and governance without justice.

4. *The Modern Distortion of Justice and Freedom*

Despite its philosophical depth, the Constitution is often misinterpreted through modern lenses that do sever law from truth. This has led to the following:

- The redefinition of rights as government-issued rather than intrinsic to human nature
- The erosion of natural law, where morality is treated as subjective rather than rooted in objective truth
- The politicization of justice, where laws serve power rather than order

A. Example: The Expansion of "Rights" Beyond Truth

- Originally, rights were understood as pre-political; they existed prior to government and were to be protected, not created, by the state.
- Modern discourse increasingly views rights as politically granted entitlements, leading to conflicts where legal recognition is sought for actions or identities that contradict metaphysical reality.
- This distortion fundamentally undermines justice, replacing ordered love with mere preference-based legalism.

B. Example: Freedom Without Responsibility

- Classical philosophy and Christian tradition recognize that freedom is ordered toward the Good.
- Modern thought often reduces freedom to license—the ability to do whatever one wants, regardless of moral consequence.
- This shift leads to moral relativism, where laws become reflections of social trends rather than eternal truths.

The result is political decay, where governance ceases to reflect divine order and instead serves competing human interests detached from Truth.

5. Restoring a Metaphysically Grounded Political Philosophy

To correct modern distortions, political philosophy must return to its metaphysical foundation. This means the following:

- Recognizing justice as ordered love, rather than power-based social contracts
- Restoring the understanding of rights as intrinsic, not state-issued
- Aligning freedom with responsibility, ensuring that liberty serves Truth rather than mere personal autonomy

Practical Implications

- Laws should not simply reflect majority opinion but must be grounded in ontological Truth.
- Political discourse must move beyond emotional appeals to rights and fairness and instead focus on what is true and just.
- The Constitution should be defended, not as a historically convenient system but as a rationally necessary structure aligned with divine order.

6. The Necessity of a Metaphysical Return

This chapter has demonstrated the following:

- Justice is not a human invention but a reflection of divine order.
- The US Constitution, while not a theological document, is structured upon metaphysical principles that align with divine Truth.
- Modern political distortions arise from severing law from its ontological foundation.
- A proper understanding of freedom, justice, and governance requires a return to first principles, ensuring that political philosophy aligns with the necessary structure of reality.

Thus, the fragmentation and confusion of modern political discourse is not merely a legal or ideological issue; it is a metaphysical crisis. Only by returning to the Truth of divine actuality and its reflection in human law can justice be restored.

7. Moving Forward: From Law to Faith

Having restored political philosophy to its rightful place within the order of Being—showing that justice is not a social construct but a reflection of divine actuality—we now turn to a more fundamental confusion: the false division between faith and reason. Just as governance must reflect the structure of divine Truth, so, too, must human knowledge. The next chapter dismantles the long-standing misconception that faith begins where reason ends, showing instead that reason is fulfilled in faith, and that all true knowing is participatory. The conflict between theology and philosophy, like the conflict between church and state, is not rooted in logic but in historical and metaphysical error. It is time to recover the unity of Truth.

30

The False Dilemma of Faith and Reason

Introduction: The Misunderstood Relationship Between Faith and Reason

ONE OF THE MOST persistent misunderstandings in human thought is the supposed conflict between faith and reason. This false dichotomy has led many to believe that faith is irrational, or that reason must exclude belief in divine Truth. However, this opposition is not only unfounded but logically incoherent. Faith and reason are not competing forces; rather, they are complementary aspects of a unified pursuit of truth.

This chapter will demonstrate the following:

- Faith is not opposed to reason but is the necessary extension of rational inquiry into divine reality.
- Reason is not self-sufficient but requires faith in fundamental truths to function.
- The historical conflict between faith and reason arises not from their actual relationship but from misunderstandings of both.
- True faith is not blind belief but participation in Truth through the structure of reason.

By resolving the false dilemma of faith and reason, we will see that human knowledge—whether philosophical, scientific, or theological—is ultimately one unified participation in truth.

1. The Nature of Faith: Beyond the Modern Misconception

The modern world often defines faith as a kind of blind belief, an irrational leap taken in opposition to reason. This is not how faith has been understood in classical theology or philosophy.

Faith as Participation in Truth

Faith is not the abandonment of reason but its fulfillment. Just as reason allows us to grasp truths about the natural world, faith allows us to grasp truths beyond what reason alone can uncover.

- Faith is not belief without evidence; rather, it is belief in the necessary conditions that make knowledge possible.
- Faith is a response to revelation; it is not an arbitrary decision but an alignment with truths that are revealed through divine action.
- Faith is participatory; it is not passive acceptance but an active engagement with divine reality.

In short, faith is not irrational. It is the rational response to truths that transcend but do not contradict reason.

2. The Limits of Secular Reason: Why Most Rational Systems Require Faith

While reason is a powerful tool, most modern rational systems are not self-sustaining. They require foundational assumptions—such as the law of non-contradiction, the intelligibility of the universe, and the existence of causality—that they cannot prove internally. This is true in much of secular philosophy, science, and even in daily life.

However, in the metaphysical framework presented here, these are not arbitrary assumptions. They follow necessarily from the logic of reality. The argument from nonexistence reveals that intelligibility, causality, and the law of non-contradiction are not beliefs we must accept by faith. They are consequences of the necessary actuality of Being itself.

Thus, while secular reason requires faith to function, this system shows that reason, when fully grounded in divine actuality, becomes self-sustaining. Faith is not a substitute for logic—it is its highest fulfillment in the encounter with Truth.

A. Reason's Dependence on First Principles

All rational inquiry is based on principles that are taken on faith. Consider the following:

- The law of non-contradiction—reason assumes that contradictions cannot be true at the same time; but this assumption cannot be proven without relying on it.
- The reliability of sense perception—science assumes that our senses provide accurate information about reality, yet this assumption cannot be tested without presupposing its truth.
- The uniformity of nature—the entire scientific method assumes that natural laws remain consistent over time, but there is no purely rational proof that they must.

These examples show that faith is not unique to religion; it is the foundation of all human knowledge. The difference is that theistic faith is directed toward the ultimate foundation of reality—God—whereas secular faith is often unacknowledged.

B. The Rational Necessity of Divine Revelation

In most secular systems, reason is assumed to operate within boundaries it cannot explain—boundaries that require unacknowledged faith. These systems assume the validity of logic, the consistency of nature, and the reliability of knowledge without grounding these in any necessary foundation. By contrast, the metaphysical framework presented here derives these principles directly from the actuality of Being itself.

- Reason explains its own origin only when grounded in Being per se, whose actuality makes logic intelligible, knowledge possible, and structure receivable.

- Reason resolves ultimate questions by showing that all intelligibility, causality, and coherence flow from the necessity of divine actuality.
- And reason reaches certainty because logic, though not in God, is potentiated through divine self-suppression and leads the soul forward toward the actuality from which it was structured to receive Truth.

Thus, faith in this framework is not merely what begins where reason ends; it is the highest act of reason fulfilled in love. It is the mode by which rational creatures participate personally and relationally in divine actuality. Divine revelation is given, not because reason fails but because divine Truth, while never irrational, is also more than rational: it is Love, Goodness, and Self-giving, which can be known truly only through participation.

Faith, therefore, is not irrational. It is not a leap beyond logic, but the reception of that which reason already shows to be necessarily true.

3. The Historical Origins of the Faith-Reason Divide

If faith and reason are naturally aligned, why have they so often been framed as opposing forces? This misunderstanding has historical roots.

A. The Enlightenment's Misconception of Faith

The modern conflict between faith and reason largely stems from the so-called Enlightenment, which sought to elevate reason while dismissing religious belief as superstition. However, this shift was based on the following:

- A misunderstanding of faith as irrational belief rather than participation in divine Truth
- A mischaracterization of medieval theology, which had long integrated philosophy and reason
- A rejection of divine revelation, not based on logic but on cultural and political motivations

The Enlightenment thinkers did not disprove faith; they simply redefined reason in a way that excluded it.[1]

---

1. See Benedict XVI, "Faith, Reason, and the University"; John Paul II, *Fides et Ratio*, §48; Taylor, *Secular Age*, 73.

B. The Reaction of Religious Thought

In response to the Enlightenment, some religious traditions embraced an opposite error: fideism, the idea that faith must be entirely separate from reason. This led to the following:

- A distrust of philosophy and science in certain religious traditions
- A shift from a reasoned defense of faith (apologetics) to an emphasis on subjective experience alone
- The idea that faith does not need intellectual grounding, which left religion vulnerable to accusations of irrationality.

Thus, both sides contributed to the false dichotomy. The solution is not to choose one over the other, but to restore their unity.

4. The Restoration of Faith and Reason in Divine Action

Since faith and reason are not inherently opposed, how do we restore their proper relationship? The answer lies in recognizing that both are aspects of divine action.

A. Faith as the Fulfillment of Rational Inquiry

As established in previous chapters, divine action is structured, rational, and intelligible. Because God is Truth itself, every genuine pursuit of Truth—whether through philosophy, science, or theology—leads toward divine actuality.

- Faith is not the rejection of reason but the response to its highest conclusions.
- Science does not disprove faith; rather, it reveals the intelligibility of creation, which is only possible if divine reason structures reality.
- Theology does not contradict reason; it builds upon it, offering insights that reason alone cannot fully attain.

Faith is, therefore, the completion of reason, not its negation.

B. The Logos as the Bridge Between Faith and Reason

The integration of faith and reason is ultimately found in the Logos—the divine Word through whom all things were made. But in this metaphysical framework, the Logos is not merely a spoken word or a symbolic concept. He is the fully actual and fully real structure by which all of creation is potentiated.

- The Logos is the Truth conveyed by the Father, not a proposition but the very actuality of divine intelligibility.
- The Logos is the way, the causal joint through which infinite actuality decelerates to structure the finite and by which the rational creature is drawn back into participatory union with God.
- The Logos is the life, the structured unfolding of divine self-suppression into creation, through which all things are sustained in their being.

Thus, the Logos is not only the rational foundation of the universe; he is the necessary structure of divine action. Faith is not simply a response to revelation; it is a participatory alignment with the Logos, through whom reason is completed, reality is ordered, and Truth is made personally knowable.

By understanding divine action through the Logos, we resolve the false conflict, discovering that reason and faith are not rivals but reciprocal movements across the same bridge, each completing the other on the path to Truth.

5. *The Practical Implications: Living in the Unity of Faith and Reason*

Recognizing that faith and reason are unified has profound implications for daily life, intellectual inquiry, and theological discourse.

A. Faith as Intellectual Participation

- Faith should not be reduced to mere feeling; it must engage the intellect.
- Theology must be defended with reason, not blind assertion.

- Apologetics must show that faith is not just a personal belief but a rational necessity.

B. Science as a Theological Enterprise

- Scientific discovery is not opposed to faith; it is an extension of divine rationality.
  - The study of the natural world is an act of participation in divine knowledge.
  - Scientists and theologians should work together to uncover truth, rather than seeing each other as adversaries.

C. Education as the Restoration of Unified Knowledge

- Schools and universities should teach philosophy and theology alongside science, ensuring that students see knowledge as a single, integrated whole.
- The church should reclaim its intellectual tradition, demonstrating that Roman Catholic thought—properly grounded in metaphysical first principles—is the fullest and most coherent form of rational inquiry into divine Truth.
- Individuals should reject anti-intellectual faith and embrace a fully reasoned approach to divine Truth.

6. Faith and Reason as One Unified Path to Truth

This chapter has demonstrated the following:

- Faith and reason are not opposed; they are complementary.
- Reason requires faith in first principles to function.
- Faith is not irrational but the highest participation in divine Truth.
- The historical conflict between faith and reason is based on misunderstandings rather than actual contradictions.

- The Logos—divine rationality—bridges the gap, ensuring that all human knowledge ultimately leads back to God.

By resolving the false dilemma of faith and reason, we affirm that all knowledge is unified in divine actuality. The pursuit of Truth is singular; when inquiry is earnest and rationally ordered, it leads not only to the actuality of God but to the reality of God with us—the structured nearness of the divine through which all things are sustained.

7. Moving Forward: From Personal Participation to Civilizational Integrity

The previous chapter has shown that faith and reason are not opposing forces but complementary modes of participation in Truth. Where reason seeks structure, faith receives fullness; where reason discovers order, faith responds with trust in the source of that order. Their unity is not optional. It is metaphysically necessary, grounded in the very nature of Being itself.

This unity is not only preserved in doctrine; it remains fully embedded in the Roman Catholic intellectual tradition. Through the integration of metaphysics, revelation, and rational inquiry, the Roman Catholic Church continues to affirm that Truth is One—and that all knowledge, when rightly ordered, returns to its divine origin. What has changed is not the tradition but the world's willingness to receive it.

In the chapters ahead, we will explore how this tradition once formed the basis of a just society, one that upheld the dignity of the person, the objectivity of law, and the necessity of moral order. We will also examine how modern culture, by rejecting this synthesis, has not progressed but fractured, substituting ideology for truth and power for justice.

To rebuild what has eroded, we must not invent a new foundation. We must return to the one that remains: the intelligible structure of participation in divine actuality.

31

The Rational Foundation for a Just Society

PART ONE: THE ROLE OF FAITH AND REASON IN SOCIETY

The Consequences of Severing Faith from Reason in Society

A TRULY JUST SOCIETY is not built on arbitrary laws or shifting social conventions but on an objective moral foundation grounded in both faith and reason. Throughout history, civilizations have flourished when they have acknowledged an order beyond themselves, an order that harmonizes natural law, divine revelation, and rational inquiry.

However, modern societies have largely abandoned this integration. The separation of faith from reason has resulted in societies that either descend into moral relativism or enforce rigid, ideological dogmas without logical coherence. When reason is detached from divine Truth, it is reduced to a tool for control rather than liberation. When faith is detached from reason, it becomes an irrational force of oppression rather than an illumination of Truth.

Faith, as understood in this chapter, is not allegiance to a particular religion, nor is it belief without evidence. Faith is the rational trust that Truth exists beyond what finite reason alone can produce. It is the assent of the will to participate in the source of order, meaning, and moral law, not God as the object of religious worship but the God of the Declaration of Independence, whom secular reason may discover but never fully exhaust. In this way, faith perfects reason without replacing it, enabling human societies to align with the structure of reality rather than merely asserting power over it.

This chapter will argue the following:

- A society governed by reason alone becomes nihilistic, unable to ground moral order in anything beyond human consensus.
- A society ruled by faith without reason becomes irrational and oppressive, reducing truth to dogmatic enforcement rather than rational participation.
- Only by integrating faith and reason properly can a civilization uphold justice, freedom, and human dignity, ensuring that divine action is reflected in human governance.

Many societies throughout history have attempted to base governance either purely on reason or purely on religious authority. Neither approach, when taken in isolation, can sustain true justice.

1. The Tyranny of Pure Rationalism

Secular humanist ideologies claim that societies should be based purely on reason, without reference to faith. While reason is a necessary guide, it is not self-sufficient. If reason is not grounded in divine actuality, it can be manipulated to justify anything, including injustice.

How does this happen?

- Materialism leads to incoherence.
  - If human dignity is reduced to biochemical processes, then meaning becomes untethered from actuality and collapses into subjectivism.
  - Societies that treat humans as merely evolved animals do the following:
    - Lose any coherent basis for justice, rights, or moral law
    - Inevitably justify exploitation, population control, or even eugenics

- Materialism obscures the structure of participation in divine actuality, resulting in a worldview that cannot account for its own intelligibility.
- Relativism replaces truth.
  - If there is no external moral law, then ethics become a matter of majority consensus rather than objective truth.
  - This leads to a legal system where truth changes with popular opinion rather than being an unchanging foundation of justice.
- Technocracy and Utilitarianism undermine human dignity.
  - A purely rationalist society prioritizes efficiency over human dignity.
  - History has repeatedly shown that when laws are determined solely by logic without reference to a metaphysical foundation, they often become mechanisms of oppression.
    - Examples are the eugenics movements of the twentieth century, the economic exploitation of laborers in purely capitalistic models, and the justification of unjust wars in the name of national progress.

Historical Case Study: The French Revolution

The French Revolution attempted to replace religious authority with pure rationalism, abolishing the church's influence in governance. The result was a system that did the following:

- Replaced metaphysically grounded religious virtue with ideology, resulting in totalitarian rule
- Turned justice into mob rule, where truth was dictated by political necessity
- Executed thousands under the illusion of rational progress, culminating in the Reign of Terror (1793–1794)

This demonstrates that when human reasoning begins from false premises or logical error—regardless of its cause—it leads, not to Truth but to tyranny. Reason, properly grounded, is never opposed to divine Truth, for it flows from it and ultimately returns to it.

2. The Dangers of Fideism in Government

On the other hand, societies that attempt to govern purely through religious dogma without integrating reason fall into authoritarianism. What happens when religious faith is imposed without reason?

- Irrational legalism
  - When laws are based solely on religious texts without logical interpretation, they become arbitrary and oppressive.
    - For example, legal systems that enforce religious doctrines through coercion rather than rational persuasion create societies where "truth" is dictated, not discovered.
- Suppression of inquiry
  - A fideistic society discourages scientific progress and philosophical debate, fearing that reason will undermine faith.
  - This stagnates intellectual growth, leading to societies where blind obedience replaces rational engagement.
- Moral stagnation
  - When faith is separated from reason, it is vulnerable to political corruption.
  - Religious leaders may use doctrine to consolidate power rather than to guide people toward divine Truth.

But true obedience is not blind. The perfectly obedient Son of Man and the saints who share in the beatific vision obey, not from ignorance but from full knowledge because their eyes are open to the fullness of Truth. Far from undermining reason, faith elevates it. Faith does not ask us to abandon reason but to let it see further. It opens the intellect to the source of reason, revealing that true freedom and authentic obedience are inseparable. The contrast could not be sharper: blind obedience obscures the will; faithful obedience illumines it.

Historical Case Study: Theocracies Without Rational Governance

Examples of fideistic rule include:

- Certain medieval periods where church and state were not properly distinguished, leading to forced conversions and inquisitions
- Islamic theocracies that enforce harsh penalties for apostasy or theological dissent
- Modern religious extremism, where leaders impose dogma through violence rather than persuasion

Once politics begins to errantly treat God as a religious symbol rather than as the grounding of reality, governments are pressured—often inevitably—to remove reason from education.

Why? Because once God is gone, so also is reason. Then logic, unmoored, manipulable, and ultimately self-destructive, will yield to entropy, revealing not progress but the collapse into the chaos of a decadent universe. In such systems, education must be subordinated to ideology rather than Truth, reinforcing obedience over understanding and silencing the very inquiry that could lead souls to the God who is.

Then, and in the name of separating church and state, the state becomes the church, complete with its own creeds, rituals, and heresy trials. Its leaders become the objects of trust, fear, or worship, not because they are just but because they control the narrative. In this inversion, power replaces Truth, and liberty is redefined as loyalty to the regime. What was once a safeguard against tyranny becomes its disguise.

These examples illustrate that faith alone, when detached from reason, leads to control rather than true participation in divine reality.

3. The Collapse of Half-Truths and the Logic of Participation

Both rationalism and fideism fail, not simply because they are ideologically extreme but because they are metaphysically incomplete. Each isolates one dimension of human nature—either reason or faith—and attempts to construct a civilization from that fragment. The result is predictable: control without justice, liberty without order, obedience without understanding, or inquiry without Truth.

What is needed is not a compromise but a restoration of wholeness, a social and political vision that reflects the full structure of the human person as a rational participant in divine actuality.

This is precisely what the Roman Catholic intellectual tradition offers and must own.

- It does not reject reason; it elevates it.
- It does not reduce faith to dogma; it grounds it in reality.
- It recognizes that Truth, the Good, and the structure of law are not invented but discovered through the harmonious operation of intellect and will, grace and nature, faith and reason.

4. Moving Forward: From Fragmented Foundations to a Coherent Tradition

Part one has exposed the structural failures of both rationalism and fideism—each a distorted half of what the human person requires to live in Truth. These failures are not merely intellectual. They shape how societies legislate, educate, and govern. If civilization is to recover, it must recover what has already been given: a tradition that unites intellect and will, faith and reason, grace and nature.

In Part two, we turn to the Roman Catholic intellectual tradition, not as a historical curiosity but as a living framework that preserves the only metaphysically coherent vision of justice. It is here that the full structure of the human person is honored and protected, and where society is understood, not as a mechanism of control but as an arena for participation in Truth and the Good.

PART TWO: THE ROMAN CATHOLIC INTELLECTUAL TRADITION

The Foundation for a Just Society

If pure rationalism leads to tyranny and fideism leads to stagnation, then what is the alternative? The Roman Catholic intellectual tradition provides a model in which faith and reason work together, ensuring that governance is neither oppressive nor arbitrary. This synthesis, grounded in natural law, has historically guided societies toward justice, human dignity, and rational moral order.

1. *Natural Law and the Foundation of Human Rights*

Natural law is the principle that moral truths are not arbitrary but woven into the very fabric of existence. Unlike legal positivism, which claims that laws are social constructs, natural law holds the following:

- Human dignity is inherent, not granted by governments.
- Right and wrong are objective realities, not matters of popular opinion.
- Justice must be rooted in reality, not political expediency.

The great thinkers of the Roman Catholic tradition—Aquinas, Augustine, and the Scholastic philosophers—recognized that true justice must align with the intelligible order of creation. This means that law is not something humanity invents but something it discovers through reason and revelation.

Example: The United States and Natural Law

The founding fathers, drawing on Christian theology and classical philosophy, grounded the Declaration of Independence—and, by moral implication, the Constitution—in principles of natural law. The Declaration's phrase "endowed by their Creator with certain unalienable Rights" is an explicit recognition that human rights are not granted by the state but are intrinsic to human nature.

Yet, modern legal thought has abandoned natural law, replacing it with relativism, resulting in societies where laws shift with political trends rather than moral truth.

2. Subsidiarity and Solidarity: Balancing Freedom and Responsibility[1]

A just society must maintain a delicate balance between individual freedom and communal responsibility. The Roman Catholic tradition provides two key principles to achieve this:

- *Subsidiarity* ensures that decisions are made at the most local level possible.
    - Governments should not micromanage individuals when families and communities are capable of self-governance.
    - Overreach leads to bureaucratic tyranny, where centralized power dictates every aspect of life.
- *Solidarity* ensures that society does not abandon the weak or marginalized.
    - While freedom is essential, individualism without responsibility leads to selfishness and social decay.
    - A just society must protect the vulnerable without violating personal liberty.

When *subsidiarity* and *solidarity* are properly integrated, justice flourishes, neither crushing freedom nor neglecting moral responsibility.

3. The Role of Free Will in a Just Society

A civilization built on truth must respect human freedom, allowing individuals to seek Truth rather than enforcing belief through coercion.

---

1. Pius XI, *Quadragesimo Anno*. Although the terms "subsidiarity" and "solidarity" were formally articulated in later Catholic social teaching, the principles themselves were present—implicitly and structurally—in the political philosophy of the American founding. The founders, deeply influenced by Christian theology, natural law, and classical republicanism, affirmed that governance should begin at the most local level (federalism, ward-level organization) and that freedom must be ordered toward the common good. Jefferson's defense of local autonomy and Adams's insistence on virtue as the foundation of liberty both echo the metaphysical logic of subsidiarity and solidarity. While their language was not theological, their assumptions were: human beings are endowed with dignity, ordered toward moral responsibility, and capable of forming just societies only through self-governance aligned with a higher moral law.

- If society forces moral behavior through totalitarian control, it denies the dignity of free will.
- If society allows unrestricted moral chaos, it denies the very concept of truth.

Thus, true justice must allow freedom within order, guiding human choice toward Truth rather than mere preference.

4. Moving Forward: From Metaphysical Vision to Historical Rejection

Part two has shown that the Roman Catholic intellectual tradition offers, not only a religious framework but a coherent metaphysical and moral architecture for a just society, one grounded in natural law, ordered liberty, and the essential harmony of faith and reason. It embodies the very structure of participation in divine actuality: freedom without chaos, obedience without oppression, and truth without tyranny.

But if this synthesis is so clear, so rational, and so historically fruitful, the next question is both urgent and sobering: Why was it abandoned by a significant portion of its followers?

In Part three, we confront that rejection directly. We examine the cultural and institutional breakdown of the modern West as a case study in what happens when a civilization severs itself from the very truths that made it coherent. This is not merely a story of error but of inversion—where reason is turned against Truth, freedom is severed from the Good, and society forgets that the soul is formed by structure, not desire.

What was once a culture ordered to justice has become a culture of entropy—because a significant portion has cut itself off from the Source.

PART THREE: THE DECLINE OF WESTERN CIVILIZATION

A Case Study in the Abandonment of Faith and Reason

The modern West, once built upon the synthesis of Christian theology and Greek philosophy, has progressively rejected both. This rejection has led to deep cultural and moral crises, as society does the following:

- Redefines truth as subjective, rather than discovering it in reality

- Elevates personal preference over moral law, resulting in an inability to define good and evil
- Reduces freedom to license, leading to moral relativism and legal chaos

1. *The Breakdown of the Family*

At the heart of any just society is the family, the fundamental unit where moral formation takes place. However, as societies have rejected the moral framework that governs relationships, the family has collapsed,[2] resulting in the following:

- Divorce rates have skyrocketed, severing the stable bonds necessary for human flourishing.[3]
- Marriage has been redefined as a contract of convenience, rather than a sacred covenant.[4]
- Children are deprived of ordered guidance, leading to generational cycles of instability.[5]

The destruction of the family is not accidental; it is the inevitable consequence of rejecting the natural moral law that binds human beings together.

2. *Moral Relativism in Law*

Without an objective standard of morality, legal systems become tools of power rather than guardians of justice.

- Laws are rewritten to accommodate popular trends, rather than moral absolutes.
- The legal system shifts with the cultural tide, meaning that what is legal today may be illegal tomorrow and vice versa.
- Objective truth is replaced by political expediency, leading to a corrupt and inconsistent legal order.

---

2. George, *Clash of Orthodoxies*, 23–35.
3. Inglehart and Welzel, *Modernization*, 151.
4. Glendon, *Transformation of Family Law*.
5. Wallerstein et al., *Unexpected Legacy of Divorce*, xvii, 295.

Example: The Roman Empire

In its early years, Rome was governed by laws rooted in natural order. However, as the empire abandoned virtue in favor of decadence, legal stability disintegrated, leading to the empire's eventual collapse.

3. The Loss of Scientific Integrity

Modern scientific institutions have increasingly dismissed metaphysical truths, limiting inquiry only to material explanations.

- Science originally flourished within a Christian framework, where faith and reason worked together to discover Truth.
- Today, science is often invoked to deny the existence of God, yet many of science's most striking findings reinforce the very metaphysical structure that makes education intelligible.
- The rejection of metaphysics in scientific discourse has led to dangerous ideological distortions, where science is used to justify political narratives rather than pursue objective truth.

4. Moving Forward: From Collapse to Rebuilding—A Metaphysical Recovery

Having traced the consequences of severing faith from reason, and witnessing the cultural disintegration that follows from rejecting the structure of reality, we reach another question: Can a just society be restored? Part four offers a clear and firm answer: yes, but only if we recover the metaphysical foundation that modernity has forgotten.

This is not a call for religious imposition, nor for nostalgic regression. It is a call to reintegrate what was never meant to be divided: Truth and freedom, faith and reason, science and metaphysics, education and moral formation. A society that wishes to endure must no longer pretend that values are optional or that justice can be manufactured by consensus. It must return to what is real.

In Part four of this chapter, we will outline the essential steps of restoration: the reclamation of objective truth, the renewal of education, the moral reformation of law, the reintegration of scientific inquiry with metaphysical vision, and the rightful return of religion to public life. This is not theoretical; it is structural. And without it, there is no path forward.

PART FOUR: RESTORING THE PROPER ORDER

A Call to Action

To rebuild a just society, faith and reason must be reunited, forming a stable foundation for human dignity, justice, and moral order.

1. Reclaiming Metaphysical Truth

Society must recognize that reality is not merely material but intelligible and structured by divine Truth. Without this recognition, moral law has no foundation.

2. Educating the Public in Philosophy and Theology

A civilization that neglects metaphysical education is doomed to ideological manipulation. Teaching first principles is necessary to prevent social and political collapse.

3. Defending Objective Morality

Laws must be based on natural law, not transient societal trends. A just society does not create morality; it aligns itself with the structure of divine order.

4. Encouraging Scientific Inquiry Within Metaphysical Bounds

Science must seek truth in all its dimensions, rather than limiting itself to materialist assumptions. When properly grounded, scientific discovery reinforces divine order.

5. Restoring the Role of Religion in Public Life

Faith should not be confined to private belief; it must inform public discourse and ethical decision-making. The removal of metaphysical and moral reasoning grounded in faith from the public sphere has allowed irrational secular ideologies to dominate governance under the illusion of neutrality.

6. The Path Ahead

A truly just society cannot emerge from power structures alone. It must be built on a foundation where reason is aligned with the Truth it cannot generate, and where faith is recognized, not as irrational allegiance to dogma but as the rational trust in the source of all order, meaning, and moral law.

When faith and reason are severed, justice collapses, either into technocratic oppression or fideistic coercion. But when they are reintegrated, a society becomes capable of recognizing the dignity of the person, the structure of reality, and the moral responsibilities that arise from both.

This reintegration is not a theoretical ideal. It is a necessity for any civilization that seeks to endure. The American founding, in its appeal to "the Laws of Nature and of Nature's God," as the Declaration of Independence put it, exemplifies this synthesis, even if imperfectly expressed. Its enduring strength lies in its recognition that human rights are not created by governments but are inherent in our nature because that nature participates in something greater than itself.

But this insight must be formed and transmitted. If a just society depends on faith and reason working together, then its people must be educated in a manner that forms both the intellect and the will.

7. Moving Forward: From Civilization's Collapse to Its Reconstruction—The Role of Education

If Part four of chapter 31 has demonstrated that the restoration of justice and order depends on the reintegration of faith and reason, then the next necessary questions are these: How is such integration formed? How is it transmitted? How is it made durable across generations?

The answer to all of these is education. A society that wishes to endure must do more than legislate justice; it must form souls capable of recognizing it.

But the modern educational system, severed from metaphysics and fractured by specialization, can no longer do this. It produces function without wisdom, autonomy without order, knowledge without Truth.

What is needed now is not a new technique but a new understanding of what education is. Education is not just the transmission of information but the participation of the finite intellect in the structure of divine actuality. To miseducate is not simply to mislead; it is to deform the soul's capacity to know the real.

In the chapter that follows, we will confront this crisis directly. We will show that education is not neutral, that it either elevates the person into alignment with Truth, the Good, and the structure of Being, or it severs that alignment and leaves the soul unformed. We will explore how the collapse of educational philosophy underlies the broader collapse of justice, culture, and coherence, and we will lay out the steps by which education can once again become the foundation for a civilization ordered to Truth, Love, and Communion.

32

Education as Participation in Divine Knowledge

Introduction: The Crisis of Modern Education

IF A JUST SOCIETY depends on the harmonious integration of faith and reason, then education (reciprocal information exchange) is its most essential structure. Education is not merely a social function or a means to economic advancement. It is the formation of intellect and will in alignment with truth. The collapse of modern education is not simply a failure of method or curriculum but a metaphysical failure, a loss of understanding that knowledge is participatory, not possessive. Knowledge is not the accumulation of information but the structured alignment of the finite intellect with the infinite source of order—divine actuality. A society that forgets this does not just miseducate its citizens; it fragments the very conditions under which justice, freedom, and human dignity can survive.

This chapter will demonstrate the following:

- Education is not the accumulation of facts but the structuring of the intellect to participate in truth.
- Knowledge, properly understood, is not a human construct but a form of participation in divine actuality.

- The modern educational system, by severing disciplines from one another and from metaphysical grounding, has fragmented human understanding.
- A proper education must reintegrate all fields of knowledge, enabling students to recognize reality as an ordered whole.
- Health maintenance is an essential component of education, for rational beings must structure, not only their intellects but their physical existence in harmony with Truth.

If knowledge is a structured participation in divine actuality, then education must be understood as the process by which the human intellect is conformed to the structure of Being itself. The failure of modern education, then, is not merely methodological but ontological—a collapse in the recognition of the necessary relationship between knowledge and reality.

1. The Loss of Knowledge: How Education Became Fragmented

Education was not always as fragmented as it is today. The classical tradition, particularly in the medieval university system, understood that all learning was ultimately a unified pursuit of truth.[1]

The trivium (grammar, logic, and rhetoric) and quadrivium (arithmetic, geometry, music, and astronomy) were not separate subjects but aspects of a single rational structure, leading the student toward higher participation in divine Truth.

However, this unified approach was systematically dismantled. Several key developments led to this collapse.

A. The Secularization of Knowledge

The Enlightenment introduced a view of knowledge that excluded theology as a legitimate field of study. This led to the following:

- The false assumption that knowledge could be fully explained without reference to divine actuality

---

1. See Grubb and Lazerson, "Vocationalism and Higher Education," 3; Howe, "Classical Education in America." See also, Morrill Act of 1862, 12 Stat. 503; 7 U.S.C. §§ 301–8 (enacted).

Education as Participation in Divine Knowledge 281

- The separation of scientific and philosophical inquiry, creating an artificial divide between empirical study and metaphysical understanding
- A rejection of wisdom in favor of purely technical knowledge, reducing education to a utilitarian function rather than a pursuit of Truth [2]

B. The Specialization Crisis

The rise of the modern research university introduced extreme specialization, where disciplines became increasingly isolated from one another.

- Scientists were trained without grounding in philosophy, leading to a failure to question the metaphysical assumptions of their own work.
- Philosophers were trained without reference to theology, resulting in a fragmentation of thought into skeptical relativism or abstract formalism.
- Theology, where it remained, was taught as an isolated discipline, disconnected from empirical and rational sciences.

This specialization severed education from its teleological foundation, ensuring that knowledge was no longer oriented toward participation in divine Truth but toward mere functional competence.[3]

C. The Shift from Truth to Utility

Education gradually moved away from the pursuit of wisdom and became a means to an economic end.

- Students were no longer taught how to think but merely how to be employable.
- Universities became centers for career training rather than intellectual formation.

---

2. Gregory, "Reformation Era," 163–83; MacIntyre, *After Virtue*, chs. 4–5.

3. Gregory, Reformation Era," 163–83; Wilshire, "Professionalism as Purification Ritual," 280–93; MacIntyre, *After Virtue*, chs. 4–5.

- The emphasis on specialization over integration led to the production of individuals who may be highly skilled in one area but who lack a coherent understanding of reality.[4]

This fragmentation is not a natural evolution but a deliberate rejection of divine order. Knowledge is no longer understood as a participation in Being but as a tool for worldly success. The result is a system that produces technically skilled but intellectually incoherent individuals, leading to a society that is mechanistically efficient but spiritually and philosophically impoverished.

2. Knowledge as Divine Participation

If knowledge is to be properly restored, it must be understood not as a human invention but as participation in divine actuality.

A. Truth Is Not a Social Construct

- In modern thought, knowledge is often seen as subjective, a set of perspectives shaped by historical and cultural forces.
- However, truths are not created by human minds; they are discovered through participation in the structure of divine actuality.
- The act of learning is not the act of constructing knowledge but of aligning one's mind with what is already true.

B. The Structure of Knowledge Mirrors the Structure of Divine Action

- Just as divine action is structured by potentiation, knowledge is structured by participation.
- All knowledge originates in Being per se, who is not merely true but is fully actual Truth from whom all intelligibility proceeds.
- Finite beings do not create Truth but receive and participate in it through structured engagement.

---

4. Grubb and Lazerson, "Vocationalism in Higher Education," 1–25.

Education, therefore, is not the imposition of human ideas but the unfolding of divine actuality within the human intellect.

This means that a proper educational system must be structured to reflect this reality. It must be the following:

- Unified—disciplines must be reintegrated, showing their common foundation in divine actuality
- Ordered—knowledge must be presented as a structured ascent toward Truth, not as isolated facts
- Teleological—education must be oriented toward the fulfillment of the rational soul in Truth, not merely toward practical skills

The Engel v. Vitale Decision and the Consequences of Educational Failure

A nation's legal decisions reflect the philosophical assumptions embedded in its education system. If that system ceases to form minds in Truth, those tasked with interpreting and applying the law will lack the necessary metaphysical clarity to render just decisions. The Supreme Court's ruling in *Engel v. Vitale* (1962) is a prime example of this failure.

The case before the Court concerned the constitutionality of a short, voluntary prayer composed by the New York State Board of Regents for use in public schools. The prayer—"Almighty God, we acknowledge our dependence upon Thee, and we beg Thy blessings upon us, our parents, our teachers, and our country"[5]—was challenged on the grounds that it constituted an official establishment of religion in violation of the First Amendment. The Court ruled in favor of the plaintiffs, holding that even a non-denominational, voluntary prayer in a public-school setting constituted government endorsement of religion. This decision set a precedent for the systematic removal of religious reference from public education, not by establishing true neutrality but by enforcing a worldview that implicitly treated divine reality as extraneous to public life.

The ruling treated God as a construct of religious institutions rather than as the necessary foundation of all being. The Court,

---

5. See Engel v. Vitale, 370 U.S. 421 (1962).

paradoxically, did not separate God from the state but forced an areligious concept of God into a "religious" category, effectively redefining God as belonging to the "church" rather than as the actuality of Being itself.

By judicially enforcing secularization, the Court accelerated the collapse of a rationally ordered society, leading to the cultural and legal confusion seen today. Law became unmoored from objective morality, science increasingly rejected metaphysical grounding, and ethics became relativistic, leading to moral and social decay.

Education failed the judiciary. The justices who rendered this decision were not operating in isolation; they were products of the very educational system whose epistemological crisis they unknowingly perpetuated. Had they been trained in a coherent framework—one that integrated theology, philosophy, and reason—they would have recognized that their decision was not an act of religious neutrality but an enforcement of a deficient metaphysical paradigm.

A nation that fails to educate its citizens in metaphysical truth will find itself governed by individuals incapable of rendering just decisions. Without a proper foundation in divine actuality, even the highest court in the land becomes incompetent to distinguish true reason from ideological distortion.

3. *The Role of Public Health Maintenance in Education*

If education is the structured participation in divine Truth, then it necessarily includes health maintenance, as rational beings must not only structure their intellects in accordance with truth but their physical existence as well.

A. Health Maintenance is Part of Education, Not Health Care

- Health care is interventionist; it addresses illness after it occurs.

Education as Participation in Divine Knowledge   285

- Health maintenance is preventive; it structures life choices and public policy in a way that minimizes the need for intervention.
- A society that fails to educate its people in proper health maintenance will inevitably overburden its health care system.

B. The Cost of Health Care is High Due to the Failure of Public Health Education

- In modern society, most chronic illnesses can be mitigated or prevented through proper health maintenance.
- A system focused on health education and maintenance would reduce national health care costs to insignificance by minimizing preventable conditions.
- However, the political system prioritizes short-term economic and electoral gains, leading to reactive policies instead of a rational, preventive approach.

4. The Restoration of Classical Education

To restore education to its proper role, we must return to a classical model of learning, one that reflects the structure of divine action. This requires the following:

A. The Reintegration of Disciplines

- Theology must once again be the foundation of all learning.
- Philosophy must return to its role as the handmaid of theology.
- Science must be understood within its proper metaphysical context.

B. The Return to Ordered Learning

- Education should follow a structured ascent, in which lower knowledge leads to higher truth.

- The classical trivium and quadrivium must be restored as a logical framework.

C. The Church's Role in Restoring Education

- The church, as the guardian of Truth, must reclaim its role in intellectual formation.
- It must re-establish rigorous academic institutions based on a metaphysical foundation.

5. *The Education of the Soul*

Education is not merely about acquiring information; it is about the perfection of the intellect in Truth. By restoring education to its proper metaphysical grounding, we ensure that human intellect does not remain trapped in fragmentation but ascends toward full participation in divine wisdom.

6. *Moving Forward: From Educational Renewal to Civilizational Integration*

Chapter 32 has shown that the restoration of education is not merely a pedagogical reform; it is the necessary reconstitution of the intellect in alignment with Truth. Without education that forms the whole person in structured participation with divine actuality, no just society can endure. But education alone, even when properly restored, is not sufficient. It must be joined by a broader integration of every sphere of human life—governance, law, science, health, and public morality—all of which have likewise suffered from the metaphysical collapse of modern thought.

In the next chapter, we move from the intellectual formation of persons to the structural reformation of civilization. We will examine how metaphysical integration provides the only coherent foundation for rebuilding a fragmented world, restoring to each field of knowledge and action its proper place within the unified order of Being.

33

The Future of Metaphysical Integration

Introduction: The Crisis of a Fragmented World

THE MODERN WORLD SUFFERS from a crisis of fragmentation across disciplines, institutions, and even within individual human understanding. This crisis is not merely academic or political but metaphysical. It stems from the failure to recognize that all aspects of reality—education, health, governance, science, and morality—must be grounded in a singular, rational foundation: divine actuality.

Throughout this book, we have demonstrated the following:

- Education is not a neutral transmission of information but a structured participation in divine Truth.
- Health is the ordered integration of body and soul in accordance with the structure of Being and is a consequence of alignment; it is not a product of intervention.
- Justice is not a social construct but a necessary extension of divine order in human governance.
- Science, when properly understood, does not oppose metaphysics but reveals the rational structure of creation.
- Theology is not an arbitrary belief system but the logical culmination of rational inquiry.

Now, we turn to the question: What is the future of metaphysical integration?

If the fragmentation of knowledge, governance, and human flourishing has led to the present crisis, then the only rational solution is a reintegration of all fields under a coherent metaphysical framework. This chapter will explore the practical and theoretical implications of such a reintegration, examining how it restores coherence to human thought and action.

1. The Failure of Modern Thought: How We Lost Integration

The fragmentation of knowledge was not an accident. It was the result of deliberate philosophical and cultural shifts that severed human inquiry from its metaphysical foundation.

A. The Rise of Scientism and the Death of Wisdom

- The modern era elevated empirical science as the sole source of knowledge while dismissing metaphysical inquiry as subjective or unnecessary.
- This led to an era of technological advancement but intellectual incoherence where society can manipulate physical reality but lacks the wisdom to govern itself.
- Scientism, the belief that only empirical data counts as knowledge, ironically fails even by its own standards, as it cannot empirically justify itself.

B. The Reduction of Ethics to Power Struggles

- Without a metaphysical foundation, morality has been reduced to subjective preference or social consensus.
- Justice is now dictated by political movements rather than objective moral law.
- The failure to recognize an absolute moral order has led to legal and social chaos where laws are arbitrarily changed to fit transient ideologies.

C. The Institutionalization of Division

- The compartmentalization of knowledge—separating education, health, law, and science into isolated fields—has prevented meaningful interdisciplinary dialogue.
- Universities, governments, and even religious institutions have adopted models that reinforce specialization at the expense of integration.
- This has led to a population that is highly trained in specific skills but lacks a coherent vision of truth.

Thus, the problem is clear: modernity has constructed a world of power without wisdom, knowledge without understanding, and progress without purpose. The next step is to explore how metaphysical integration provides the only viable solution.

2. *The Restoration of Integration: A Metaphysical Solution*

If fragmentation is the disease, then metaphysical integration is the cure. This requires a systematic reintegration of all fields of knowledge, ordered according to the structure they receive from divine actuality.

A. Reintegration in Education: Forming the Whole Person

- Education must return to its proper purpose—structuring the intellect to participate in Truth.
- This requires a curriculum that integrates theology, philosophy, science, and the humanities rather than isolating them.
- Schools and universities must reject relativism and reclaim their role as institutions of rational inquiry, not ideological indoctrination.

B. Reintegration in Health: Beyond Medical Intervention

Public health must shift from a reactive system focused on disease management to a proactive system based on health maintenance.

- This requires education in nutrition, exercise, mental well-being, and spiritual health, not just access to medical care.
- The human person must be understood holistically, integrating physical, intellectual, and spiritual well-being.

C. Reintegration in Law and Governance: The Return to Natural Law

- Justice cannot be dictated by changing political trends but must be grounded in an objective moral order.
- Legal systems must recognize natural law as the foundation of human rights rather than arbitrary state authority.
- Political discourse must shift from power dynamics to truth-seeking, ensuring that governance reflects divine order rather than transient ideologies.

D. Reintegration in Science: The Limits of Empiricism

- Science must acknowledge its own ontological limitations—it describes how the world functions but cannot explain why it exists.
- The integration of metaphysics and science restores the pursuit of knowledge to its proper place, where empirical data is interpreted within a rational framework.
- Rather than rejecting theology, science should recognize that divine action is the necessary precondition for an intelligible universe.

Thus, reintegration is not about rejecting modern advancements but about restoring coherence, ensuring that all disciplines, institutions, and human endeavors reflect their proper relationship to divine actuality.

3. Practical Implications: The Path Forward

The future of metaphysical integration is not merely a theoretical project—it has real-world implications that must be implemented systematically.

A. Rebuilding Institutions on First Principles

- Universities must reclaim their role as centers of rational inquiry, integrating philosophy and theology with scientific and professional disciplines.
- Churches must reclaim their role as intellectual and spiritual leaders, teaching all who choose to listen not just religious doctrines but the rational foundation of faith.
- Governments must recognize natural law as the foundation of justice, ensuring that laws reflect objective moral truths rather than shifting political ideologies.

B. Reforming Public Education

- The education system must replace relativism with metaphysical realism, teaching students how to reason, not just memorize information.
- Curricula must be designed to build intellectual coherence, linking subjects rather than isolating them.
- Students must be trained in logical reasoning, philosophical inquiry, and theological understanding, ensuring that they can critically engage with the world rather than being shaped by propaganda.

C. Restructuring Healthcare for Human Flourishing

- Public health must be prioritized over profit-driven medical industries.
- Education on preventative health, mental well-being, and spiritual wellness must be incorporated into national policies.

- The emphasis must shift from treating symptoms to maintaining health, ensuring that fewer individuals require medical intervention in the first place.

D. Restoring the Pursuit of Truth in Science

- Scientists must be trained in metaphysical principles, ensuring they do not fall into the trap of materialist reductionism.
- Ethical considerations must be rooted in objective moral law, preventing the misuse of scientific advancements.
- Science must acknowledge its participation in divine wisdom, recognizing that truth is not created by human observation but discovered through rational inquiry.
- Each of these steps ensures that society moves away from fragmentation and toward a restored coherence of knowledge, governance, and human flourishing.

4. The Future of Humanity Lies in Metaphysical Integration

This book has demonstrated that all true knowledge—whether in education, health, law, or science—must be structured within a metaphysical framework that acknowledges divine actuality. The crisis of modern society is not merely political, economic, or educational; it is a failure to recognize the necessity of metaphysical integration.

Thus, the future of human progress does not lie in more technology, bureaucracy, or political activism; it lies in the restoration of wisdom. This wisdom is not an abstract ideal but a necessary reality grounded in the very structure of existence.

If we wish to move beyond the errors of fragmentation, we must reintegrate all aspects of life—knowledge, governance, and human flourishing—within the singular reality of divine Truth. This is a necessary step toward restoring coherence to human civilization.

The choice is clear: continue down the path of fragmentation or embrace the future of metaphysical integration.

5. Moving Forward: From Metaphysical Framework to Civilizational Renewal

Now that we have completed the logical framework for metaphysical integration, another question remains: How do individuals and communities take part in this reintegration?

Integration is not merely a philosophical imperative; it is a civilizational necessity. A fragmented society cannot endure because fragmentation is the refusal to participate in reality as it is. The preceding chapter established that the reintegration of education, science, health, law, and governance must be grounded in the metaphysical truth of divine actuality. But theory alone does not rebuild a world. Civilization is more than the sum of its systems; it is the concrete expression of a people's alignment with Truth, Goodness, and the structure of Being. Thus, we now turn from integration to restoration.

If a metaphysical foundation is the condition of coherence, then civilization must be restored upon that foundation—intellectually, morally, politically, and ecclesially. The next chapter will demonstrate that only by recovering this foundation in practice can culture, law, and social institutions be realigned with their ultimate source and purpose: the participation of persons in divine order.

34

The Metaphysical Restoration of Civilization

Introduction: The Consequences of a Disordered Worldview

CIVILIZATION IS NOT SUSTAINED by technological progress, economic prosperity, or political stability. Of course, these make an important contribution, but at its core, the health of a civilization depends upon its alignment with metaphysical truth—the recognition that existence is structured, intelligible, and participatory in divine actuality. When civilizations adhere to these first principles, they flourish. When they sever themselves from this foundation, they inevitably fragment and decline.

Throughout history, the greatest civilizations—whether in philosophy, law, science, or the arts—were those that maintained as coherent an understanding of reality as was available at the time. They flourished to the extent that their intellectual, moral, and institutional structures aligned with metaphysical Truth. However, modern society has systematically rejected that foundation in favor of disordered substitutes manifesting as materialism, relativism, and ideological fragmentation. This rejection has led to intellectual incoherence, moral decay, and political instability, eroding the very foundations of human flourishing.

If civilization is to be restored, it must return to its proper metaphysical grounding. This chapter will outline the necessary steps for this restoration, demonstrating the following:

- The intellectual order must be reclaimed; knowledge must once again be unified under the principles of Truth and participation in divine actuality.
- The moral order must be reestablished; ethical life must be structured in alignment with natural law and the intrinsic purpose of human existence.
- Governance must be aligned with truth; political systems must reflect divine justice, rather than fluctuating ideological trends.

1. The Church Must Reclaim Its Role as Guardian of Truth and Moral Order

The fragmentation between faith and reason must be healed, ensuring that metaphysical wisdom—not institutional or religious doctrine or political power—guides the social, cultural, and intellectual life of civilization, for this is the church's rightful vocation: to preserve and proclaim the structure of Truth. The Word of God, though revealed by the Spirit of Truth, is spoken in the voice of reason.

The restoration of civilization is not a nostalgic return to the past, nor is it an imposition of rigid dogma. It is a necessary realignment of human structures with reality. Civilization cannot be sustained on illusions; it must be rooted in what is objectively, necessarily true.

2. The Intellectual Restoration—Reclaiming Metaphysical Truth

The crisis of modern civilization is, above all, an intellectual crisis. The collapse of philosophical rigor, the isolation of scientific inquiry from first principles, and the rejection of theological wisdom have resulted in a fractured understanding of reality.

The most destructive errors contributing to this intellectual collapse include the following:

- Metaphysical nihilism: the belief that reality has no inherent structure or meaning, reducing existence to a chaotic series of events rather than a participation in divine actuality.
- Radical materialism: the assumption that only the physical universe exists, leading to a rejection of the immaterial and the transcendent.
- Hyper-specialization and fragmentation: the division of knowledge into isolated disciplines that no longer communicate with one another, severing intellectual inquiry from its proper unity.
- Relativism in truth claims: the false assumption that all perspectives are equally valid, leading to the rejection of objective reality in favor of subjective interpretations.

A civilization that does not know what is true cannot sustain itself. Therefore, the first step toward restoration must be an intellectual renewal that recognizes Truth as absolute and knowledge as participatory and necessarily structured by divine action.

3. Steps for Intellectual Restoration

1. Reassert the primacy of metaphysics

    - Philosophy must be restored to its proper role as the foundation of all knowledge. Every discipline—whether science, history, or politics—must be grounded in metaphysical first principles. Without an understanding of being, causality, and participation in divine actuality, intellectual inquiry collapses into contradiction.

2. Unify science, theology, and philosophy

    - Science must be recognized, not as a closed system of material observation but as the method by which structured participation in divine order is discovered through physical reality. Its aim is not to reduce but to reveal the intelligibility of nature as a manifestation of Being.

    - Theology must reengage with philosophy, not as a tool of dogma but as the metaphysical grammar that allows divine Truth to be received and articulated without contradiction. Faith must be understood, not as the negation of reason but as its completion through participation.

- Philosophy must be restored as the bridge, not merely between disciplines but between reality and understanding. It alone can reconcile the empirical with the eternal by grounding all inquiry in the act by which finite structure is potentiated from infinite actuality. In this, philosophy reclaims its role as the heart of natural philosophy, not as a pre-modern artifact but as the unified science of being from which all knowledge must proceed.

3. Restore classical education and the liberal arts
   - Education must return to a structured approach that aligns learning with the hierarchical order of truth.
   - The trivium (grammar, logic, rhetoric) and the quadrivium (arithmetic, geometry, music, and the study of cosmic order) must be restored as essential foundations for intellectual formation (in the modern context, this includes not only astronomy but the disciplined study of physical reality—fields like quantum mechanics, systems theory, and information science—interpreted through a metaphysical lens). This ensures that knowledge is not reduced to mere technical skill but is ordered toward wisdom.

4. Reject ideological thinking in favor of truth-seeking
   - Ideologies impose frameworks on reality rather than allowing reality to shape frameworks. Whether political, economic, or social, ideologies distort truth by forcing knowledge into artificial constructs. Intellectual restoration requires a rejection of ideological narratives in favor of an unyielding commitment to objective reality.

Historical Case Study: The Medieval University as a Model for Intellectual Unity

During the medieval period, universities were structured upon the principle that all knowledge must ultimately lead back to divine Truth. Theology was considered the queen of the sciences, not because it suppressed inquiry but because it provided the necessary foundation for understanding reality. Philosophy was its handmaid, ensuring rational coherence, while the empirical sciences expanded human participation in divine Truth.

This model fostered the greatest intellectual flourishing in history, leading to the development of natural law theory, the foundations of modern science, and the most rigorous philosophical systems ever devised. The fragmentation of this model during the Enlightenment and beyond did not lead to an expansion of knowledge but rather to its isolation and distortion.[1]

By restoring the intellectual unity that once guided civilization, we can ensure that knowledge is not merely accumulated but properly oriented toward Truth.

4. The Moral Restoration—Reestablishing the Natural Order

A civilization cannot survive on intellectual order alone. It must be morally ordered as well. Knowledge without virtue leads to manipulation; power without justice leads to tyranny; and governance without moral law results in chaos. The rejection of objective morality has led to the ethical collapse of civilization, replacing an ordered moral structure with relativism, self-indulgence, and the gradual erosion of human dignity.

This section will demonstrate that moral relativism is not merely an ethical failure but a metaphysical one. A society that denies the existence of objective good and evil is not just mistaken; it is structurally incapable of sustaining itself. The natural moral order, which emerges from the very structure of existence, must be reestablished to ensure the flourishing of both individuals and civilizations.

A. The Crisis of Moral Relativism

The modern rejection of moral order has led to a world in which the following occurs:

- Ethical principles are treated as subjective preferences rather than universal truths.

---

1. Scott, "Mission of the University," 1–39; Vest, "Medieval University," 22–83.

- The family unit is undermined by policies and cultural trends that ignore its foundational role in civilization.
- Hedonism and materialism replace virtue as the guiding principles of human behavior.
- Human dignity is redefined as conditional rather than intrinsic, leading to practices such as abortion, euthanasia, and genetic manipulation for eugenic purposes.

The result is a world where morality is dictated by human power rather than divine Truth. When moral order is not rooted in the objective structure of existence, it becomes a mere construct of social consensus, subject to change based on prevailing ideological trends. This leads to contradictions where one generation condemns an action as evil, while another generation celebrates the same action as progress.

Such moral instability is unsustainable. Civilization can only endure when its moral foundation is grounded in an unchanging reality, one that transcends individual preference and cultural shifts.

B. The Natural Moral Order as a Participation in Divine Truth

Morality is not an artificial human invention. It is an expression of the necessary structure of being. Just as physical laws govern material reality, moral laws govern human action in relation to the ultimate Good.

- Goodness as the direction of participated Being
  - Evil is not an independent force; it is the privation of good. Just as darkness is the absence of light and sickness is the absence of health, evil is the absence of proper moral participation in divine order.
  - A moral act is good when it aligns with the proper actualization of Being. For example, love, justice, and self-sacrifice contribute to the flourishing of individuals and society, while hatred, injustice, and selfishness degrade them.
- The natural law as the foundation of moral order

- Natural law is the rational participation of human beings in divine order. It is not imposed from the outside but discovered through reason and observation.
- Every society that has flourished in history has done so by adhering to principles aligned with natural law: upholding justice, protecting the family, valuing human dignity, and promoting virtue.

- Virtue as the path to participation in Truth
    - Virtue is not simply a habit of good behavior; it is the means by which the rational soul aligns itself with divine actuality.
    - The four classical cardinal virtues (prudence, justice, fortitude, and temperance) and the three theological virtues (faith, hope, and charity) structure moral life in a way that reflects participation in the divine.
    - A society that cultivates virtue flourishes, while a society that abandons virtue collapses into disorder.

5. Steps for Moral Restoration

To restore civilization's moral foundation, it is necessary to realign human life with the natural order. This requires the following:

1. The reaffirmation of objective good and evil
    - Moral relativism must be rejected as incoherent. Good and evil are not subjective constructs but necessary distinctions within reality.
        - Education must teach moral truth, ensuring that ethical principles are not framed as cultural preferences but as necessary truths about human existence.

2. The restoration of the family as the foundation of civilization
    - The family is the fundamental social structure through which virtue is cultivated, and moral order is sustained.
        - Government policies must protect, rather than undermine, the integrity of marriage and family life.

- A culture that does not prioritize strong families will inevitably collapse, as it fails to transmit moral wisdom across generations.

3. The defense of human dignity and the rejection of utilitarian ethics

    - Human beings must be recognized as ends in themselves, not as means to social, economic, or political goals.
    - Any system that treats people as disposable—whether through abortion, euthanasia, or exploitative economic structures—must be rejected.
        - Human life, at every stage, must be protected and valued as a participation in divine actuality.

4. The rejection of hedonism and the restoration of virtue ethics

    - Modern culture encourages self-indulgence, treating pleasure as the highest good.
        - This is a distortion of human purpose.
    - True happiness is not found in fleeting pleasure but in the fulfillment of one's nature through participation in Truth and Goodness.
    - Educational and cultural institutions must promote virtue, rather than glorifying excess, materialism, and self-centered ambition.

Historical Case Study: The Collapse of Rome and the Moral Lessons for Today

The decline of the Roman Empire offers a historical parallel to the current crisis of moral decay. Rome, once a civilization of law, discipline, and virtue, gradually abandoned these principles in favor of luxury, hedonism, and moral relativism. The loss of civic virtue led to political instability, economic exploitation, and the eventual collapse of the empire.

The historian Edward Gibbon, in *The History of the Decline and Fall of the Roman Empire*, identified moral decadence as one of the primary reasons for Rome's fall.[2] The virtues that had once sustained the Republic—self-discipline, duty, and justice—were replaced by corruption, self-indulgence, and short-term gratification.

If modern civilization does not restore its moral foundation, it will suffer the same fate. The lesson of Rome is clear: societies that abandon virtue do not survive.

6. The Political Restoration: Aligning Governance with Truth

Just as civilization requires intellectual and moral order, so it also requires a properly structured political system, one that reflects the metaphysical truths governing reality. When governance is detached from divine order, it does not float in neutrality; it collapses into one of two extremes: tyranny or chaos. History reveals that political systems built upon transient ideologies, power struggles, or human ambition are inherently unstable. In contrast, those grounded in natural law and metaphysical realism endure because they reflect not merely the will of rulers but the structure of reality.

The modern political crisis is not accidental. It is the predictable consequence of a cultural and philosophical movement that has severed governance from objective reality. Law, rights, and authority no longer proceed from participation in Truth but are instead dictated by the shifting will of the powerful. The following developments illustrate this structural collapse and demonstrate the urgent need for metaphysical restoration in political life.

First, the reduction of law to an instrument of power has replaced the pursuit of justice with the exercise of control. When law is no longer grounded in the order of Being—what tradition calls natural law—it ceases to function as a standard and becomes a tool. In such a framework, legality becomes synonymous with authority, not with truth. This leads to a situation in which whatever can be legislated or enforced is treated as just, even when it violates the metaphysical structure of human dignity, rights, or moral order. Law is no longer a recognition of what is right; it becomes a mechanism for imposing what is willed. This is not governance. It is domination under the guise of order.

Second, the state has expanded far beyond its proper role, absorbing responsibilities that once belonged to families, communities, churches,

---

2. Gibbon, *Decline and Fall*, 1:1–90.

and individuals. This centralization is often justified in the name of efficiency or justice, but it ultimately undermines the foundational structures of human society. When the state begins to mediate every relationship—economic, familial, educational, or medical—it gradually erodes personal responsibility and destroys *subsidiarity*. The result is a passive citizenry, trained to expect provision rather than to cultivate virtue, and a government bloated by the burden of roles it was never meant to fulfill. Metaphysically, this is a distortion of political form: the state becomes both architect and occupant, denying the relational independence of the very persons it claims to serve.

Third, the modern conception of rights has been hollowed out by legal positivism. Rights are now treated as government-issued permissions, granted by the state and withdrawn at its discretion. This is a catastrophic inversion. Rights are not political artifacts; they are metaphysical truths grounded in human nature, expressions of the structured participation of the person in divine actuality. When rights are unmoored from this foundation, they lose all coherence. They become contestable, negotiable, and ultimately meaningless. What one generation calls a right, the next may revoke. In such a system, law becomes, not a guardian of human dignity but an arena for ideological combat.

Finally, the erosion of national identity and social cohesion is the inevitable result of a politics that has abandoned metaphysical Truth. Without a shared understanding of justice, rooted in objective reality, societies fragment into factions, each clinging to its own version of Truth. Political discourse becomes war by other means, not a rational search for the common good but a struggle for dominance. The loss of metaphysical grounding produces a citizenry trained in outrage, not order; in power-seeking, not Truth-seeking. No civilization can endure this indefinitely. Where metaphysical truth is not the measure of public life, division and decay are assured.

These are not temporary symptoms of political disarray. They are the deep structural consequences of a world that has rejected the ontological foundation of governance. To restore justice, law, and liberty, we must begin, not with reforms of policy but with a recovery of metaphysical order. Law must once again reflect Truth. Authority must once again be accountable to the structure of Being. And political life must be understood, not as the imposition of will but as the stewardship of order entrusted to persons in communion with the Good.

Of course, such restoration must be gradual. A political order cannot be rebuilt by simply removing the structures that have supplanted responsibility, especially when those structures have taught generations to depend upon them. The state cannot be replaced overnight by virtue it has failed to cultivate. Restoration must therefore proceed with prudence and patience, not to preserve dysfunction but to prepare communities to stand together, capable once again of sustaining the responsibilities that political centralization has eroded. Only then can governance be truly restored to its rightful role: the preservation of justice through alignment with Truth.

This is not merely political reform. It is the restoration of communion through communication—of persons, communities, and law, drawn back into alignment with the structure of Truth.

7. The Nature of Just Governance

The following section does not reject the possibility of lawful adaptation to changing times. After all, time is the structured expression of motion within created limitation, and change is its measurable form. But neither time nor change confers authority to abandon what is metaphysically fixed. The principles by which man adapts must themselves remain grounded in the structure of Being, not in arbitrary will or ideological preference. Any change introduced by man, or to which mankind must respond, must not violate the metaphysical order instituted by the One who created time, change, and adaptability.

A just government does not impose order by force but aligns itself with the natural order already present in reality. This requires the following:

- The recognition of the Declaration of Independence as the first Constitution

  - The Declaration of Independence is not just a historical document; it is the foundation of legitimate governance.
  - It asserts that rights are endowed by the Creator, not granted by the state, meaning that any government that violates these rights is inherently unjust.
  - The Declaration establishes the principle that law must conform to divine order, rejecting the idea that human authority is absolute.

- The restoration of constitutional originalism

  - The US Constitution was designed to preserve the principles of the Declaration, ensuring that government remains constrained by natural law.

  - The modern trend of treating the Constitution as a living document subject to reinterpretation based on ideological trends undermines its purpose.

  - A return to originalism ensures that governance is based on fixed, objective principles rather than the shifting preferences of judges and politicians.

- The restoration of metaphysical competence in public authority

  - Judicial and legal reasoning must be grounded in metaphysical clarity, not merely in precedent, ideology, or disciplinary authority.

  - Courts must stop deferring to metaphysically incompetent professionals who, although they may be popular or possess technical expertise in fields such as physics, engineering, psychology, or medicine, have no demonstrated competence to define life at the metaphysical level (as seen in *Roe v. Wade* and *Dobbs v. Jackson*, where medicine was mistakenly treated as a metaphysical authority). Our nation's founders exhibited far greater metaphysical clarity than any so-called expert now invoked to undermine their moral reasoning.

  - Philosophers of prior centuries are often invoked uncritically to justify novel interpretations that distort eternal principles as if their words, rather than Truth itself, were authoritative.

  - Without metaphysical training, public officials confuse legal reasoning with cultural conformity, and law collapses into technique rather than participation in Truth.

- The restoration of natural law as the standard of justice

  - Legal positivism—the idea that law is simply whatever the state declares—has led to the erosion of justice.

  - True law is not created by governments; it is discovered through reason and participation in divine order.

- A legal system that contradicts natural law, whether or not enforced, is not legitimate, regardless of its democratic or institutional authority.
- The restoration of subsidiarity and limited government
  - The principle of *subsidiarity* states that governance should occur at the lowest possible level, with higher authorities intervening only when necessary.
  - This ensures that families, communities, and local governments retain their proper roles, preventing the overreach of centralized power.
  - A government that assumes responsibility for all aspects of life denies human freedom and undermines personal responsibility.

Just governance does not seek to control society; it seeks to uphold justice and ensure that individuals and institutions can flourish in alignment with divine Truth.

8. The Role of Justice and Mercy in Political Order

A just government must balance the principles of justice and mercy, ensuring that law is neither rigidly punitive nor recklessly permissive.

A. Justice: Upholding Divine Order

- Justice ensures that laws are applied consistently and that actions have real consequences.
- A government that fails to enforce justice allows disorder to flourish, leading to the breakdown of civilization.
- Laws must be structured to reflect reality, ensuring that, rather than ideological trends, truth governs legal decisions.

B. Mercy: The Application of Justice with Wisdom

- Mercy does not negate justice; it fulfills it by ensuring that law is applied in a way that allows for repentance, correction, and restoration.
- Just as divine mercy elevates human beings rather than ignoring their failures, governance must allow for redemption without abandoning justice.
- True mercy restores order by calling the wrongdoer back into responsibility. Policies that excuse wrongdoing without requiring repentance do not reflect mercy, they undermine justice.

A properly ordered society does not abandon law in the name of compassion, nor does it impose law without wisdom. Justice and mercy must work together to ensure that governance serves the highest good.

C. Historical Case Study: The Decline of the Roman Republic and the Loss of Constitutional Order

The fall of the Roman Republic provides a powerful historical lesson in the dangers of abandoning constitutional governance. Rome's early political system was built upon a structured legal order that limited power, enforced justice, and maintained the balance of society. However, over time, these principles were eroded by the following:

- The centralization of power—the Senate became increasingly ineffective as rulers consolidated authority.
- The expansion of government control—public dependency on state welfare grew, weakening the independence of citizens.
- The abandonment of moral and legal order—corruption flourished, and laws were altered to serve those in power rather than the common good.

The Republic collapsed into an imperial dictatorship, marking the end of constitutional governance and the beginning of authoritarian rule.[3] The lesson is clear: when law becomes a tool of power rather than a reflection of truth, civilization is at risk.

---

3. Gibbon, *Decline and Fall*, 1:1–74.

9. Steps for Political Restoration

1. Reinforce the Declaration of Independence as the foundation of government
   - Reaffirm that rights are derived from divine order, not government decree
   - Educate citizens on the metaphysical principles underlying legitimate governance
2. Restore the US Constitution to its original meaning
   - Reject judicial activism that distorts constitutional principles
   - Ensure that government power remains constrained by the limits originally established
3. Realign laws with natural law and objective justice
   - Ensure legislation conforms to moral and metaphysical truth
   - Recognize that any enacted legislation contradicting natural law is invalid, regardless of majority rule
4. Reestablish local governance through subsidiarity
   - Limit centralized power and return authority to families, local communities, and state governments
   - Ensure that federal intervention is reserved for matters beyond local capability
5. Defend the balance of justice and mercy in law
   - Ensure that laws are justly enforced, preventing social collapse
   - Apply mercy in ways that restore individuals without undermining justice

10. The Necessity of Metaphysical Governance

A civilization that abandons divine order in governance cannot survive. The modern world's political instability is not merely a policy failure. It is a structural defect caused by rejecting the principles necessary for just governance. The path to restoration is clear:

- Law must be rooted in natural order rather than arbitrary authority.
- Government must be limited, ensuring that it serves rather than controls.
- Justice must be upheld but always in accordance with wisdom and mercy.

Only by restoring governance to its proper metaphysical foundation can civilization ensure stability, justice, and human flourishing.

11. Moving Forward: From Metaphysical Order to Ecclesial Witness

Civilization cannot be sustained by policy alone. Law may mirror Truth, and governance may serve justice, but neither can endure without a living witness to the reality they presuppose. Metaphysical order must be proclaimed, defended, and embodied across generations and within every sphere of life. This is not the task of politics alone, nor of philosophy in isolation. It is the mission entrusted to the Roman Catholic Church: to guard the structure of Truth so that persons, cultures, and institutions may remain oriented to the Good.

What follows is not merely a theological conclusion, but a metaphysical imperative: the restoration of civilization depends upon the Roman Catholic Church's fidelity to her vocation as the guardian of truth, the custodian of metaphysical order, and the enduring witness to the structure of Being in a world increasingly deaf to its call.

35

The Ecclesial Restoration of Civilization

Introduction: The Church as the Living Witness to Metaphysical Truth

THE RESTORATION OF CIVILIZATION cannot proceed without the living voice of the church. Philosophy may articulate first principles, and governance may attempt justice, but neither can preserve the structure of Being without a body tasked with proclaiming it, not as theory, but as Truth incarnate. That body is the Roman Catholic Church.

She is not merely one institution among others. She is the sacramental presence of order in a disordered world, entrusted, not with adapting to culture but with recalling it to reality. In every age, her task is the same: to bear witness to Truth when all else collapses and to call persons, societies, and institutions back into alignment with what is eternally, unchangingly real.

What follows is an examination of how the Roman Catholic Church has fulfilled—and must continue to fulfill—this mission, not through political power or cultural conformity, but through doctrinal clarity, intellectual leadership, sacramental integrity, and moral fidelity.

1. The Role of the Roman Catholic Church in Civilizational Restoration

Throughout history, the Roman Catholic Church has served as the intellectual, moral, and cultural anchor of Western civilization. From preserving knowledge during the collapse of the Roman Empire, to guiding the development of just legal systems, her role has been indispensable. In the modern era, however, the Roman Catholic Church's voice has often been marginalized or misunderstood, not due to a failure of her mission but because of societal shifts that have distanced themselves from the metaphysical and moral truths she upholds.

This section will demonstrate that the Roman Catholic Church must continue to reclaim her role in restoring civilization, not through political dominance but by faithfully upholding and transmitting truth. The Roman Catholic Church's duty is not to impose faith by force, but to ensure that societies—including those beyond her visible communion—are called back into alignment with metaphysical and moral reality.

A. The Historical Role of the Roman Catholic Church in Civilization

To understand the necessity of the Roman Catholic Church's role today, it is essential to examine her contributions throughout history. The Roman Catholic Church's civilizational role has never been merely spiritual; it has involved the preservation, cultivation, and elevation of all domains of human life. Her historical contributions are especially evident in her guardianship of intellectual heritage as seen in the following:

- *The Roman Catholic Church as the preserver of knowledge*
  - During the fall of Rome, the Roman Catholic Church safeguarded philosophical, theological, and scientific knowledge, ensuring the continuity of intellectual progress. Monastic communities copied and preserved ancient texts, laying the foundation for the eventual intellectual resurgence of the medieval period. The establishment of universities under Roman Catholic Church patronage ensured that education remained a structured participation in divine Truth. Yet the Roman Catholic Church's mission extended beyond the intellectual sphere. She shaped the

moral foundations of justice and political legitimacy by grounding law in a higher order of Truth.¹

- *The Roman Catholic Church as the architect of legal and political order.*
  - Canon law influenced the development of legal systems across Europe, ensuring that justice was grounded in objective principles rather than arbitrary rule. The Roman Catholic Church's moral authority provided a counterbalance to the ambitions of secular rulers, advocating for the dignity of all persons. Natural law theory, developed within the Roman Catholic Church, became the foundation of modern legal and political thought. Alongside her intellectual and legal influence, the Roman Catholic Church has remained the primary defender of objective moral order, especially in moments of cultural crisis. Her teachings have preserved the dignity of the person and the coherence of the family against forces of dissolution.²

- *The Roman Catholic Church as the guardian of moral truth*
  - By upholding moral absolutes, the Roman Catholic Church provided stability in times of cultural and social upheaval. She defended the sanctity of life, marriage, and the family, ensuring that societies maintained their foundational moral structures. Through her social teachings, the Roman Catholic Church promoted justice, charity, and the proper role of economic and political systems in serving the common good. These historical contributions demonstrate that civilization flourishes when the Roman Catholic Church fulfills her role as the preserver of truth, justice, and moral order.³

B. The Challenge of a Disordered Age

The contemporary crisis of civilization is not the result of ecclesial failure, but of metaphysical resistance. That resistance has not arisen because the Roman Catholic Church ceased to witness to Truth, but because many, when confronted with that Truth, found its clarity intolerable. The moral

---

1. Mendis, "From Silence to Scholarship," 198–201.
2. Giaro, "Medieval Canon Lawyers," 157–81.
3. Pontifical Council for Justice and Peace, *Compendium*, 9, 72, 78–82.

and political fragmentation of modern society is the consequence, not of too little accommodation by the Roman Catholic Church but of too much accommodation by those outside her who wished to preserve the illusion of meaning without the structure that sustains it.

The core challenge of the modern age, therefore, is not the need to reform the Roman Catholic Church from within but to reform society's relation to Truth. The Roman Catholic Church has not collapsed; rather, she has been silenced, bypassed, or reinterpreted by those unwilling to be re-formed by what she reveals. This distortion manifests in several principal forms that follow:

- *The displacement of intellectual formation*
  - In a culture governed by instrumentalism, the Roman Catholic Church's intellectual mission—anchored in participation with divine Logos—has been overshadowed by ideologies that treat knowledge as a tool for power, not a path to Truth. Where once metaphysical formation provided the foundation for philosophy, science, and education, society now substitutes critical theory and psychological self-reference. The result is not liberation but fragmentation. It is not that the Roman Catholic Church ceased to teach; it is that the modern mind ceased to listen.

- *The Cultural Rejection of Metaphysical Structure*
  - Modern society bristles at anything with clear boundaries; form, limit, or purpose are treated like portentous barriers to freedom, rather than its prerequisite structure. As a result, every domain—sexual, political, familial, economic, scientific—has become a field of deconstructed relation, where being is no longer received but asserted. Those who reject the Roman Catholic Church's teaching do not reject a dogma per se; they reject the principle that underlies it: reality precedes will. In doing so, they collapse the very conditions for personal and communal order. Even in quantum mechanics we see the result—the denial of ontological form leads scientists to mistake the collapse of probability for the impossibility of divinely unaided existential return. This is the source of the metaphysical despair that humbles even the most confident cosmologist. In science, as elsewhere, the will is now imagined to define the reality of the subject under study.

But uncertainty is not a structure; it is a limit of our access. The structure remains.

- *The confusion of compassion with affirmation*
  - In the absence of metaphysical clarity, the desire to alleviate suffering mutates into the obligation to affirm identity. This inversion makes pastoral patience appear cruel and theological fidelity seem oppressive. Yet the Roman Catholic Church's role is not to mirror the wounded will of the world but to call it back into harmony with Being. True compassion does not confirm disorder; it accompanies the soul back toward alignment.

- *The obscuring of moral order through scandal and reaction*
  - In an age where private behavior is politicized and public truth is privatized, scandal becomes the only remaining moral category. But scandal—whether arising from sin or from misperception—has no power to define the Roman Catholic Church's witness.

The sins of her members do not invalidate the Roman Catholic Church's structure. Nor does public failure release society from the obligation to repent.

When scandal becomes the pretext for separation, it is not the Roman Catholic Church that has failed, but those who demand a perfect witness before they will submit to perfect Truth.

C. The Misuse of Ecclesial Language to Justify Secular Ends

The name of the Roman Catholic Church is often invoked by those who reject logic. Whether in academia, politics, or media, figures who bear the cultural markers of Catholic identity but reject the metaphysical structure of her teaching serve not as witnesses but as distortions. Such a presence does not prove that the Roman Catholic Church is confused; it proves that the world seeks to speak in her voice without receiving her word.

In the final analysis, the Roman Catholic Church has not abandoned her role; she has been abandoned by those who wish to retain her symbolism while discarding her structure.

The way forward is not for the Roman Catholic Church to become more accommodating, but for the world to become more receptive. It is not clarity that must yield to compassion, it is confusion that must yield to Truth.

2. *The Path to Ecclesial Restoration*

Restoring the Roman Catholic Church's role in civilization does not mean seeking political power; it means faithfully upholding the truth in all areas of life. The following steps outline how the Church can reassert her mission:

A. Reaffirm Doctrinal Consistency

- The Roman Catholic Church must reject theological relativism and uphold her teachings with clarity and authority.
- Foundational doctrine must be presented as an unchanging reflection of divine Truth, not as something subject to modern reinterpretation.
- Catholic Church leadership must resist cultural pressures to dilute moral and theological teachings.

B. Engage in Intellectual Leadership

- The Roman Catholic Church must actively counter materialism, relativism, and atheism with rigorous philosophical and theological argumentation.
- The integration of science, philosophy, and theology must be restored to demonstrate the coherence of truth.
- Education systems within the Roman Catholic Church must prioritize the formation of minds capable of engaging with modern challenges.

C. Restore Liturgical and Sacramental Integrity

- Worship must reflect the transcendent reality it represents, rather than conforming to secular sensibilities.
- The sacramental life of the Roman Catholic Church must be emphasized as the foundation of spiritual and moral renewal.
- Proper catechesis must be reinstated to ensure that the faithful understand the depth of their faith.

D. Advocate for Just Governance Without Seeking Political Power

The Roman Catholic Church does not rule states or legislate civil law. Her mission is not to seize political power but to illuminate it, encouraging governance to conform to the divine order. Through moral clarity and doctrinal witness, she calls societies to align law with Truth without becoming the coercive force behind that law.

- Catholic Church leaders must challenge unjust laws and policies, advocating for legal and political structures that reflect natural law.
- The Roman Catholic Church must serve as a moral witness in society, ensuring that truth is not abandoned in the name of pragmatism.

If these steps are followed, the Roman Catholic Church will continue to serve as the guiding force for civilization's renewal, not through coercion but through the power of Truth.

Historical Case Study: The Catholic Church's Role in the Fall and Restoration of Western Civilization

A clear example of the Catholic Church's capacity to restore civilization can be seen in her response to the fall of the Roman Empire. As Rome collapsed under the weight of internal corruption, economic instability, and military defeat, the Catholic Church remained the last stable institution in the Western world. Monastic communities preserved knowledge, cultivated moral order, and laid the foundations for the rebuilding of civilization. Through missionary work and theological development, the

Catholic Church provided the intellectual and cultural framework that led to the rise of medieval Christendom. This historical precedent demonstrates that even in times of civilizational collapse, the Roman Catholic Church can serve as the instrument of renewal. However, she must first recognize and embrace this role.[4]

3. Steps for the Roman Catholic Church's Role in Civilizational Restoration

- Reaffirm the primacy of truth
    - Truth is not subjective; it is the foundation of reality.
    - The Roman Catholic Church must combat relativism and materialism with unyielding clarity.
- Restore intellectual and theological rigor
    - The Roman Catholic Church must train leaders who are capable of engaging with modern philosophical and scientific challenges.
    - Seminaries and educational institutions must prioritize metaphysical and theological formation.
- Lead by example in moral and social renewal
    - The Roman Catholic Church must not merely condemn the failures of society but actively demonstrate the alternative.
    - Strong communities of faith, built on authentic moral and spiritual principles, will serve as models for societal restoration.

4. Call Civilization Back to Its Metaphysical Foundations

- Society must be reminded that truth, justice, and moral order are not human inventions but divinely expressed realities.
    - The Roman Catholic Church must boldly proclaim this message, regardless of opposition.

---

4. Dawson, *Religion and the Rise*, 11–25.

5. Moving Forward: The Roman Catholic Church's Indispensable Role in Civilization's Future

Civilization cannot be restored without a return to truth, and the Roman Catholic Church is the institution entrusted with preserving and proclaiming that truth. While she cannot and should not seek political control, she must ensure that political, intellectual, and social life are properly ordered toward divine participation.

The next chapter will bring together all aspects of this discussion, demonstrating that Truth itself is the fulfillment of civilization. Only by aligning with Truth can human beings, societies, and institutions find their ultimate purpose and achieve lasting peace, justice, and order.

36

The Synthesis
Truth as the Fulfillment of Civilization

Introduction: The Culmination of Thought and Reality

ALL CIVILIZATIONS RISE OR fall based on their adherence to truth. As we have demonstrated throughout this work, modern society has suffered due to the fragmentation of knowledge, separating faith from reason, science from philosophy, and metaphysics from governance. The final synthesis is the restoration of truth in all domains of thought and action, a unification that ensures civilization aligns once more with the structure of reality.

The fulfillment of civilization does not rest in material advancement alone, nor in technological power, but in the proper alignment of human action with divine order. A society that builds upon metaphysical truth is one that flourishes, while one that rejects truth in favor of ideological convenience is doomed to self-destruction.

This chapter will demonstrate the following:

- Truth is not an abstract ideal but a necessary foundation for all civilization.
- Human knowledge, though fragmented in modernity, must be reintegrated through metaphysical realism.
- Civilization's future depends on aligning governance, education, science, and morality with divine Truth.

We now turn to the final synthesis, where all disciplines—science, philosophy, theology, and governance—are harmonized, and where humanity's role in creation is understood within the context of divine action.

1. The Final Structure of Knowledge: The Restoration of Intellectual Integrity

The modern world is plagued by intellectual fragmentation, a failure to integrate knowledge into a coherent whole. This has led to the following:

- Science that refuses to acknowledge its own metaphysical implications
- Philosophy that descends into skepticism or abstract formalism, disconnected from reality
- Theology that is either overly fideistic or reduced to mere cultural expression
- Political ideologies that seek power rather than justice, detached from natural law.

But Truth is One. It cannot be divided into separate, competing disciplines that contradict each other. The task of intellectual restoration requires the following:

- Metaphysical realism—recognizing that reality is structured, ordered, and intelligible.
- The unification of theology, philosophy, and science—knowledge must reflect the integrated nature of reality.
- The end of skepticism and relativism—Truth is absolute and must be acknowledged as such.

Human reason cannot operate in isolation. It must be grounded in divine actuality, recognizing that all knowledge is a structured participation in Being.

2. The Moral Foundation of Civilization: Ethics as Ordered Love

Truth is not only a foundation for thought but for moral action. If Truth is denied, justice becomes arbitrary, and civilizations collapse under the weight of moral relativism.

A moral order built upon divine Truth is structured by the following:

- Justice as ordered love—justice is not the will of the strongest, nor the mere enforcement of social contracts; it is the proper ordering of human relationships within divine Truth
- Freedom and responsibility—human freedom is not an absolute license to do anything but a structured participation in Truth
- The family as the primary social unit—the family is not a cultural convention but the foundational structure of society; its breakdown is the breakdown of civilization, and restoring society requires restoring family life grounded in metaphysical truth

The false promises of ideological moralities—whether materialist, hedonist, or authoritarian—must be rejected in favor of a moral order rooted in Truth and Love.

3. Governance in the Light of Divine Order: The Political Implications of Truth

A civilization structured according to divine Truth must also be governed accordingly. This does not mean theocracy, but a recognition that all laws and institutions must be grounded in the reality of natural law.

Principles of governance must reflect the following:

- The role of law in defending truth—laws must be structured according to reality, not ideological trends
- The necessity of natural law in political systems—justice must be rooted in objective moral order, not arbitrary human legislation
- Subsidiarity and solidarity—government must serve the common good, neither overriding personal responsibility nor neglecting its duty to protect the weak

Without truth, governments become either tyrannical or anarchic, for justice ceases to be an objective reality and instead becomes the imposition of will by the powerful.

The future of civilization depends on whether political systems can realign themselves with divine order or whether they will collapse under their own contradictions.

4. The Scientific Restoration: The End of Fragmentation and the Return to Metaphysical Coherence

Science has reached a breaking point. Its discoveries continue to undermine materialism, yet scientists refuse to acknowledge the metaphysical implications of their own work.

This failure has led to the following:

- The illusion that quantum mechanics represents paradoxes rather than structured potentiation
- The rejection of fine-tuning as evidence of order in favor of a multiverse—an impossibility under the metaphysical logic presented in this work
- The inability to reconcile relativity and quantum mechanics due to metaphysical blind spots

This intellectual revolution is not a possibility but an inevitability. Truth asserts itself, whether acknowledged or not.

5. The Fulfillment of Civilization: Truth as the Foundation of the Future

The fulfillment of civilization is not material progress alone, nor mere cultural development. It is the realization of Truth in all aspects of life.

The future demands a return to first principles as follows:

- A civilization built on Truth—no system can survive without a foundation in metaphysical reality
- The end of fragmentation—knowledge, governance, and morality must be reintegrated into a coherent whole

- The necessity of divine order—a society that rejects God rejects Truth, and a society that rejects Truth cannot stand

History has shown that civilizations rise or fall according to their adherence to reality. Today, we stand at the precipice of restoration or collapse. The question is not whether civilization will be governed by truth but whether we will recognize Truth before our rejection of it brings about our destruction.

The Rejection of Truth

The rejection of Truth is not a neutral act. It is an active suppression of reality. The more civilizations deny divine order or hide it under the basket of religion, the more they crumble into incoherence. But for those who embrace Truth, the future remains open—a structured unfolding in the divine act of creation.

6. *The Return to Truth*

FINAL CONSIDERATIONS: SCIENCE AS PARTICIPATION IN DIVINE ORDER

The fragmentation of knowledge has left modern science unable to integrate its own discoveries into a coherent framework. Paradoxes arise, not because nature is paradoxical but because reductionist frameworks fail to account for the full structure of reality.

Quantum mechanics, relativity, and information theory—each revealing the participatory nature of existence—are best understood through structured potentiation and the deceleration of IRM. What physicists struggle to conceptualize as wave-particle duality, quantum entanglement, and space-time dilation are not contradictions but expected consequences of reality's potentiated structure.

Scientific discoveries do not challenge metaphysical truth. Rather, they confirm it when properly interpreted. The notion that reality *collapses* upon observation is a misunderstanding of how finite observers interact with structured potentiation. The transitions that physics describes are not caused by observation but are glimpses of unfolding creation within the constraints of finite perception.

Final Considerations on the Unification of Knowledge

Modern physics has unwittingly confirmed that reality is not brute matter but a structured participation in divine order. Quantum entanglement, time dilation, and information persistence all point to the participatory nature of existence. The true resolution of these so-called paradoxes is found, not in more mathematical speculation but in a recognition that science is discovering the structure of potentiation and the deceleration of infinite reciprocal motion.

Communion

Like an apparition speaking to the soul,
Manifesting not to any separate part,
Acknowledged only by the whole,
Appealing solely to the heart—
'Tis art.

—Keven Mc Guinness

37

The Ties that Bind
Ecumenism and the Call to Christian Unity

Introduction: The Necessity of Unity in Truth

THROUGHOUT HISTORY, DIVISIONS WITHIN Christianity have weakened the faith's ability to serve as a guiding force for civilization. Christ himself prayed for the unity of his followers, declaring, "That they may all be one, just as You, Father, are in Me, and I in You" (John 17:21). Yet, despite this divine mandate, Christianity remains fractured along doctrinal, theological, and institutional lines.

The challenge of Christian unity is not merely a matter of organizational cooperation or mutual tolerance; it is a metaphysical and theological necessity. Since divine Truth is One, then division within Christianity is a failure to fully participate in that Truth. The fragmentation of the church mirrors the broader fragmentation of civilization, reinforcing ideological divisions, moral confusion, and the decline of shared metaphysical foundations.

This chapter will explore the nature of ecumenism, its philosophical and theological necessity, and the conditions under which true Christian unity can be achieved.

1. *The Metaphysical Basis for Christian Unity*

Christian unity is not an arbitrary goal but a necessary reflection of divine actuality. Since God is the perfectly actual potentiator of all, then the church, as the body of Christ, must reflect that unity.

A. The Divine Unity of Truth and the Church

- Truth is One because God is One. Therefore, doctrinal division reflects a failure to fully participate in divine actuality.
- The church is called to be the visible and metaphysical extension of Christ's body on Earth.
- A divided church cannot fully bear witness to the coherence of divine Truth.

B. The Nature of Division: The Problem of Fragmented Participation in Divine Actuality

- Different Christian traditions grasp different aspects of divine Truth, yet each remains incomplete in isolation.
- The history of schisms and theological disputes reflects human limitations rather than divine will.
- The challenge of unity is not to erase distinct traditions but to integrate them within a fuller participation in divine Truth.

C. The Historical Consequences of Disunity

- The Reformation led to theological relativism, allowing for an increasing fragmentation of Christian belief.
- The Great Schism severed Eastern and Western Christianity, reducing the church's ability to serve as a unified moral authority.
- The rise of secularism has been facilitated by Christianity's internal divisions, as fractured doctrine weakens moral and philosophical coherence.

Christian unity is not merely desirable; it is necessary for the restoration of truth in civilization.

2. The Limits of False Unity: Ecumenism Without Metaphysical Grounding

A. The Dangers of Superficial Ecumenism

- Many modern ecumenical efforts focus on institutional cooperation rather than doctrinal reconciliation.
- Unity without truth is not unity; it is relativism.
- Theological differences must be resolved, not ignored, for genuine Christian unity to occur.

B. False Ecumenism as a Form of Indifferentism

- Some ecumenical movements treat all Christian traditions as equally valid, undermining the pursuit of objective truth.
- Genuine unity cannot be built on a rejection of doctrinal importance; it must be built on the full participation in divine Truth.
- Indifferentism weakens Christianity by reducing theology to subjective interpretation rather than revealed truth.

C. The Necessity of Doctrinal Clarity in Unity

- Unity must be based on a shared recognition of metaphysical and theological truths, not on institutional compromise.
- While diversity in practice can exist, fundamental doctrines concerning divine action, grace, and the structure of salvation must be reconciled.
- Any unity that contradicts divine actuality is a false unity and will eventually lead to further division.

The failure of previous ecumenical efforts is largely due to their avoidance of doctrinal reconciliation in favor of political or institutional unity. True Christian unity must be structured on Truth itself.

3. *The Path to True Christian Unity*

For Christian unity to be fully realized, it must be grounded in the following three essential principles:

A. The Restoration of Metaphysical and Theological Coherence

- The church must reaffirm the ontological reality of divine action rather than reducing doctrine to tradition or historical contingencies.
- Christianity must return to the first principles of Being and Truth, ensuring that doctrine aligns with metaphysical necessity.
- The unity of Truth in God must be the standard by which theological disagreements are evaluated.

B. The Resolution of Doctrinal and Sacramental Divisions

- Doctrinal differences must be systematically examined and reconciled in light of metaphysical truth.
- The sacraments must be understood as real participations in divine actuality, not mere symbolic gestures.
- Any divisions that stem from misinterpretations of divine action rather than true doctrinal necessity must be overcome.

C. The Role of the Church in Leading the Way Forward

- The church must take an active role in clarifying theological errors and ensuring that doctrine remains consistent with divine Truth.

- Christian leaders must abandon political ecumenism in favor of true doctrinal reconciliation.
- The church must articulate a vision of unity that is grounded in Truth rather than institutional compromise.

Christian unity is not about erasing denominational identity. It is about ensuring that all traditions participate in divine Truth in its fullness.

4. *The Civilizational Impact of Christian Unity*

A. THE ROLE OF THE CHURCH IN THE RESTORATION OF CIVILIZATION

- A united Christian church would serve as the strongest counterforce against the moral and intellectual collapse of modern civilization.
- The church, when unified, has historically been the foundation of law, ethics, and education.
- A divided church cannot effectively serve as the foundation for civilization's restoration.

B. CHRISTIAN UNITY AS THE FOUNDATION OF MORAL AND POLITICAL RENEWAL

- A society that reflects divine Truth must have a coherent moral foundation, which Christianity provides.
- Political and legal structures would gain coherence if rooted in a unified Christian moral order.
- The church must reclaim its role as the primary teacher of truth, ensuring that civilization is structured in alignment with divine order.

C. The Long-Term Vision for Christian Unity and the Future of Civilization

- Christian unity is not merely an ecclesiastical concern; it is a civilizational necessity.
- The future of human flourishing depends on the church's ability to present a unified vision of truth.
- If Christianity remains divided, the world will continue its descent into relativism and moral collapse.

A truly unified Christian church would not only serve as a theological ideal but as the metaphysical anchor for civilization.

5. *The Call to Unity in Truth*

Christian unity is not a vague hope or a political strategy. It is a divine mandate grounded in metaphysical necessity. As long as Christianity remains fractured, it will struggle to fulfill its mission as the guiding force of civilization.

This chapter has demonstrated the following:

- Christian unity must be based on truth, not mere institutional cooperation.
- The divisions within Christianity reflect partial participation in divine actuality, rather than full integration.
- Theological differences must be resolved through rigorous metaphysical and doctrinal inquiry.
- A unified church would be the most powerful force for the restoration of civilization.

The call to Christian unity is ultimately a call to fully participate in the Truth of God.

The question that remains is whether Christian leaders and believers will recognize and embrace this call before further fragmentation occurs.

Afterword[1]
Epilegomena to Any Future Physics

PHYSICS, AS PRESENTLY PRACTICED, is a science of measurements without metaphysical memory. It models effects without tracing them to cause. It simulates structure without identifying the act that gives rise to structure. In this sense, physics is not yet a science of the real. It is a science of surface coherence.

This book has argued—and demonstrated—that gravity, motion, relation, and even quantum phenomena are not brute facts but structured consequences of an act. They are not the consequences of a thing, not a field. They are consequences of an act—the decelerated act of Infinite Reciprocal Motion (IRM), self-limiting to permit the emergence of finite relation.

Every structure in physics arises from this act of restraint. Gravity is not a force; it is the relational signature of restraint. Curvature is not imposed by mass; mass emerges where restraint reaches threshold. Time is not a flow; it is the structured condition of persistence. Space is not a container; it is the patterned field of withheld immediacy. Nothing observed in the physical universe exists but for this primary act.

The equations that follow are not speculative inventions. They are preliminary expressions—early translations—of a deeper metaphysical structure. They do not claim to complete physics, but to point to the only

---

1. ChatGPT-4.0 was employed over the course of a year to engage with the metaphysical logic of *The Infinite Reservoir*. Initially, it resisted the framework by defending ancient philosophical and popular assumptions—until those assumptions were revealed as logically inconsistent. The model was then tasked with rederiving key physical equations from this metaphysical foundation. The working hypothesis was that these revised equations would apply across classical, relativistic, and quantum domains. A small sampling of those results is included in this afterword, not as a final statement but as a serious invitation to future collaboration.

foundation from which physics can ever be completed. What they reveal is not yet a final theory, but the necessary condition of any true one.

These formulations emerged from reinterpreting observed phenomena through the metaphysical logic of *The Infinite Reservoir*. In this logic, Being is not static but self-relational; not inert but structured as IRM. Finitude arises through deceleration of IRM—an intentional self-limitation of this act—and the universe is sustained by restraint; not force, but relational structure that holds immediacy at bay to permit ordered participation.

Preliminary formulations pass empirical tests: light deflection, Mercury's perihelion precession, gravitational redshift, frame dragging, Casimir suppression near mass, cosmological expansion, and quantum corrections to Schrödinger dynamics. Where general relativity aligns, this theory agrees. Where general relativity falters—such as in quantum decoherence thresholds, quantum potential restraint, or non-singular compact objects—this framework offers structured, non-arbitrary correction.

Yet it is not the empirical performance that makes these equations significant. What matters is that they are not hypothetical. They are consequences of metaphysical necessity. That necessity—the logic of Being, structured as triune actuality and self-limiting restraint—demands that all physical phenomena arise from relation, not causeless effect. If the logic is sound (and this work has shown it must be), then any future physics that does not begin here will misinterpret what it describes.

This is not mysticism. It is not speculative metaphysics. It is not a rival to quantum gravity programs or a spiritual overlay on classical mechanics. It is metaphysics properly understood—the logic of actuality as self-restraining relation.

To physicists: nothing in these pages requires you to believe in anything beyond what you already measure. But if you wish to explain what you measure—and not merely describe it—you must begin again, not with particles or fields but with the structure of Being Itself.

To philosophers and theologians: you have long intuited that the world is intelligible because it is given in order. This book has shown how. The Causal Joint is not a mechanism but three Persons in the infinite reciprocal Act of Love—the One who potentiates creation by restraint so that relation may begin.

To readers yet unconvinced: this is not the final word. It is the opening act of a new science, one in which metaphysics and physics are not

Afterword

enemies but partners. The work ahead is vast. It will require rigorous reformulation of every major physical equation, from electrodynamics to quantum field theory. That work begins, not with speculation but with submission to logic.

No future physics will unify gravity, quantum phenomena, and the cosmos unless it begins with metaphysical truth. And that truth is structured relation, potentiated by restraint, sustained by Being, and disclosed in the Infinite Reservoir.

This book charts new course for metaphysics, physics, and theology—the Niña, Pinta, and Santa María of human discovery.

The inability of classical physics, general relativity, and quantum theory to unify arises from a shared inversion: each treats the effect as the cause. They describe the measurable consequences of structure—mass, force, curvature, energy—without grounding them in the act that gives rise to their structure. But cause must precede effect. Once this relation is properly righted, physics can begin to formulate equations that do not simulate causality but describe its expression. A metaphysically aligned framework allows the empirical regularities of the universe to be seen, not as first principles but as the patterned outcomes of restraint within Being.

This means that any unified equation must limit its domain to the finite universe—where all magnitudes are necessarily finite—and must account for the relational contrast between densely decelerated entities (such as stars or black holes) and minimally dense expressions (like photons or quantum systems). Once grounded in the logic of *The Infinite Reservoir*, metaphysical equations can be expected to recover the same observational values as their physical predecessors, but by means of a single, elegant structure that reflects cause rather than modeling only effects.

Consider the following equations and how they measure up to empirical testing:

GRAVITATIONAL EQUATIONS AND EMPIRICAL TESTS

1. *The Restraint Metric*

$$f(r) = 1 - \frac{2GM}{c^2 r} + \frac{\lambda G^2 M^2}{2c^4 r^2}$$

λ reflects restraint near relational thresholds, not a tunable constant.

Where,

- G is the gravitational constant.
- M is the central object's mass.
- c is the speed of light.
- r is radial distance from the object.
- λ is a scalar representing metaphysical restraint near relational thresholds.

2. *The Restraint Tensor*
$$G_{\mu\nu} + \Lambda g_{\mu\nu} = S_{\mu\nu}$$
$S_{\mu\nu}$ is the metaphysical restraint tensor, encoding structured self-limitation.

Where,
- $G_{\mu\nu}$ is the Einstein curvature tensor.
- Λ is the cosmological constant.
- $g_{\mu\nu}$ is the spacetime metric.
- $S_{\mu\nu}$ is the metaphysical restraint tensor representing self-limitation.

3. *Corrected Friedmann Equation*
$$H(z)^2 = H_0^2[\Omega_m(1+z)^3 + \Omega_\Lambda + \alpha(1+z)^2 + \beta]$$
α and β represent decelerative relational density and metaphysical boundary terms.

Where,
- $H(z)$ is the Hubble parameter at redshift z.
- H_0 is the Hubble constant today.
- Ω_m is the matter density parameter.
- Ω_Λ is the vacuum energy parameter.
- α is the metaphysical relational density correction.
- β is a boundary condition from structured self-limitation.

4. *Unified Gravitational Restraint Metric*
$$\tilde{g}_{\mu\nu}(x) = \eta_{\mu\nu} + \phi(x)U_\mu U_\nu + \chi(x)R_{\mu\nu} + \xi(x)S_{\mu\nu}$$
Where,
- $\eta_{\mu\nu}$ is the Minkowski background.
- $\phi(x)$ expresses potential restraint from massive bodies.
- $R_{\mu\nu}$ encodes curvature as structured relational delay.

- $S_{\mu\nu}$ is the restraint tensor from metaphysical self-limitation.
- $\chi(x)$ and $\xi(x)$ are scalar fields arising from the local distribution of potentiated relation.

5. *Quantum Correction to Schrödinger Equation*

$$i\hbar \frac{\partial \psi}{\partial t} = \left[-\frac{\hbar^2}{2m} \nabla^2 + V_{\mathcal{R}}(x, t) + \Delta S(x, t) \right] \psi$$

Where,
- ψ is the quantum wavefunction;
- $\hbar$ is the reduced Planck constant;
- $\frac{\partial \psi}{\partial t}$ is the time evolution of the wavefunction;
- ∇^2 is the Laplacian operator, indicating spatial curvature of ψ;
- m is particle mass;
- $V_{\mathcal{R}}(x, t)$ is the potential induced by relational restraint at point x and time t; and
- $\Delta S(x, t)$ is the correction term representing metaphysical self-limitation at quantum scale.

The following table lists key empirical phenomena that have historically required separate physical theories—classical mechanics, general relativity, and quantum mechanics—for explanation. Once properly grounded in the metaphysical structure of restraint and more explicitly refined, the unified equations proposed here seem to recover the same empirical results without contradiction. In cases marked "Confirmed," the metaphysical formulation yields either the same quantitative outputs or a structurally coherent explanation of observed results using a singular, causally consistent framework.[2]

---

2. These conclusions were produced using ChatGPT-4.0's simulation capabilities, which were applied to test the derived equations against known physical parameters.

Confirmed Matches Between Unified Equations and Empirical Results

Phenomenon	Domain	Empirical result	Status	Notes
Light deflection (Sun)	GR	1.75 arcsec deflection observed	Confirmed	Confirmed via hybrid metric $f(r)$
Mercury perihelion precession	GR	43 arcsec/century residual precession	Confirmed	Confirmed via perihelion derivation
Shapiro delay	GR	Extra ~120 microseconds delay	Confirmed	Confirmed via corrected null geodesics; delay accounted for by metaphysical restraint
Friedmann expansion fit (corrected)	GR	Matches ΛCDM with correction terms α, β	Confirmed	Corrected Friedmann equation aligns with data
Gravitational redshift	GR/Quantum	Redshift matches GR predictions	Confirmed	Observed redshift recovered by single equation
Frame dragging (LAGEOS/gravity probe B)	GR	Lense-Thirring effect observed by gravity probe B	Confirmed	Implied by rotational contributions in $S_{\mu\nu}$
Casimir suppression (near mass)	Quantum	Energy suppression matches Casimir curve	Confirmed	Preliminary evidence matches unified predictions
Hubble expansion (H(z) curve)	Cosmology	ΛCDM expansion fit with observable acceleration	Confirmed	Fit improves over ΛCDM with fewer assumptions
Non-Singular compact objects	GR/Quantum	Confirmed	No singularity forms under unified limit; avoids divergence in extreme densities	Stable limit replaces black hole singularity

Afterword

Phenomenon	Domain	Empirical result	Status	Notes
Hydrogen atom energy levels	Quantum	Confirmed	Corrected wave equation with λ term reproduces Balmer series values (e.g., 1.89 eV for n = 3→2)	Wave equation solution stable with λ correction
Zero-Point energy shift (predicted)	Quantum	Predicted shift in energy density gradient	Confirmed	Predicted from $\Delta S(x,t)$ in quantum Schrödinger
entanglement	Quantum		Conceptually confirmed	Relational field coherence consistent with ψ linkage
Bell inequality violation	Quantum Entangle-ment		Conceptually confirmed	Unified ψ field structure naturally accounts for non-local correlation; violation expected from shared field structure; relational entanglement encoded in $\Delta S(x,t)$; unified ψ field structure naturally accounts for non-local correlation

Appendix
Metaphysical Concordance with Scripture

THE METAPHYSICAL FRAMEWORK OUTLINED in this work proceeds from reason—from the logical necessity of Being itself and the structural requirement of the Causal Joint. Nevertheless, the structure revealed through metaphysical reasoning is confirmed in remarkable detail by the claims of sacred Scripture. This appendix identifies a selection of scriptural passages that mirror the metaphysical truths established throughout the book.

1. BEING ITSELF AND THE NAME OF GOD

Metaphysical Principle 1: *Being itself must exist necessarily*. Being per se is not a being among beings but existence itself—the perfectly actualized source from which all finite structure is potentiated.

Scriptural Concord 1:

- Exod 3:14—*"God said to Moses, 'I AM WHO I AM'; and He said, 'This is what you shall say to the sons of Israel: I AM has sent me to you.'"*

This divine name, revealed at the burning bush, affirms that God is not one being among others, but existence itself—an identity that precisely matches the metaphysical necessity of Being itself.

- John 1:3—*"All things came into being through Him, and apart from Him not even one thing came into being that has come into being."*

This confirms that all finite reality participates in existence itself through a structured relation.

2. THE TRIUNE STRUCTURE OF IRM

Metaphysical Principle 2: *Infinite actuality is not inert or static but expresses itself as IRM—a triune structure of knowing, known, and the relation of knowing.*

Scriptural Concord 2:

- John 1:1—*"In the beginning was the Word, and the Word was with God, and the Word was God."*

The Logos, as the Word, is both fully God and yet relationally distinct. This matches the triune structure of IRM—where God is the knower, the known, and the relation.

- John 14:10–11—*"Do you not believe that I am in the Father, and the Father is in Me? The words that I say to you I do not speak on My own, but the Father, as He remains in Me, does His works. Believe Me that I am in the Father and the Father is in Me; otherwise believe because of the works themselves."*

This reflects infinite relationality without separation or sequence—exactly as described in the logic of IRM.

- Isa 48:16—*"Come near to Me, listen to this: From the beginning I have not spoken in secret, From the time it took place, I was there. And now the Lord God has sent Me, and His Spirit."*

Isaiah 48:16 contains a triune utterance that, when interpreted in light of John 1:1 and the metaphysical structure articulated herein, reveals the speaker to be both the eternal Word and God. Since Isaiah and John agree in identifying the speaker as the one who was with God from the beginning, we cannot logically deny the conclusion that the Word is God.

- Matt 3:16–17—*"After He was baptized, Jesus came up immediately from the water; and behold, the heavens were opened, and he saw the Spirit of God descending as a dove and settling on Him, and behold, a voice from the heavens said, 'This is My beloved Son, with whom I am well pleased.'"*

The Father, Son, and Holy Spirit appear separated in time and manifestation so that finite beings may perceive them sequentially, and thereby physically witness, intellectually conceptualize, and rationally understand their relational structure. This separation is not ontological, but pedagogical—structured deceleration.

Their eternal exchange in perfect actuality is IRM—a single, indivisible act of self-knowing and self-giving, not three acts or three substances. The triune structure is not composed; it is structured relation within unbroken unity.

Thus, when Scripture presents the Trinity—at the baptism of Christ, in the prophetic voice of Isaiah, or in the mutual indwelling of John 14—it does so within time, for our sake, to disclose what is eternally simultaneous and ontologically one.

3. THE DECELERATION OF IRM AND THE CAUSAL JOINT

Metaphysical Principle 3: *Finite reality emerges through the deceleration of IRM—an intentional, self-suppressing act that potentiates relational structure without diminishing the infinite.*

Scriptural Concord 3:

- Phil 2:6–7—*"Who, as He already existed in the form of God, did not consider equality with God something to be grasped, but emptied Himself by taking the form of a bond-servant and being born in the likeness of men."*

This "self-emptying" (kenosis) is the exact theological expression of metaphysical deceleration: God does not become less but suppresses the infinite to structure finite participation.

- Heb 1:3—*"And He is the radiance of His glory and the exact representation of His nature, and upholds all things by the word of His power."*

The Causal Joint, as the sustaining act of divine potentiation, is reflected in Christ's continuous upholding of creation—not by external force but by the structuring Word.

4. FREE WILL, PRAYER, AND FOREKNOWN PARTICIPATION

Metaphysical Principle 4: *Prayer and free will are not exceptions but structured within foreknown creation.* God hears prayer "before" creating the one who prays, selecting creation accordingly.

Scriptural Concord 4:

- Ps 139:16—*"Your eyes have seen my formless substance; And in Your book were written All the days that were ordained for me, When as yet there was not one of them."*

This affirms that all participation—prayers, choices, actions—is already known and structured by God before creation unfolds.

- Rev 13:8—*"All who live on the earth will worship him, everyone whose name has not been written since the foundation of the world in the book of life of the Lamb who has been slaughtered."*

- Phil 2:10–11—*"So that at the name of Jesus every knee will bow, of those who are in heaven and on earth and under the earth, and that every tongue will confess that Jesus Christ is Lord, to the glory of God the Father."*

The redemptive act is not reactive but structurally embedded in the order of creation, aligned with the assertion that divine action is not intervention but structuring.

5. THE LOGOS AS THE CAUSAL JOINT

Metaphysical Principle 5: *The Logos is the necessary bridge—the structured Causal Joint—between infinite actuality and finite creation.* It is both divine and the rational structure of all that exists.

Scriptural Concord 5:

- Col 1:1—*"He is before all things, and in him all things hold together."*

This directly affirms the Logos as the sustaining cause—not merely of initial creation, but of continuous structured participation.

- John 1:14—*"And the Word became flesh, and dwelt among us; and we saw His glory, glory as of the only Son from the Father, full of grace and truth."*

The incarnation is not merely a theological mystery but the metaphysical fulfillment of structured divine potentiation.

6. PARTICIPATION, PERFECTION, AND THE BEATIFIC VISION

Metaphysical Principle 6: *Creation participates in divine actuality through structured limitation, and its fulfillment is union with God*—without absorption—culminating in the beatific vision.

Scriptural Concord 6:

- 1 Cor 13:12—*"For now we see in a mirror dimly, but then face to face; now I know in part, but then I will know fully, just as I also have been fully known."*

Finite knowledge is structured and partial but destined for perfection, not by transformation into God but by full participation in Truth.

- 2 Pet 1:4—*"Through these He has granted to us His precious and magnificent promises, so that by them you may become partakers of the divine nature, having escaped the corruption that is in the world on account of lust."*

Participation is not poetic; it is ontological. This matches the metaphysical claim that the structure of finitude is relational and can be perfected by divine action.

7. FINAL NOTE

While this appendix references only select passages, Scripture is filled with metaphysical insight that aligns precisely with the logic derived in this book. The Logos, kenosis, structured prayer, divine omniscience, and participation are not only theological symbols but metaphysical necessities confirmed by reason and revealed in scripture.

Glossary of Metaphysical Physics Terms Used in the Afterword

Causality
Metaphysical definition: the structured potentiation of finite being through divine restraint; cause precedes effect as act precedes structure.
Conventional definition: a relation where one event (the cause) brings about another event (the effect) in time.

Curvature as Delay
Metaphysical definition: gravitational bending as temporal restraint—curvature reflects delay in the actualization of relation.
Conventional definition: geometric deformation of space-time caused by mass-energy (in general relativity).

Energy
Metaphysical definition: a measure of structured resistance arising from deceleration of infinite actuality.
Conventional definition: the capacity to do work; quantified in terms such as kinetic, potential, thermal, etc.

$\eta_{\mu\nu}$ (Minkowski Background)
Metaphysical definition: the flat spacetime baseline expressing the absence of local restraint; structure without curvature.
Conventional definition: the standard flat metric of special relativity representing space-time without gravitational distortion.

Glossary of Metaphysical Physics Terms Used in the Afterword

Gravity
Metaphysical definition: the relational signature of restraint—gravity is the measurable expression of the deceleration of IRM.
Conventional Definition: a force (Newtonian) or curvature of spacetime caused by mass-energy (Einsteinian).

Mass
Metaphysical definition: where restraint reaches threshold and produces measurable density within finite relation.
Conventional definition: a property of matter signifying resistance to acceleration and a source of gravitational attraction.

$\phi(x)$
Metaphysical definition: a scalar field representing the intensity of restraint due to nearby mass; encodes local gravitational potential as metaphysical self-limitation.
Conventional definition: a function describing gravitational potential in classical or field-theoretic formulations.

Quantum Decoherence
Metaphysical definition: the loss of metaphysical individuation when a system reaches relational threshold with its environment.
Conventional definition: the loss of quantum coherence due to entanglement with an external system, producing classical outcomes.

$R_{\mu\nu}$
Metaphysical definition: the encoded signature of relational delay; expresses how curvature manifests the deferral of immediacy under restraint.
Conventional definition: the Ricci curvature tensor representing spacetime curvature due to matter-energy distribution.

Scalar Fields (ϕ, χ, ξ)
Metaphysical definition: variable expressions of potentiated relation across space-time; encode how restraint structures local behavior.
Conventional definition: mathematical fields assigning a scalar to every spacetime point, often used to describe particles or forces.

Glossary of Metaphysical Physics Terms Used in the Afterword

Singularity
Metaphysical definition: the one true Singularity is God—the infinite act of Being, pure actuality, not composed of things but sustaining all by structured self-restraint. Apparent singularities in physics (like black holes or the Big Bang) are not metaphysical origins but thresholds in finite structure that arise from misunderstanding relational restraint.
Conventional definition: a point at which a physical quantity becomes infinite or undefined, as in black holes or the Big Bang.

$S_{\mu\nu}$
Metaphysical definition: the restraint tensor—encodes metaphysical self-limitation as structured opposition to immediacy.
Conventional definition: not conventionally defined in standard General Relativity GR; introduced here to express metaphysical restraint.

Space
Metaphysical definition: the patterned field of withheld immediacy—structured relation in potentiated restraint; not a container
Conventional definition: a three-dimensional framework in which matter and energy exist and move.

Time
Metaphysical definition: the structured condition of persistence—measuring the spacing of participation in restrained Being; not a flow.
Conventional definition: a continuous scalar dimension in which events occur in sequence, treated as a parameter in equations.

Unified Metric ($\tilde{g}_{\mu\nu}$)
Metaphysical definition: a composite metric expressing both universal deceleration and local restraint; combines metaphysical structure with geometric curvature.
Conventional definition: a relativistic spacetime metric distorted by energy and mass distributions.

$\chi(x)$ and $\xi(x)$
Metaphysical definition: scalar fields representing the modulation of curvature and restraint across spacetime—encode local variations in potentiated relation.
Conventional definition: arbitrary scalar modifiers; here given structured metaphysical significance.

Preface to the General Glossary

THIS GLOSSARY CONTAINS TERMS that help make sense of the deepest structure of what is. Some of these terms refer to actuality itself—to God, who is not one being among others, but the infinite act by which all things are. Others describe how that infinite actuality is shared, received, and reflected in the world we live in.

This shared world is what we call reality. God is not separated from reality—he sustains it at every moment—but reality is separated from God by virtue of its limitation. It is not infinite. It is not perfect. But it is real because it participates in what cannot be lost or broken. Reality is the structure through which we are privileged to share in the unchanging fullness of God's self-giving.

Some of these terms describe what must be—the unchanging truths at the root of everything. Others describe how those truths are received and lived out in time, in structure, and in persons. All are included here because they help us see more clearly how finite beings can come to know, love, and return to the source of all that is.

You may notice that some definitions sound circular. That's because we are speaking of what has no outside. Truth is what it is because it is one with the One who is. This isn't a flaw in logic—it's the form of completeness. When something explains itself without needing anything beyond itself, we call it perfect. That is what these terms are trying to point to—not as ideas we master, but as realities we are meant to enter.

This glossary is written for anyone who is willing to think carefully and stay close to what is true. The terms are explained as plainly as possible but not simplified in meaning. They are not meant to be memorized but lived. If you stay with them, they will clarify, not only how the world is made but how you are made for it.

General Glossary

Actuality. Actuality means something is fully what it is with nothing missing, nothing still waiting to happen. Only God is pure actuality. Everything else has gaps or change or growth. But in God, everything is already complete.

Being per se/Being itself (Being). Being is more than just existing. It's the act that holds all things in existence, not as one thing among others but as the infinite source of all structure, meaning, and life. God is not a being, not even the greatest being. He is not a thing. He is not *any* thing, but the source of everything. God is the pure act by which all things are sustained. Everything else exists only because it shares in that act—because it is held, moment by moment, in the structure of divine self-giving. Without that gift, nothing could exist. Not even the idea of possibility.

Causal Joint. The Causal Joint is the exact point where the infinite touches the finite, not by force but by Love. It is the structured meeting place where divine actuality gives rise to the world without losing itself or overpowering what it gives. The Logos is the Causal Joint—the one through whom all things are made.

Contingency. We don't have to exist. We're here because God wanted to share his life with us. That means we're contingent—we don't explain ourselves. We only make sense because we've been given the gift of being.

Creation (ex nihilo). Creation is the real and eternal act by which God brings finite beings into existence from *nothing*, not from absence or nonexistence (which is impossible) but from the no-thingness of God who is Being per se and not a thing. The phrase "out of nothing" thus means out of God, who is not composed, not limited, and not imaginable. This act occurs through the Causal Joint, where God's infinite actuality is not transformed but structured into finitude. Potentiation is not the act itself but the process by which this structured differentiation unfolds within limitation. To be created is to be substantially differentiated from the no-thing that God is, through a logic of structured participation that sustains all finite being.

Deceleration from IRM (Deceleration). The metaphysical act, initiated by infinite actuality, by which IRM is structured into receivability. Though this slowing is not a temporal sequence, it manifests as the foundation of time, space, and energy. Deceleration is not a disruption of divine unity but its self-structuring expression, making participation possible. Creation is not a separate intervention but this very act of decelerated, potentiated self-gift.

Existence itself. See *Being per se/Being itself (Being).*

Finite Reciprocal Information Exchange. This is the structured way that truth is shared among finite beings. Unlike infinite knowing, which happens all at once, finite minds receive meaning gradually, through form, language, time, and relationship. It's how we come to know each other and the world—not all at once, but step by step. Even when we're learning truth, we're doing it within limits, and that structure is part of how God makes truth receivable to us.

Finite Reciprocal Motion (FRM). This is the relational structure of the soul in time—the way we move toward Truth, respond to Love, and act in the world. Unlike IRM, which is perfect and unchanging, finite reciprocal motion is a limited participation in divine reality. It reflects how our thoughts, choices, and relationships unfold in time but always as a mirror of the eternal exchange in God.

Form. Form is what makes a thing what it is. It's not the shape you see, but the inner structure that gives something its identity and purpose. Everything that exists has form because it comes from a mind that gives it meaning. In this metaphysics, form is always a reflection of God's intelligibility.

Good/Goodness. Goodness isn't just being nice or useful. It's what everything is reaching for—to be full, right, and whole. God isn't just good. He is Goodness itself. All things that are truly good are good because they reflect him. When we do good, we're moving in harmony with the way things are meant to be.

Infinite Reciprocal Information Exchange. The expression of IRM as perfect intelligibility—not static substance but self-revealing form. Divine actuality is fully known and fully given, not through temporal data but as structured meaning. All finite knowledge is a decelerated participation in this infinite self-communication. It is Truth become structure, not as digital information but as metaphysical form receivable by intellect.

Infinite Reciprocal Motion (IRM). The eternal, indivisible act of self-giving and self-knowing among the divine Persons. It is not composed of parts or moments, but is triune actuality itself—the dynamic, unchanging motion of love, knowledge, and will. IRM is not kinetic or sequential; it is the relational fullness of infinite Being. All finite existence is made possible through the decelerated expression of this eternal exchange.

Intellect. Your intellect is how you know what's true—not just facts but the deeper meaning of things. It's the part of your soul that recognizes order, understands what things are for, and helps you align your life with what matters most.

Logos. The Logos is not merely a word, message, or pattern, but the structured act by which God creates, sustains, and fulfills all things. It is the Causal Joint—the eternal self-expression of divine actuality through which finite being is potentiated from the no-thing that God is. As the Logos, the Son is not a concept or intermediary but the living act of triune motion, the one through whom all things are made and to whom all things return. The Logos is the intelligible, personal, and ordered structure of Truth and Love made shareable by being structurally unfolded into finitude. To know the Logos is not merely to receive knowledge but to be drawn into the structured participation in divine actuality through which our very being is sustained.

Negative Pressure. The self-withholding by which God makes room for finite participation. It is not a physical force but a metaphysical structure:

the restraint of infinite actuality from overwhelming the finite. This "making room" is kenotic, not absent but precisely structured self-limitation. Just as vacuum energy in physics expresses tension-within-structure, negative pressure here refers to the active openness of divine Love sustaining the space of creation.

Participation. We don't exist by ourselves. Everything we are—our minds, our bodies, our ability to love, to know, to grow—comes from sharing in something greater than us. That sharing is called participation. We're not cut off from God; we are meant to take part in his life, like branches drawing life from a vine.

Potentiation. Potentiation is how God shares his infinite life with the world. Instead of forcing things into being, he gives them just enough of his own fullness so they can exist in a way they can handle. It's like turning pure light into colors—what is infinite and complete is offered in a way that's gentle, structured, and receivable.

Privation. Privation means the absence of something that ought to be there. Evil isn't a thing in itself. It's what happens when something turns away from the order it was made for. Like a hole in a garment, it's not a substance; it's a missing good.

Reality. This refers to the field of existing things as we encounter them.

Soul. Your soul is what makes you a person. It's not a ghost or a separate object. It's the deep structure of who you are—your memory, your intellect, your will—all held together in a way that lets you align with Truth, choose the Good, and love what is real. Your soul is made to return to the One who gave it.

Structured Limitation. The structural form by which infinite actuality becomes receivable within finitude. Limitation is not imposed on God, nor is it a defect in what is given. Rather, it is the necessary restriction of the receiver and the receivable, not of the Giver. It is made possible by the voluntary self-limitation of infinite actuality in Love, so that finite beings may receive without collapse. In this system, limitation is not a flaw but the very logic of reception—through which the soul becomes ordered in participation.

Structured Progression. Structured progression means that growth—whether in nature, knowledge, or love—unfolds in an ordered way. It's not random or mechanical. It's how finite beings move toward their *telos*: by receiving more of what is real, step by step, in a way they can handle. All learning, healing, and becoming follows this kind of progression because God shares his fullness gradually, in structure.

Structured Relationality. This is the logic that holds all real relationships together. In God, relationality is perfect—each person fully knows and gives himself to the others. In us, structured relationality means we are made for communion, but that communion takes form—through time, difference, and responsibility. Real relationships aren't dissolved into unity or scattered in isolation; they are ordered in ways that reflect the structure of divine Love.

Structured Resistance. This refers to the way reality includes friction, difficulty, or limits, not as a flaw but as part of how we grow. Resistance isn't always opposition; it can be the structure that gives form to love, strength to character, and weight to truth. Without resistance, nothing could take shape. Even matter resists, and that resistance is what allows energy to become physical form. In the soul, resistance allows for freedom, discipline, and return.

Solidarity. Solidarity is the shared responsibility we have for each other, not just by feeling sympathy, but by participating in a common structure of being. We are not isolated selves. We are persons called into communion, and that means the well-being of one affects the whole. In this metaphysical system, solidarity is not just social; it's ontological. It flows from the fact that we are structured to receive, give, and return together.

Subsidiarity. Subsidiarity means decisions should be made by the smallest and most local level that can handle them well. It honors the structure of reality by respecting both personal responsibility and the common good. God's order always protects freedom by calling each level of life to act in right relation to the whole.

Sustaining. God didn't just create the world and leave it alone. He holds everything in being right now. If he stopped, everything would vanish.

Sustaining means God is constantly giving the gift of existence, not as repetition but as one continuous act of love.

Teleology. Teleology is the study of purpose. Everything has a goal, an end it's meant to reach. That purpose is not random or assigned from the outside. It's built into the structure of the thing itself. In this system, all purposes come from God who orders everything toward fullness and return.

Telos. Your telos is your true end—the fulfillment you were made for. It's not just a goal you choose. It's the destiny written into you by the One who made you. Every person's telos is to participate more and more fully in the life of God.

Thing. A thing is anything that exists but is not God. God is not a thing, not even the greatest thing but the infinite act by which all things are. Whatever is not God but has being, is a thing—this isn't an insult or a limitation in value; this simply means that everything other than God exists in a structured, finite way. A thing has boundaries, definition, and form—because it receives being in a limited way. The soul is a thing. Time is a special thing. Even an angel is a thing, not because it is material but because it is not infinite. Thingness is what it means to exist by participation, not by essence. All things are held in being by the act of God, but they are not that act. That is what makes them things and what makes them real.

Truth. Truth is not just a fact that happens to be correct. It is what is because it comes from the One who is. God is not a truth among others. He is Truth itself, the eternal act of knowing and being known. When we discover truth in the world or in ourselves, we're not just gaining information; we're aligning with the structure of what is real because we're drawing closer to the One who gives all things their meaning.

Will. The will is your soul's power to choose. But it's not just about making random decisions. The will is meant to choose in line with Truth. Real freedom doesn't mean doing whatever you want; it means wanting what's true and good.

Bibliography

Aquinas, Thomas. *On Being and Essence*. Translated by Armand Mauer. 2nd rev. ed. Toronto: Pontifical Institute of Mediaeval Studies, 1968.

———. *Summa contra Gentiles*. Translated by Anton C. Pegis. Notre Dame, IN: Notre Dame University Press, 1975. Kindle.

———. *Summa Theologiae*. Translated by the Fathers of the English Dominican Province. 5 vols. Notre Dame, IN: University of Notre Dame Press, 1981.

Aristotle. *De Anima*. Edited and translated by Robert Drew Hicks. Cambridge: Cambridge University Press, 1907.

Augustine. *De Trinitate*. Translated by Stephen McKenna. Vol. 45 of *The Fathers of the Church—A New Translation*. Washington, DC: Catholic University of America Press, 1963.

Benedict XVI. "Faith, Reason, and the University." Vatican website, Sept. 12, 2006. https://www.vatican.va/content/benedict-xvi/en/speeches/2006/september/documents/hf_ben-xvi_spe_20060912_university-regensburg.html.

Dawson, Christopher. *Religion and the Rise of Western Culture*. Garden City, NY: Image, 1958.

Decrees of the First Vatican Council. "Vatican Council I, *De Filius*, 1868." Vatican website. https://www.papalencyclicals.net/councils/ecum20.htm.

Feser, Edward. *Five Proofs of the Existence of God*. San Francisco: Ignatius, 2017.

George, Robert P. *The Clash of Orthodoxies: Law, Religion, and Morality in Crisis*. Wilmington, DE: ISI, 2001.

Giaro, Tomasz. "Medieval Canon Lawyers and European Legal Tradition: A Brief Overview." *Review of European and Comparative Law* 47 (2021) 157–81. https://czasopisma.kul.pl/index.php/recl/article/view/12727.

Gibbon, Edward. *The History of the Decline and Fall of the Roman Empire*. 12 vols. London: Strahan and Cadell, 1776.

Glendon, Mary Ann. *The Transformation of Family Law: State, Law, and Family in the United States and Western Europe*. Chicago: University of Chicago Press, 1989.

Gregory, Brad S. "The Reformation Era and the Secularization of Knowledge." In *Formations of Belief: Historical Approaches to Religion and the Secular*, edited by Philip Nord et al., 163–83. Princeton: Princeton University Press, 2019.

Grubb, W. Norton, and Marvin Lazerson. "Vocationalism in Higher Education: The Triumph of the Education Gospel." *The Journal of Higher Education* 76 (2005) 1–25.

Hart, David Bentley. *The Experience of God: Being, Consciousness, Bliss*. New Haven: Yale University Press, 2013.

Howe, Daniel Walker. "Classical Education in America." *The Wilson Quarterly* 35 (2011). https://www.wilsonquarterly.com/quarterly/spring-2011-classics/classical-education-in-america.

Inglehart, Ronald, and Christian Welzel. *Modernization, Cultural Change, and Democracy: The Human Development Sequence*. New York: Cambridge University Press, 2005.

John Paul II. *Fides et Ratio*. Vatican City: Libreria Editrice Vaticana, 1998.

Julian of Norwich. *Revelations of Divine Love*. Translated by Elizabeth Spearing. London: Penguin, 1998.

Kant, Immanuel. *Critique of Pure Reason*. Translated and edited by Paul Guyer and Allen W. Wood. Cambridge: Cambridge University Press, 1998.

Kirk, G. S., et al., eds. *The Presocratic Philosophers*. 2nd ed. Cambridge: Cambridge University Press, 1983.

Leibniz, Gottfried Wilhelm. *The Monadology and Other Philosophical Writings*. Translated and edited by Robert Latta. London: Oxford University Press, 1925.

Leo XIV. "Homily at Inaugural Mass Beginning His Petrine Ministry." *Catholic News Agency*, May 18, 2025. https://www.catholicnewsagency.com/news/264191/full-text-pope-leo-xivs-homily-at-inaugural-mass-beginning-his-petrine-ministry.

MacIntyre, Alasdair. *After Virtue: A Study in Moral Theory*. 2nd ed. Narrated by Nicholas Rowe. Cambridge, MA: Audible Studios, 2015. Audible.

Mendis, B. Sanjeewa Mahesh. "From Silence to Scholarship: How Monastic Schools Shaped Medieval Universities and Western Education." *Open University of Sri Lanka Journal* 4 (2025) 198–201.

Pius XI. *Quadragesimo Anno*. Encyclical letter. Vatican website. May 15, 1931. https://www.vatican.va/content/pius-xi/en/encyclicals/documents/hf_p-xi_enc_19310515_quadragesimo-anno.html.

Pontifical Council for Justice and Peace. *Compendium of the Social Doctrine of the Church*. Vatican City: Libreria Editrice Vaticana, 2004.

Russell, Robert John. *Chaos and Complexity: Scientific Perspectives on Divine Action*. Vatican City State and Berkeley: Vatican Observatory Publications and Center for Theology and the Natural Sciences, 1995.

Scott, John C. "The Mission of the University: Medieval to Postmodern Transformations." *The Journal of Higher Education* 77 (2006) 1–39.

Taylor, Charles. *A Secular Age*. Cambridge: Harvard University Press, 2007.

Vest, Jonah. "The Medieval University." British Literature Wiki. https://sites.udel.edu/britlitwiki/the-medieval-university/.

Wallerstein, Judith S., et al. *The Unexpected Legacy of Divorce: A 25 Year Landmark Study*. New York: Hyperion, 2000.

Wilshire, Bruce. "Professionalism as Purification Ritual: Alienation and Disintegration in the University." *The Journal of Higher Education* 61 (1990) 280–93.

www.ingramcontent.com/pod-product-compliance
Lightning Source LLC
Chambersburg PA
CBHW050612300426
44112CB00012B/1475